Who Rules the Universities?

Who Rules the Universities?

An Essay in Class Analysis

by David N. Smith

Monthly Review Press
New York and London

Library of Congress Cataloging in Publication Data
Smith, David N 1952–
Who rules the universities?
Includes bibliographical references.
1. Universities and colleges—United States.
2. Social classes—United States. I. Title.
LA227.3.S58 378.73 73-90075
ISBN 0-85345-320-9

Monthly Review Press
62 West 14th Street, New York, N.Y. 10011
21 Theobalds Road, London WC1X 8SL

First Printing

Manufactured in the United States of America

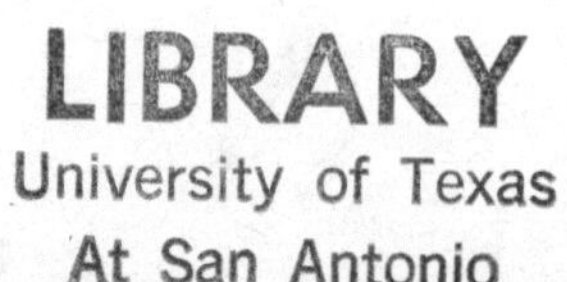

To my parents, for their warmth and honesty,
and my sister, for her comradeship.

Acknowledgments

My friends and comrades have contributed greatly to the writing of this book, not only through their criticisms of the text but through their active comradeship in political struggle—the crucible in which the majority of the ideas presented here were initially forged. Without the abundant arguments and insights, criticisms and ideas offered by my friends, this work would have been a far poorer one.

In particular I am deeply grateful to Dean Manders, Peter Shapiro, David Winet, Bill Martin, Marla Kraus, Steve Izen, John Judis, Jerry Morgan, Marty Harwayne, Elliott Smith, Richard Lichtman, Jeff Blum, Paul Heft, David Plotke, Ray Barglow, and Mark Ashley for their penetrating, thoughtful, and surprisingly varied criticisms of the manuscript. If their criticisms were not always entirely harmonious with one another, they were nonetheless invaluable to me as indications of perspectives which would otherwise have remained only dimly imaginable.

Of the many people who helped me in similar ways in the context of discussion and political debate, I would like to mention especially Scott Kerrihard, Bill Kononen, Laura Bennetts, Linda Dauterman, Rich Gallegos, Laurel Smith, and Vi Smith. Harry Braverman of Monthly Review also gave freely of his knowledge and wisdom, and Rhoda Slanger proved to be the perfect copy editor, rigorous and demanding yet a pleasure to work with. Finally, I would like to thank Daisy

Goodman, who typed most of the first draft while on strike in 1972, and Jon Harwayne, for his photography.

This work, although entirely mine in conception and elaboration, must be understood as the fruit of political and theoretical struggles which have engaged the efforts of countless members of the "New Left." It would not have been possible without their truly pathbreaking activism—nor can it be considered a success if it fails to inspire similar activism. Dare to struggle, dare to win!

Contents

Introduction 11

Part 1: Ruling-Class Control

1. The Regents 19
2. The Ruling Class 37

Part 2: The Genesis of Ruling-Class Control

3. The Genesis of Ruling-Class Control 61
4. The Robber Barons 66
5. Carnegie and Rockefeller 94
6. The State and College-Educated Labor 112

Part 3: The Meaning of Ruling-Class Control

7. Capitalism and the Universities 139
8. The Myth of the Middle Class 173
9. The Changing Composition of the Working Class 185
10. Problems of Class Analysis 202

Part 4: An End to Ruling-Class Control

11. The Student Revolt 225
12. Future Contradictions 253
13. The Struggle for Socialism 269

Introduction

It has become an almost traditional part of the rhetoric of the student left in the past decade to declare that the university system is controlled by big businessmen and war profiteers who use the universities for *their* private gain and *our* shared loss. It has become almost traditional to declare that the universities are subservient to the powerful profit interests of the capitalist class; but aside from a few genuinely pathbreaking studies, little proof of this contention has been offered.[1] My purpose in writing this book has been to reaffirm the arguments and principles of the student left by providing systematic proof of their substantial accuracy. I have tried to demonstrate the many points at which social reality converges with the spirit and substance of the radical viewpoint and, although I have explicitly tried to avoid balancing on the razor's edge of "academic neutrality and objectivity," the facts and figures presented here can be tested for accuracy with little difficulty.

Above all else, this book should be understood as an essay in class analysis. In the course of writing it, I have attempted a difficult synthesis of two different but related modes of argument: on the one hand, I have tried to present a popular argument analyzing the past and present reality of capitalist domination of the universities; on the other hand, I have tried to make the class identity of students and college graduates *intelligible* in the context of my analysis of capitalist domination of higher education. As will become clear, the relationship between ruling-class control of the universities and the class status of students is tangible and, ultimately, visible.

In order to present a persuasive argument about the reality of capitalist hegemony in the sphere of higher education, I found it necessary to explore and document not only the history but the logic of ruling-class control of the universities. In each different historical period in the evolution of the universities (and there have been three such periods in modern times—cf. chapters 4-7), the capitalist class has used its power over the universities to achieve different goals. In the present era, for the first time, capitalist control of the universities has had vital implications for the development of the working class in America, and, consequently, for the development of an accurate analysis of class relations. In the contemporary period, what capitalism requires most of all from the universities is the creation and socialization of a new force within the working class: college-educated workers. Needing new kinds of workers, the capitalist class has moved, during the last thirty years, to transform the universities from small schools educating the children of the ruling class into colossal factories for the training and socialization of young, educated workers. The working class has thus expanded, diversifying as the needs of capitalism have diversified. No longer can we view the working class simply as the classic industrial proletariat of Marx's time. For as capitalism changes, and the working class changes accordingly, our class analysis must expand and deepen in order to remain in step with reality. If our theory remains static, we will inevitably lose touch with the unceasing forward motion of social development.[2]

My central argument is that college-educated workers are members of an expanded working class which has been called into being by a capitalist class faced with new needs in a new historical situation. In the light of an argument of this kind, it is possible to understand both capitalism and the role of workers in new and valuable ways. It is also possible to gain a deeper understanding of the meaning of the student revolt. It would be false, however, to pretend that the basic assumptions in this analysis are not controversial. My argument clashes not only with the logic of popular wisdom—that there are no major class differentiations in the United States and that most people are members of a loosely defined "middle class"—but also with the wisdom of "orthodox Marxists," who argue that the working class today is what the working class has always been, and that college graduates are members of a middle class located in some intermediate position between capital and labor. I intend to show that neither analysis is sufficient for an understanding of the real class relations in society. The liberal analysis obscures reality rather than illuminates it, while the orthodox Marxist interpretation violates the essential principles of Marx's definition of class.

With an understanding of the development of key contemporary class relationships as my central theme, illustrated by the historical growth and progress of the universities, I make a serious if provisional effort, in the second half of the book, to define the working class in structural terms, showing how it has expanded and diversified as the historical focus of capitalism has expanded and diversified. My goal here is not an analysis of the subjective problems of class consciousness, although my three final chapters address these problems. Although I recognize that an understanding of these problems is vital to any fully developed political analysis, at this point my goal is to define the working class in *objective* terms, in terms of its *structural* role in the capitalist process of production. For I believe that class is an objective phenomenon related to the structural organization of the production process, and that it must be understood in that light before a sufficient theory of class consciousness is possible.[3]

The book begins with a single question: "Who rules the University of California?" The answer—that the University of California is controlled by a powerful and wealthy Board of Regents which rules in its own interest—raises a new set of questions, which are analyzed in the second chapter. Are the Regents typical or atypical of university trustees? Are they exceptional for their wealth and power, or are they members of an identifiable ruling class which controls *all* the major American universities? The answers to these questions—that the Regents are not atypical of university trustees but are in fact members of an American ruling class—leads us to ask, and answer, another set of questions. In the third, fourth, fifth, and sixth chapters I explore the genesis and development of ruling-class control of the universities in order to document the historical process which paved the way for the existing state of university power relations. Finding that the nature of ruling-class control has differed in every period, in the seventh chapter I explore this historical process in terms of the changing needs of capitalism. Discovering that the universities and their central social products—college-educated workers—are of vital importance to contemporary capitalism, in the eighth, ninth, and tenth chapters I confront the crucial question of class and the class identity of students and college-educated workers. While the problems raised in these chapters are not easily resolved, they cannot be evaded. They are important not only in a theoretical sense but in a practical, political sense as well, for if students and college-educated workers are to develop the revolutionary class consciousness necessary for the elimination of class exploitation and the creation of socialism, they will need a theory that makes sense of their experience in society and enables them to understand the class nature of their oppression and struggle.

In the last three chapters I touch upon some of the problems of consciousness and struggle which the diversification of the working class entails. I present an analysis, first, of the student revolt, and, second, of the relationship between college-educated workers and other sectors of the working class in the context of the larger struggle for socialism. This analysis is not intended to be exhaustive. Instead, I have tried to suggest paths of interpretation which strike me as having fruitful possibilities. If my work on these themes fails to provoke both controversy and further analysis, then it will have fallen short of its goals.

My argument, in a nutshell, is that if students—as apprentice workers—or workers of any kind are ever to lead full lives, then revolutionary struggle must be waged against both capitalism and the capitalist ruling class which controls the universities. "If you don't believe me," as Upton Sinclair wrote in a study of the universities and the ruling class more than fifty years ago, "just come along and let me show you—not merely the skeleton of the beast, but the nerves and the brains, the blood and the meat, the hide and the hair, the teeth and the claws of it."[4]

Notes

1. See, for example, the following three pamphlets: "Who Rules Columbia?" (New York: North American Congress on Latin America [NACLA], 1968); David Horowitz, "The Universities and the Ruling Class," 1969; Bettina Aptheker, "Big Business and the Universities" (New York: Institute for Marxist Studies, 1966).

2. For good Marxist critiques of contemporary society, see the journals *Socialist Revolution, Monthly Review,* and *New Left Review* in particular. For a superb radical bibliography, see *Counter Course,* ed. Trevor Patman (Middlesex, England: Penguin, 1972), pp. 297-389.

3. This is not to say, however, that Stanley Aronowitz is wrong when he observes that "the history of the working class is the unfolding

of its collective subjectivity as much as of its objectivity." Aronowitz's book, *False Promises: The Shaping of American Working Class Consciousness* (New York: McGraw Hill, 1973), was published too late for me to be able to integrate his ideas into my own analysis, but it appears to be directly parallel to this book as a work on class analysis. From a brief glance through it, and on the basis of hearing him speak, I can say that it looks like the most promising work on class consciousness in several years.

4. Upton Sinclair, *The Goose Step* (Pasadena, Calif.: published by the author, 1923), p. 17.

Part I
Ruling-Class Control

1
The Regents

Individual Portraits: A Regents' Meeting

Uniformed policemen stood guard at the entrance to the University of California Extension Center in San Francisco on September 17, 1971, the day on which the Regents last raised tuition officially. A few dozen cameras clicked quietly under the murmur of animated conversation coming from the audience. As a stream of people slowly filed into the hall, lights were focused on the large square table at the front of the room and the Regents took their seats, with University of California President Charles Hitch, Chairman of the Regents William French Smith, and Governor Ronald Reagan facing the audience. With a blow from his gavel and a few mumbled words, Smith called the meeting to order; conversation subsided and the dozen or so photographers melted into the audience.

Sitting under a large California flag, the secretary, one of only three women at the table, read off the names in a crisp voice. At the conclusion of roll call, Hitch, puffing on a cigar, outlined the major topics of discussion. When he raised his eyebrows and looked around at the other Regents for approval, he was only half surprised to see Norton Simon raise his hand to object. Simon—whose firm, Norton Simon, Inc., is the 120th largest industrial corporation in the nation, with sales amounting to over $1 billion a year—launched into an attack on Governor Reagan. Simon had run against the incumbent George Murphy in the last Republican senatorial primary and had been defeated. His intense dislike for Reagan was evident. In a gravelly voice, he came to the point bluntly: "With all due respect, gentlemen, I would like to suggest that Ronald Reagan do something other than run the University of California during his term of office." Reagan, taking off his glasses, looked around the table in mock surprise, saying, "But I thought *Norton* was running it!" inspiring gales of laughter from the other Regents.

The sad truth is that *both* Reagan and Simon have a hand in running the University. As two of the twenty-four Regents, they share with their colleagues ultimate control over the educational lives of ninety thousand students. The reality of the Regents' power—and its potentialities—became clear during the course of the meeting.

For two long hours after the initial flurry of thrusts and counter-thrusts, the meeting moved placidly forward, with Board members making random comments here and there but little of importance being discussed. Edwin Pauley, with a bleak expression on his heavy, chiseled face, seemed on the verge of falling asleep. A sixty-eight-year-old oil man, Pauley is the founder of Pauley Petroleum, which has a sales volume of $12-15 million annually.[1] A Regent since 1940, Pauley was national treasurer and secretary of the Democratic party during the early forties, but found himself in the eye of a political hurricane in 1947 when President Truman nominated him as Undersecretary of the Navy under James Forrestal. Corruption was charged, Congressional hearings were held, and Pauley didn't get the position. Although his national political career was over, Pauley remained a power in California politics and has been known to fly legislators to Regents' meetings in his private plane (as did Samuel Mosher of Signal Oil, who resigned from the Board of Regents in 1969 for reasons of health).

Edward Carter, prim-faced and grim, his white hair parted

in the middle like an old-fashioned dandy, kept a sour expression on his long pink face for most of the meeting. The president and co-owner of Broadway-Hale Stores, with an annual sales volume in excess of $650 million, Carter is plugged into almost every source of power in the state. Among his many interests is his position on the board of directors of the powerful Irvine Foundation, a position which Regent Simon highlighted when he commented accusingly, after a significant roll-call vote: "I would like to point out that Regent Carter changed his vote twice after a different vote from the chairman, who is attorney for the Irvine Foundation." Carter stiffened at this remark but didn't reply, his pink face growing pinker. Only once during the meeting did Carter smile—a thin, radiant, white picket-fence smile which lighted his face but lasted only a moment.

On the whole the Regents were quiet that day. Frederick G. Dutton, a former Assistant U.S. Secretary of State and one of four liberals on the Board, sported sideburns. Another liberal, William Coblentz, a former consultant to Secretary of State Dean Rusk, wore a colorful tie. The rest of the Regents were conservatively dressed, and their conversation was even less interesting than their clothes. As a result, my mind wandered, collecting impressions of the various men. John Canaday, executive consultant with Lockheed Aircraft and a former vice-president of the California Manufacturers Association, was pudgy, white haired, and quiet.[2] Dean Watkins, co-owner and chairman of the Watkins-Johnson Company—manufacturers of electronic devices, including the electronic battlefield, with annual sales of $32 million—was blunt and stumbling, with the quick, toothy grin of a football coach. William Matson Roth, described by *San Francisco Chronicle* columnist Herb Caen as "Bill Roth of the Matson millions," puffed a cigar during the meeting and raised occasional questions in a deep, smooth voice. Like Dutton and

Coblentz, Roth is a significant figure in the Democratic party, and is, after Simon, the fourth and last of the liberals on the twenty-four member Board of Regents.

Joseph Alexander Moore, Jr., who is listed in the *Social Register,* is president and director of the Moore Investment Company, the Moore Dry Dock Co., and the Semya Construction Co. Speaking only occasionally during the meeting, usually with a complacent half-smile on his aquiline face, Moore has the bearing and features of an aristocrat, resembling British Conservative leader Edward Heath. An important national figure in the Republican party, Moore is also a director of Edward Carter's Emporium-Capwell Stores (a subsidiary of Broadway-Hale), the Crocker-Citizens National Bank, the Fibreboard Corporation, and several lesser companies. He voted conservatively on every issue that came up.

Elinor Heller, who sits on several corporate boards in her own right, became a Regent upon the death of her husband, Edward Heller of Wells Fargo, who had been a Regent before her. Looking like an aging gun moll, her hair bobbed in 1920s style, she chatted frequently during the lengthy meeting with Ronald Reagan, who sat next to her. Reagan, when he wasn't speaking, either looked down at his notes or peered tight-lipped over his glasses. When he did speak, his smooth, rapid, rubber-silk voice usually managed to carry the day.

Robert O. Reynolds, a professional football player during the 1930s, said little during the meeting but voted conservatively on every issue. As president of the California Angels baseball team and a director of ten corporations (including the Los Angeles Rams and Poly Fibers, Inc.), Reynolds is a significant figure in the California economy and a member of thirteen of the state's leading social clubs.

Another consistently conservative vote was cast by Catherine Hearst, whose elaborate coiffure was as rigid as her position on most issues. Her husband Randolph is second in command of the Hearst media empire founded by his father,

William Randolph Hearst. According to her official biography, Catherine Hearst "is the current embodiment of the close association which has existed over the years between the Hearst family and the University of California."

Another Regent with connections in the media is William E. Forbes. Formerly a high-ranking executive of CBS television, Forbes is president of the influential Southern California Music Company. His silence during the meeting was matched by that of DeWitt A. Higgs, a prominent and extremely conservative lawyer.

The chairman of the Regents, William French Smith, is Ronald Reagan's personal lawyer and was appointed to the Board by Reagan himself. Smith is a director of Crocker Bank, Pacific Telephone and Telegraph, Pacific Lighting Corporation, Pacific Mutual Life Insurance, and Norton Simon, Inc. Norton Simon himself is a self-made millionaire whose renowned art collection has been valued at $150 million.[3]

Regent John H. Lawrence, whose term expired in 1972, has been associate director of the Lawrence Radiation Laboratory at the University of California and a consultant to the Atomic Energy Commission. Regent Christian Markey, whose one-year term as president of the Alumni Association also expired in 1972, was notable during the meeting for his youthfulness and talkativeness and the fact that he occasionally voted on the liberal side of an issue.

In the audience, the new chancellor of the Berkeley campus, Albert Bowker, sat smiling and pudgy faced, his silver hair fashionably disheveled. The audience itself was made up of pink-faced men in business suits, with a few bearded students here and there. It was a quiet and attentive audience when the issue of tuition finally came up.

Chairman Smith, beginning the discussion with a few inconsequential remarks, played idly with a rubber band during the debate, frowning whenever objections were raised. Most of the Regents had little to say about the proposed increase in student tuition except "yes" when the time came to vote. Nevertheless, some of the more liberal members did come up with a few objections. Dutton, blunt and accusing, interrupted Hitch at one point to say, "Mr. President, I would like to say that those are just generalizations and platitudes. . . . Yesterday we were discussing increasing our expenditures on cement; but consideration of students' monetary problems always comes in last. . . . The institutional burden of fees always falls on middle- and lower-income students." Hitch, who was Robert McNamara's Assistant Secretary of Defense from 1961 to 1964 before succeeding Clark Kerr as president of the University, replied calmly, his slow syllables evenly spaced. Calling upon a succession of University vice-presidents who jumped up to make reports, he entertained droning questions from several of the Regents—duck-voiced W. Glenn Campbell of the prestigious Hoover Institute on War, Revolution, and Peace; Elinor Heller; and several others. Testimony was then presented by one of several student body presidents attending the meeting, urging the Regents emphatically not to support the proposed tuition increase. The Regents listened politely, thanked him for his opinion, and then prepared to vote. At this point Norton Simon broke in again, referring to the "illegal procedures" at Irvine, pointing out that the federal government is considering prosecuting the Irvine Foundation for ecological damage to the Pacific coastline, and ending by exclaiming, "No wonder the students have to pay increased fees—we have to take care of too many companies, too many corporations, too many wealthy individuals." It is only ironic that millionaire Simon should have been the one to say this.

When the roll call vote came to Reagan, with the proposal winning by an overwhelming margin, the governor smiled, paused, and then commented: "Since the bill will come to me eventually, I'll abstain." His comment was greeted with general laughter—and students now pay $4 million a year additional tuition for the privilege of acquiring an education at the University of California.

The Regents' Powers

The decision to fire Angela Davis in 1969 came neither from her fellow faculty members nor from the administration, but from the Regents of the University of California. The final decision to change from the semester system to the quarter system in the early 1960s came not from faculty, students, or the campus community at large, but from the Regents, in direct opposition to the expressed wishes of all seven of the campus-based faculty organizations then functioning. Similarly, the decision to keep ROTC on campus a few years ago came from the Regents. Ultimate power over the University of California and its nine campuses resides, in fact and in law, in the hands of the twenty-two men and two women who make up the Board of Regents.

At the height of the Free Speech Movement in 1964, Edward Carter, then chairman of the Regents, issued the following statement outlining the powers of the Board: "The Constitution of the State of California clearly charges the Regents with full and ultimate authority for conducting the affairs of the University of California. This they exercise principally through their appointed administrative officers and by delegation of certain specific but revocable powers to properly constituted academic bodies."[4] Thus the Regents' sphere of influence extends from the smallest details of administrative concern to the largest questions confronting the University. It is within their power to cancel a rally or raise tuition, to fire a professor or increase University complicity in war research. Moreover, although they don't make administrative decisions for the University on a day-to-day basis, they nonetheless do have the power to choose the men who make those decisions. The president and vice-presidents of the University, the chancellors, and so on, are little more than the "administrative lieutenants" of the Regents, chosen by them and ultimately responsible to them.[5] As Thorstein Veblen pointed out, "The academic head [of the University] commonly holds office by choice of the governing board. Where the power of appointment lies freely in the discretion of such a board, the board will create an academic head in its own image."[6]

According to Vernon Stadtman, the official historian of the University, the Regents have "near-absolute power": "With this near-absolute power," he argues, "the Regents can and do alter the size and mission of the University in response to the needs of the state and the growth of knowledge. None of the University's remarkable expansion, nor any of its distinction in diverse endeavors, could have been achieved without Regental consent. Much of it occurred through Regental initiative."[7] An analysis of this kind, however, ascribing final power over the University to the Regents, flies directly in the face of the now popular argument advanced most articulately by David Riesman and Christopher Jencks in their recent book, *The Academic Revolution.* In this work; Riesman and Jencks describe what they contend is the true "academic revolution" of recent times—"the rise to power of the academic profession."[8] No longer is power concentrated primarily in the hands of university trustees, they argue; in fact, the opposite is true. According to their hypothesis, teachers now rule and trustees play an "increasingly ceremonial role" in running the universities.

This argument deserves our further attention for at least two reasons: first, because it is, to my knowledge, the only major argument so far advanced denying the fundamental power and importance of university trustees; and second, because it has been accepted by many critics of higher education. It is thus necessary for us to assess its validity.

Riesman and Jencks argue their case with a surprising lack of confidence and enthusiasm. Yielding few new insights or understandings, their equivocating and frequently contradictory arguments are neither rigorous nor grounded in historical data. Intending to convince us of the truth of their viewpoint, they end by doing the opposite.

They begin by declaring that in the early years of the century many battles were fought between trustees and faculties over "the shape of the curriculum, the content of particular courses, or the use of particular books. The professors (for instance, Veblen) lost most of the publicized battles, but they won the war. Today faculty control over these matters is rarely challenged, and conflict usually centers on other issues."[9]

This is their key thesis. They support it in the following manner: "The faculty, for example, have sought the right to choose their colleagues. While they have not usually won this right in the formal sense of actually making appointments themselves, their recommendations are sought at all reputable colleges and universities, and heeded in nine cases out of ten. Faculty committees are, it is true, sometimes overruled." They continue: "As long as faculty members stick to problems defined by their disciplines, they almost never run into public controversy except in the most provincial milieus. And while administrators or trustees sometimes reject faculty recommendations, they almost never foist their own candidates on an unwilling faculty."[10]

Concretely, what real powers do faculty members have? Riesman and Jencks answer, grimly oblivious to the ripening contradictions in their analysis: "College professors," they argue, "have not for the most part won significant *formal* power, either individually or collectively, over the institutions that employ them. On paper the typical academic senate is still a largely advisory body whose legal jurisdiction is confined to setting the curriculum and awarding degrees.

Departments, too, have little *formal* power except sometimes over course offerings and requirements. Budgets and personnel, for example, are in principle subject to 'higher' review, and ultimate control mostly remains where it has always been—with the administration, the lay trustees, and in some cases the legislature."[11]

With "formal power" and "ultimate control" still vested in the higher authorities, what power remains in the hands of the faculty? After this much has been said, are we still to believe that teachers rule? In their attempt to worm their way out of this dilemma, Riesman and Jencks unwittingly deal a fatal blow to their theory. They say: "The trustees, however, are seldom what they once were. Most are more permissive than their nineteenth- or early twentieth-century predecessors."[12] In other words, faculty members have power because the trustees *permit* them to control certain aspects of teaching and administration! Insofar as they conform to the desires of the trustees, faculty members are allowed to participate in lower-level decision-making. Insofar as they stick to their disciplines and leave the waters of controversy untroubled, their advice will be respected and even heeded. This, in short, is the fabled "academic revolution." It is on the basis of this analysis that Riesman and Jencks conclude, with a muffled clash of cymbals, that "those with access to public or private money still throw their weight around at times. But the overall trend seems to us toward moderation and an increasingly ceremonial role for trustees."[13]

If this analysis appears facile and unconvincing in general, it is even less convincing when one considers the University of California in particular. James Benet, a journalist who has spent fourteen years covering Regents' meetings for various publications, comments that "the Regents have neither hesitated nor found it difficult to move into any of the areas supposedly barred to them." He cites numerous Regental wishes forcibly imposed on student and faculty constituencies, including one striking instance in which faculty members made a concerted effort to place a single, non-voting representative on the Board. "The Board rejected this proposal without the slightest appearance of anxiety over faculty wrath. And finally, the Regents rejected a mild proposal that the President of the University might be permitted to decide how much students should be allowed to participate in departmental meetings, thus barring any student participation at all." Benet provisionally concludes that "if these constituencies or the university administrators really had substantial power, one might have expected it to be demonstrated during such episodes. In fact, however, all these groups have been impotent in the face of Regents' decisions. . . . We cannot agree, therefore, with the statement of Jencks and Riesman that 'the overall trend seems to us toward moderation and an increasingly ceremonial role for the trustees' . . . [for] the Regents are tenaciously resisting any lessening of their power."[14]

A Collective Portrait

What kind of people become Regents, and *how* do they become Regents? Are they representative of the community at large, or do they represent special interests? Are they rich or poor? Racially and sexually balanced, or exclusive? Radical, liberal, or conservative?

Answers to these questions are not hard to find. Each of the two women on the Board is known by her husband's name and one of them, Mrs. Edward Heller, was appointed to the Board on the death of her husband, a Regent before her. Twenty-three of the twenty-four regents are white. The one black member, Wilson Riles, is an ex-officio member; he is on the Board only because he is the elected State Superintendent of Public Instruction. He is also the first non-white member of the Board in history. With the exception of the four ex-officio members on the Board (Reagan, Lt. Gov. Ed Reinecke, State Assembly Speaker Bob Moretti, and Riles) and University President Charles Hitch, each of the Regents was appointed by a governor of California. With the exception of two interim Regents, each serving two-year appointments, all are full-term Regents serving sixteen-year appointments. Their median age is approximately sixty; the youngest full-term Regent is forty-seven, the oldest is sixty-eight.

Nor is there any doubt about the economic status of the Regents: some are staggeringly wealthy—at least ten are millionaires—and all are extremely well off. According to a study conducted by the American Association of Universities, the median annual income of university trustees in general is $50-75,000, and the Regents of the University of California are among the crème de la crème of university trustees.[15] Where does this vast wealth come from?

On the whole, it comes from the Regents' extensive corporate holdings and consequent powerful positions in the economy. Twenty Regents (excluding the four ex-officio politicians on the Board) sit on a total of sixty corporate boards —an average of three apiece. These corporations include Western Bancorporation, the nation's largest bank holding company, with twenty-three subsidiaries and over $11 billion in assets; Crocker-Citizens National Bank, the nation's twelfth largest; United California Bank, the nation's fifteenth largest; the Stanford Bancorporation, which is affiliated with Union Bank, the nation's twenty-second largest; American Telephone and Telegraph; Pacific Telephone and Telegraph; Broadway-Hale Stores, one of the nation's largest department store chains—Emporium-Capwells and Neiman-Marcus are two of its subsidiaries; Western Airlines; Pacific Lighting Corporation, "the largest gas sytem in the country, with over three million meters in homes and industry"; Crocker National Corporation; Southern California Edison Company; Pacific Mutual Life Insurance; Del Monte, Inc.; Northern

Pacific Railway; Fibreboard Corporation; Lockheed Aircraft, the nation's top defense contractor; the Los Angeles Rams; the California Angels; Pauley Petroleum, Inc., owned by Regent Edwin Pauley; the gigantic Norton Simon, Inc. (owned by Regent Norton Simon), which controls Hunt & Wesson Foods, the McCall Corporation, Canada Dry, and Glass Containers Corporation; Moore Investment Company, owned by Regent Joseph Moore; Watkins-Johnson Company, co-owned by Regent Dean Watkins; Matson Navigation, owned by Regent William Matson Roth's family; the Hearst Corporation—which owns nine newspapers, four radio and television stations, Avon Books, and numerous national magazines, such as *Good Housekeeping, Popular Mechanics,* etc.—owned by Regent Catherine Hearst's family; and so on, over the course of a list spanning thirty-six additional corporations.

The Regents have numerous connections with one another outside the Board. Regents Moore, Smith, and Roth are on the board of Crocker-Citizens National Bank. Regents Simon and Roth and former U.C. Berkeley Chancellor Roger Heyns and former U.C.L.A. Chancellor Franklin Murphy are all on the board of Norton Simon, Inc. Regents Carter and Moore both sit on the board of Emporium-Capwells Stores. Regents Watkins and Heller are both on the board of Stanford Bank. There are indirect connections as well: Regent Smith is a director of the Pacific Lighting Corporation, along with Regent Carter's Broadway-Hale partner Prentis Cobb Hale. These examples could be multiplied almost endlessly. The facts speak for themselves: (1) most of the Regents belong to an interlocking directorate of corporate wealth and power that exercises immense influence on the state and, to a lesser extent, on the nation; and (2) their relationships with one another flow through many channels and cross many shining tables in addition to those of the Board of Regents of the University of California.

The Regents' collective story does not end with the enumeration of their corporate holdings. They also exercise a pervasive and continuing influence on society through their "charitable" activities. Edward Carter is a director of the Irvine Foundation (which controls a large percentage of the real estate in Orange County) and is also on the board of directors of the Defense Department-affiliated Stanford Research Institute, the Brookings Institute, and the extremely important Council for Financial Aid to Education.[16] He is president of the Santa Anita Foundation and a member of the powerful Committee for Economic Development.[17] He is chairman of the Los Angeles Art Museum, a trustee of Occidental College, an advisor to the Stanford, Harvard, and U.C.L.A. business schools, and a director of the San Francisco Opera Association. Other Regents include two additional members of the Committee on Economic Development; one member of the enormously important Council on Foreign Relations;[18] one member of the Carnegie Commission on Higher Education, of which former U.C. President Clark Kerr is chairman; the director of the Hoover Institute on War, Revolution, and Peace; one member of the National Association of Manufacturers; a trustee for the Institute of Defense Analysis, which is formally linked to the Defense Department; a fellow at Harvard; a trustee for the Institute of Advanced Study at Princeton; a trustee of Reed College; a trustee of the Carnegie Institution; a member of the San Francisco Chamber of Commerce; a member of the San Francisco Board of Education; the chairman of the San Francisco Planning and Urban Renewal Commission; the president of the San Francisco Museum of Art; two directors of the San Francisco-area educational television station, KQED; one trustee of the Los Angeles County Zoo; one director of the Cancer Research Institute; trustees of four hospitals and three museums; the director of the John F. Kennedy Memorial Library; the winner of the 1961 "Industrialist of the Year" award; a director of the Girl Scouts; and so on, apparently without end. There is almost no important institution not connected in some way with one or more of the Regents.

Politically, the Regents are highly conservative. Norton Simon, one of the few "liberals" on the Board, is a Republican. Most of the other Regents are generally in political sympathy with ex-officio Regent Ronald Reagan. Frederick G. Dutton, probably the most liberal of the Regents, was executive director of the platform committee at the 1964 Democratic National Convention which nominated Lyndon Johnson. Dutton was subsequently director of research and planning for Johnson's presidential campaign. Previously, he had been an advisor to President Kennedy and secretary to the Cabinet, and more recently he was a member of the inner circle of McGovern advisors. Many other Regents have also been powerful figures in state and national politics. Edwin Pauley, for example, has been described as the "hulking old man who ran Harry Truman's campaign in 1948."[19] William Matson Roth was a special representative of the White House for trade negotiations from 1963 to 1969. Elinor Heller is a former member of the National Executive Committee of the Democratic Party. Joseph Alexander Moore, Jr., was a member of the Republican National Finance Committee in 1953. William Coblentz has been, among other things, special counsel to the Governor of California. Moreover, Coblentz and Roth were co-directors of the Muskie for President campaign in California in 1971-72, and Roth entered the 1974 California gubernatorial race in 1973. Wesley Glenn Campbell is a member of a White House Presidential Committee and a former advisor to the Senate. John H. Lawrence has been a consultant to the Atomic Energy Commission, which was headed until recently by former U.C. Chancellor Glenn Seaborg.

And so it goes. This partial list, which doesn't even include the political activities and positions of the four professional politicians on the Board, indicates the kinds of political activities engaged in by the Regents. Given these activities, it's no surprise that the Regents are consistently conservative in defining and setting University policy. For, as Hubert Beck pointed out a generation ago, "Boards whose members have high stakes in the existing economic and social system can hardly be expected to approve educational or social adjustments that aim at basic or major reforms as contrasted with those that are palliative in nature; neither can they be expected to support any other approach to these issues than the traditionally conservative one for which they are famous."[20]

Socially the Regents belong to a thin upper crust of wealth and prestige. Several Regents are listed in the *Social Register.* All except multimillionaire Norton Simon are college graduates, and they graduated from the best schools: eight attended the University of California, four Harvard, three Yale, three Stanford, two Occidental, one Oxford, one Duke, one Mills, and one DePauw. They belong to a total of thirty-nine "society" clubs, including the ultra-exclusive Los Angeles Country Club (two Regents are members), the Bel Air Bay Club (two members), the California Club (one member), and the Burlingame Country Club (four members). The Bohemian and Pacific Union clubs of San Francisco are probably the two most exclusive clubs in Northern California. Six Regents belong to the Bohemian Club. The Pacific Union, which is considered to be a cut above the Bohemian and is, according to G. William Domhoff, among the twenty most exclusive clubs in the country, has four Regents as members.

The Regents, then, are people not only of great wealth but of great power, socially, economically, and politically. Having thus demonstrated that they belong to a select group of men who occupy the highest positions in our economic and political life as well as control our universities, we have gone a long way toward proving that the Regents are a segment of the ruling class. Now we must show that the Regents are not atypical of college trustees in general. When that is accomplished, we will at least tentatively have established that college trustees are a part of the ruling class: an identifiable group of men who control the major institutions in our society, from the corporations to the universities, and who benefit from the continued existence of corporate capitalism and the oppressive social relations capitalism generates and requires. We will then need to discuss why the ruling class needs control of the universities and how it got such control.

Notes

1. All facts and figures in this chapter are for September 17, 1971, the time of the Regents meeting.

2. Most data about the Regents in this chapter are from *Standard and Poor's Industrial Index, Who's Who, Who's Who in the West,* and similar publications.

3. James Benet, "California's Regents: Window on the Ruling Class," *Change,* February 1972, p. 21. Also, see the book prepared for the Parke-Benet Galleries auction of May 7-8, 1972, "Property of the Norton Simon Foundation (Chinese Porcelain, Italian Majolica, European Porcelain, Works of Art, Decorations, Furniture, Paintings, Carpets & Tapestries, and Old Master Drawings and Paintings from the private collection of Norton Simon)."

4. Cited in the official history by Vernon Stadtman, *The University of California, 1868-1968* (New York: McGraw Hill, 1970), p. 464.

5. Troy Duster, "The Aims of Higher Learning and the Control of the Universities," University of California, Berkeley, booklet (n.d.), p. 5.

6. Thorstein Veblen, *The Higher Learning in America* (New York: B. W. Huebsch, 1918), p. 59.

7. Stadtman, op. cit., p. 501.

8. David Riesman and Christopher Jencks, *The Academic Revolution* (New York: Doubleday, 1968), p. xvi.

9. Ibid., p. 15.

10. Ibid.

11. Ibid., p. 16 (emphasis added).

12. Ibid., pp. 15-16.

13. Ibid., p. 16.

14. Benet, op. cit., pp. 26-27.

15. Ibid., p. 23.

16. See chapter 6 for the full story of the CFAE.

17. According to G. William Domhoff, the CED has been instrumental in shaping national foreign policy. Its members, who are "expressly limited to businessmen and implicitly to representatives of the biggest and most important corporations in the country," have originated many aspects of American foreign policy, including parts of the Marshall Plan, and have included among their ranks thirty-eight men who have served important governmental roles, some at the Cabinet level (such as Charles E. Wilson, who was Eisenhower's secretary of Defense after being president of General Electric). Three Regents are members of the CED, and University of California Vice-President John Perkins is a fourth member. G. William Domhoff, "Who Made American Foreign Policy? 1945-1963," in *Corporations and the Cold War,* ed. David Horowitz (New York: Monthly Review Press, 1969).

18. For detailed information on the CFR, see Domhoff, op. cit., pp. 28-36.

19. James Ridgeway, *The Closed Corporation* (New York: Random House, 1968), p. 139.

20. H. P. Beck, *Men Who Control Our Universities* (New York: King's Crown Press, 1947), p. 145.

2
The Ruling Class

Americans do not trust their money to a lot of professors and principals. . . . Americans put their money under the control of business men at the head of the Universities."[1]

Andrew Carnegie

The Regents of the University of California, with their vast economic power, their significant political influence, and their social prominence, are not atypical of the trustees of most major colleges. The majority of college trustees throughout the nation are financially powerful, politically influential, socially prominent, old, white, male, and Protestant. The trustees and regents of the major universities are even richer, more conservative, and more powerful than their counterparts among the trustees of lesser colleges, and, because of their greater importance, are more tightly integrated in the military-industrial web of modern capitalism. These assertions are neither arbitrary nor unfounded; each of them is borne out by the three major studies of this question conducted so far.

Beck's Findings

In 1947, Hubert Beck published the results of an exhaustive study of the social composition and economic status of the boards of trustees of the thirty "largest, richest, and most respected" universities in the nation.[2] The year he chose to examine was 1934-35; the conclusions he reached were unequivocal.

1. An Examination of Earlier Studies. Beck began his study by examining the results of three earlier, less extensive investigations conducted by Scott Nearing, Evans Clark, and J. A. Leighton.[3] In 1917 Nearing had concluded that "college and university boards are almost completely dominated by merchants, manufacturers, capitalists, corporation officials, bankers, doctors, lawyers, educators, and ministers. These nine occupations contain a total of 1,936 persons, nearly four-fifths of the total number of trustees. . . . A new term must be coined to suggest the idea of an educational system owned and largely supported by the people but dominated by the business world."[4] In 1923 Clark reached essentially the same conclusion: "We have allowed the education of our youth to fall into the absolute control of a group of men who represent not only a minority of the total population but have, at the same time, enormous economic and business stakes in what kind of an education it shall be."[5] Leighton, a leading member of the American Association of University Professors, provided further empirical support for this position when in 1920 he conducted a study of the twenty-five leading universities. "Boards of trustees," he concluded, "are composed chiefly of members of the vested interests and the professions—bankers, manufacturers, commercial magnates, lawyers, physicians, and clergymen. It is a somewhat rare thing to find on a board a representative of either the teaching profession or scientific research. Still rarer to find a representative of the industrial workers!"[6] Beck, although by no means a radical, found that the results of his own study thoroughly and dramatically confirmed these earlier conclusions.

2. **Age, Race, Sex, Religion.**[7] After analyzing biographical data on more than seven hundred trustees, Beck found that in 1934 their median age was fifty-nine (almost exactly the same as the current median age of the Regents). Only 4 percent of the trustees Beck studied were under forty years of age; 78 percent were fifty or older and almost half were over sixty. Moreover, the older trustees held a disproportionately large number of the leading positions on the boards examined. Roughly 97 percent of the trustees were men—and "no indication was found that any of these boards included a Negro member." Only 5 percent of the trustees studied had not progressed beyond high school in their education—in striking contrast to the more than 89 percent of the general population at that time which had not gone beyond high school. Eighty-seven percent of the trustees studied were Protestant—"an overwhelming majority," in Beck's words. Catholics constituted as much as 11 percent of the total primarily because Catholic University was included in the study; 70 percent of all the Catholic trustees examined were from Catholic University. A fraction over 1 percent of the trustees were Jewish—yet fully 43 percent of the total number belonged to two relatively small Protestant denominations (the Episcopalian and Presbyterian churches) which, combined, totaled only 7 percent of the general population at the time.

Why was this the case? Eduard Lindeman, in his book *Wealth and Culture,* explains: "Where there is no state church the various economic classes distribute themselves among religious bodies according to a class-conscious principle. In one sense, therefore, church affiliation, in our society, constitutes an index of class structure. In most American communities, for example, the Episcopal and Presbyterian Churches represent wealth and privilege."[8] This, however, is only indirect proof of the wealth and power of the university trustees of the period. Far more direct proof can be found in the data Beck collected on the economic status of the trustees: their occupations, earnings, and links with big business.

3. Income. Beck found that in 1924, the only year for which relatively complete data could be found, "the average income of those with known taxable incomes" was $102,000 and "the average salary of others with known salaries" was $49,000. Unfortunately, the incomes for several hundred of the trustees could not be determined, but even if these are assumed to have been zero, the average annual income for the 734 trustees would still have been $35,000—in a year in which the average worker earned $1,563! Furthermore, in 1934, at the height of the depression, the trustees' average income was approximately $61,000—at a time when the average worker's income was $1,000 a year and the breadlines were miles long and growing longer.[9] University trustees were *sixty times as well off as the average worker* in 1934!

But more than that: in 1924, according to Beck, people with taxable million-dollar incomes were at least 1800 times as common among university trustees as among all "gainful workers." The same ratio was found for people with yearly incomes of over $500,000. Moreover, of all trustees examined in Beck's study, 7.5 percent had annual incomes above $100,000—a 600:1 ratio in terms of the general population. Even government statistics of the period verify that trustees and their families belonged to a wafer-thin layer at the top of the upper crust of wealth and power. The upper 1 percent of families in 1935-36 earned $10,000 or more, the upper 0.5 percent earned an average of $15,000; and only 0.1 percent of the nation's families—one one-thousandth—earned $35,000 a year; yet the trustees earned considerably more. Their income, in other words, clearly placed them at the top of the economic pyramid. Where did this wealth come from?

4. Occupation.[10] A decisive majority of the trustees Beck studied had significant connections with big business. Bankers, brokers, and financiers constituted 15.4 percent of the trustees surveyed. "In disproportionately large numbers, bankers from the great nationally prominent banks had been selected." At the California Institute of Technology, 39 percent of the trustees were bankers or financiers, and at fourteen of the thirty universities studied, bankers comprised 10 percent or more of the board of trustees. All told, bankers were found to be "53 times as prominent numerically on these 30 boards as among the general working population." In the realm of industry, "manufacturing entrepreneurs and executives—the owners and officials—were equally as prominent on the boards of these 30 leading universities as were the bankers and financiers." Comprising 15.5 percent of the membership of the boards studied, these "captains of industry" had a proportional representation forty-four times greater than their percentage of the total population. "Within this manufacturing group," Beck adds, "owners were about three times as numerous as officials." Moreover, "The enterprises represented were usually large and powerful. They included, for example, United States Steel, du Pont, General Electric and General Motors." Other kinds of businessmen—insurance officials, real estate agents, etc.—comprised 10.6 percent of the membership of the boards of trustees.

Together, bankers, industrialists, and miscellaneous businessmen constituted 41.5 percent of the total number of trustees studied. Lawyers and judges, comprising 25 percent of all university trustees, were the single largest occupational group on the boards, "125 times as numerous" on boards of trustees as they were in the general population. Beck and several other early students of power relations in the university (most notably George S. Counts and Earl J. McGrath[11]) considered lawyers to be an integral part of the business establishment whose interests and social outlook paralleled that of businessmen. McGrath in particular—after establishing, in his 1936 study of the question, that businessmen constituted 52.2 percent of the trustees of the twenty leading universities, with lawyers comprising 21.5 percent—concluded that ". . . the control of higher education in America, both public and private, has been placed in the hands of a small group of the population, namely, financiers and businessmen. From two-thirds to three-fourths of the persons on these boards in recent decades have been selected from this group. It is fair to include the lawyers among this group," he states, "because the biographical material examined indicates that, especially in recent years, a majority of these lawyers have been associated with large corporations; indeed, in many instances they have been presidents or directors of such organizations."[12]

Beck's findings confirm this statement. Close to 50 percent of the lawyers and other professionals on the boards of trustees at the time of his study were also officers or directors of business enterprises, and roughly 15 percent of them "were officers or directors of one or more of the 400 largest corporations in the nation." Beck emphasizes the significance of these percentages by commenting that "the businessmen, the bankers, and the lawyers together constituted such a high percentage of total board membership [during the period 1860 to 1930] that by acting in concert they readily could have controlled most board decisions throughout this period."

Bankers, industrialists, and lawyers thus comprised 66.5 percent of the trustees Beck placed under scrutiny in his definitive study. That still leaves almost a third of the trustees unaccounted for. What did they do for a living?

The largest remaining occupational group of trustees consisted of "professionals" (doctors, editors, engineers, etc.), who comprised 11.8 percent of the trustees and whose interests were identified by Beck and McGrath with the business sector in much the same way the lawyers' interests were. Clergymen, the largest single group of trustees during the seventeenth and eighteenth centuries and most of the nineteenth century, constituted only 6.6 percent of the trustees in 1934 and were concentrated almost entirely on the boards of Catholic universities. Politicians comprised 4.9 percent of the trustees, while only 4.6 of the trustees could be considered "educators" in any legitimate sense of the word. Housewives, comprising "36.6 percent of the workers of the nation,"[13] constituted a minute fraction of university trustees: 1.6 percent *in toto*, and only 0.2 percent of the membership of the boards of private universities. Farmers and representatives of agricultural interests were allocated only 1 percent of the seats on governing boards. "All other occupational groups in the nation" were, in Beck's words, "*completely* without direct representation on these thirty boards." In other words, the white- and blue-collar working class was *totally* unrepresented on the governing boards of the universities; and students, the basic constituency of the university system, were equally powerless.

Beck concludes his presentation by underscoring some of his major theses, pointing out that "In all probability, these facts greatly understate the dominance of business leaders on these boards, for at least 47 percent of the trustees classed as professional persons were also officers or directors of business enterprises. . . ."

If we combine the governing-board representation of housewives, farmers, workers, and students, we get a total of 2.6 percent representation for "91.5 percent of the nation's workers." Diagrammatically, this appears as follows:

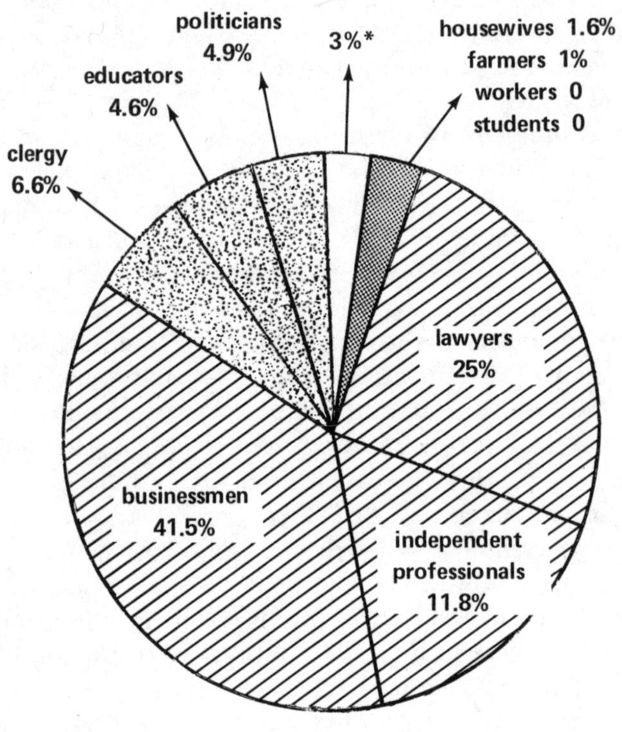

Figures based on Beck, who determined these categories.

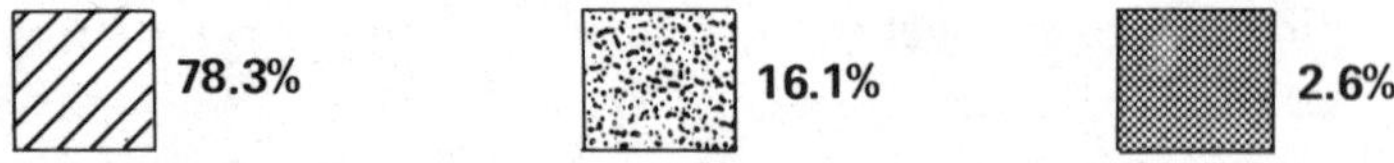

* For a small percentage of the respondents, Beck was unable to assign occupational categories.

Three further points must be made: first, that the businessmen running the university system in Beck's time were not only capitalists but the biggest capitalists; second, that they formed an interlocking directorate with interlocking class interests; and third, that Beck's data and conclusions have not grown outdated in the interval from 1935 to 1972. These three points will now be dealt with and established.

5. **Big Business.**[14] Beck measured the trustees he studied against a list of the four hundred largest industrial and financial corporations in the nation. With a note of awe, he points out that "The magnitude of the 400 largest businesses . . . is almost beyond comprehension." Citing Berle's and Means's classic study of the modern corporation,[15] Beck shows that in 1932 "the 200 largest non-banking corporations controlled . . . nearly half of all the corporate wealth in the United States."

In fact, industry and finance in the United States have been highly concentrated throughout the twentieth century. Lenin, in his superb 1916 study *Imperialism,* singled out the United States as the advanced capitalist country in which the process of concentration and monopoly formation was occurring at the greatest rate. In 1909, he showed, "Almost half the total production of all the enterprises of the country was carried on by a *hundredth part* of those enterprises! These 3,000 giant enterprises embrace 268 branches of industry. From this it can be seen that, at a certain stage of its development, concentration itself . . . leads right to monopoly."[16] By the 1930s, corporate wealth and power in the United States had become concentrated in a very small number of hands and monopolies had arisen in most major fields of production. Big businesses had become almost fully separate from smaller enterprises and dominant over them. This process has continued unabated to the present.[17]

In chapter 9 of his book, Beck presents an array of facts and figures proving conclusively that the trustees of the thirty leading universities were thoroughly immersed in the world of big business. In the next few pages I will summarize the major facts Beck presents and discuss the significance of those facts. They are truly impressive as indications of the ruling-class nature of university governing boards.

Beck found that 66 percent of the seven hundred trustees studied held at least one leading business office or directorship. Over half held at least two such positions, and fully 40 percent held three or more. "No evidence was found to indicate that the other 34 percent held any leading business office or directorship, but full biographical facts probably would have revealed scattered connections even for these trustees."

All told, the seven hundred trustees held 2,656 leading business positions, an average of almost four per trustee. The 40 percent who held more than three apiece "averaged slightly over 8 such positions in as many different business firms." Forty-seven percent of the 171 trustees Beck classified as "professionals" held a total of 576 business offices. "If professional trustees with such major business connections had been classified as proprietors, managers, and officials—as might have been appropriate—the percent in this category would have been swelled to 71."

Close to half of the four hundred leading business enterprises had representatives on the governing boards of the universities Beck studied, a total of 175 men representing 194 corporations. These 175 men—a quarter of the trustees studied—held only 50 percent of the trustees' total number of business positions, despite the fact that they averaged 7.5 business positions apiece. This clearly indicates that a large proportion of the other 75 percent of trustees studied were deeply immersed in the business world.

"Forty-six percent of the governing board members were found to hold offices or directorships, or both, in one or more . . . financial institutions." Almost a third held two or more such positions, and 16 percent held three or more. Of the two hundred largest financial corporations in the country, half of the banks and life insurance companies (and a third of all other financial institutions) had representatives among the trustees of these thirty leading universities.

A similar story can be told about the large public utility enterprises. Twenty percent of the seven hundred trustees held leading positions in such firms, occupying a total of 456 offices or directorships. Over one hundred of these positions "were held in the 96 public-utility organizations classified among the 400 largest business organizations in the country . . . 54 percent of the railroads, 49 percent of the power companies, and 60 percent of the communication companies in this select list of mammoth enterprises" had representatives among the governing board members of the thirty leading universities.

Fully half of the 734 trustees were officers or directors of an "industrial, non-financial firm." One-third held two directorships and one-fourth of the trustees held at least three major positions. "Ninety-five offices or directorships among the 104 colossal" industrial firms included in the list of the nation's four hundred leading corporations "were occupied by men who were also trustees of these universities."

As Beck concludes, "Altogether, the evidence of major university-business connections at high levels seems overwhelming. The numerous high positions of power in industry, commerce, and finance held by at least two-thirds of the members of the governing boards of these 30 leading universities would appear to give a decisive majority [of the trustees] more than ample grounds for identifying their personal interests with those of business."

Andrew Carnegie once said that the man of wealth should be the "agent or trustee of his poorer brethren."[18] Surely this was more than fulfilled in the context of the system of American higher education that existed during the 1930s. Can the same be said about the present?

Table 1

Firms	*Representatives*
U.S. Steel Corporation	3 officials, including the chairman of the board
The du Pont Company	5 directors, including the president and 3 du Ponts
General Electric Company	6 officials, including the president
International Harvester Company	5 directors, including the chairman of the board
General Motors Corporation	5 directors, including the president and chairman of the board
United Fruit Company	4 officials, including the president
Kennecott Copper Company	3 directors

Data from *Standard and Poor's Industrial Index* and *Who's Who in America.*

Duster's Findings

Almost twenty years after Beck's seminal study was published and thirty years after his target year 1934-35 had passed, Troy Duster of the University of California conducted a study very similar to Beck's designed to retest the validity of Beck's thesis and to supplement his findings with new data derived from the years 1965 and 1966.[19]

The numerical response to Duster's questionnaire was almost identical to that of Beck's. Duster received 306 completed questionnaires, out of 726 mailed; Beck had received 301 of 734 mailed.* The median age of the trustees responding to Duster's questionnaire was sixty—the same as the median age of the Regents. Their average income was between $50,000 and $75,000—comparable to the average income of the Regents, as well as to that of the trustees examined in Beck's earlier study. In terms of occupation and social status, Duster found that: "In this sample of 306, there was one labor official, but not a single working-class occupation was represented. There was one Negro, eight clergymen and ten professors. The remainder were white, in secular and successful business enterprise, and as expected, not professionally connected with higher learning." The point is unmistakable. As Duster declares, ". . . it is fair to conclude that Veblen and Beck were correct. . . ."

Unfortunately, Duster has not written as complete an account of his findings as Beck did; nevertheless, he indicates unequivocally that the trends present in Beck's day are more

* Although this might seem a low rate of return, Beck also studied all nonrespondents and Duster studied a significant sample of the nonrespondents. They found that they differed from the respondents only minimally; they were generally older (with a median age of almost seventy) and richer; "more skewed in the direction of business affiliations and related occupations" (Duster).

than characteristic of the present. Big businessmen control the major universities now as before. But Duster is unwilling to leave it at that. Beck had surmised that these representatives of corporate power would act in their own private interest as the trustees of major colleges. To test that surmise, Duster included a survey of political and social attitudes in his study. The results were revealing (if not altogether surprising).

On religious questions, fewer than 20 percent of the trustees disapproved of complete academic freedom. On political questions, over 33 percent of the trustees "expressed their disapproval of full academic freedom." The percentage of trustees unwilling to permit full academic freedom on political questions was strikingly higher at public universities (such as the University of California) than at private universities. Fully 44 percent of the trustees at public colleges stated that they would deny instructors "the right, without fear of being fired, to hold and express publicly any political position (including neo-fascist, socialist, or communist)" *even if* "the classroom is not used as a forum for the expression of those views."

Veblen long ago contended that university trustees were guided internally by what he called the "business ethic" and that they viewed the university simply as a business to be run. Although this contention was simplistic, in view of the extremely complex and subtle role played by universities in American society, Duster's data nonetheless confirms that fully a third of the trustees of major colleges endorse the statement ". . . a university is best conducted along the same principles of organization and output as a business enterprise." A striking additional fact came to light in Duster's study: "*Forty percent* of those with a business ethic believe there to be *too much* academic freedom in the United States, while only *five percent* of those without the business ideology for the university responded in this manner" (emphasis in original).

Commenting that "restriction in the forums of expression is an essential ingredient in the control of ideas," Duster points out that "an overwhelming majority of trustees support the position that the administration [and the administration alone, as agents of the trustees] should determine who shall or shall not be allowed to speak on campus." Less than a quarter of the trustees felt that even the faculty should be allowed to share this power in any way; no mention whatsoever was made of the students. Behind these beliefs, of course, lies the implicit assumption that campus speakers *should* be censored.

Duster's questionnaire was distributed while the Berkeley Free Speech Movement of 1964 was "still simmering," thus enabling him to ask the trustees what "they would have done" if they had been Regents. Ninety-seven percent of the trustees agreed that the regulations governing student political activity should not be liberalized and that the administration should not be censured for its repressive handling of the situation. "The power to hire and fire the faculty [is] a critical issue of control, and the trustees overwhelmingly place this power in the hands of the administration." Thus, their theory is consistent with their practice and their place in society. College trustees subscribe to the profit-oriented philosophy of control that one would expect from representatives of the ruling class. In short, Veblen's theoretical argument about business-minded men in control of the universities turns out to have strong empirical support.

Rauh's Findings

In 1968, Morton A. Rauh, vice president for finance at Antioch College, conducted a vast study of the eleven thousand college trustees in the United States.[20] Although Rauh's perspective was radically different from that of Beck and Duster in that he studied all trustees indiscriminately, his conclusions–based on a massive accumulation of fresh data contained in five thousand questionnaires–were very similar to theirs.

Taking into account the fact that the trustees of innumerable public and private junior colleges, Catholic institutions, etc., were included in his study, along with the trustees of more powerful colleges and universities, Rauh's conclusions are fully consistent with those of Beck and Duster. "Trustees," Rauh shows, "are predominantly male–taking all trustees combined [including those of women's colleges] 86 percent are men." Furthermore, over two-thirds of all trustees are fifty years old or older; 27 percent are over sixty and 9 percent are over seventy, while only 5 percent are under forty. In addition, "Trustees are predominantly white–taking all trustees combined [including those of black colleges], only 1.3 percent are Negro." Seventy-five percent of all trustees are Protestant (including those of Catholic colleges). Eighty-three percent of all trustees hold a bachelor's degree or higher. Fifty-eight percent are Republicans and 33 percent Democrats,* while 61 percent consider themselves "moderates," 21 percent conservatives, and only 15 percent liberals. Governor Rockefeller and President Nixon were the politicians most admired by trustees nationwide; Governor (and Regent) Reagan was the fourth most popular. Thirty-four percent of the eleven thousand college trustees are directors or

* It should be noted that this proportion is approximately the *reverse* of the national average.

major executives of corporations listed on the stock exchange. Ten percent are directors of two or more such corporations. Fifteen percent of all trustees sit on more than one college board. Only one one-hundredth of all trustees are labor-union officials; *none* are white- or blue-collar workers. The majority of trustees serve on four or more "community service" boards (the Board of Education, for example). The average income for a trustee is $40,000 a year, while that for the trustees of private universities ranges from $50-99,000.

Rauh's supplementary work on trustees' attitudes revealed the following: 81 percent of all trustees agree that "students who actively disrupt the functioning of a college by demonstrating, sitting in, or otherwise refusing to obey the rules, should be expelled or suspended"; 91 percent agree that "attendance at this institution is a privilege, not a right." A privilege, that is, that only money can buy.

The Regents of the University of California are thus exceptional as college trustees only in terms of the vast *quantity* of wealth and power concentrated in their hands. The *fact* that much wealth and power is in the hands of college trustees is not in itself exceptional. For the universities are controlled by members of the ruling class serving the interests of that class; a class of employers, of capitalists—men who profit from the labor of others (intellectual as well as physical) and whose survival as a class is bound up with its continuing control of the nation's primary institutions, of which the university is one of the most significant.

Concluding Notes

A graphic illustration of the major corporations' continuing role in directing the operation of the governing boards of the major universities can be found in an examination of the corporate connections of two Regents of the University of California, John Canaday and Edward Carter. Canaday is a full-time executive consultant with Lockheed Aircraft Company, the leading military contractor and among the top forty corporations for the past decade. Carter is, among other things, a member of the board of directors of the United California Bank, the nation's twelfth largest bank and the "flagship bank" of Western Bancorporation, the world's largest bank holding company.

Table 2

Firm	*Representatives*	*Key Universities Represented*
Chase Manhattan Bank (the nation's #1 bank)	9 directors	Harvard, Princeton, Columbia, Johns Hopkins
General Motors (the #1 industrial corporation)	7 directors, including the president	Michigan State, Pennsylvania, Duke
Standard Oil (New Jersey) (the #2 industrial corporation)	8 directors, including the president and chairman of the board	MIT (2 trustees), Harvard, Cornell, Syracuse
Ford Motor Company (#3 industrial corporation)	5 directors	Yale, Dartmouth
General Electric (#4)	11 directors, including the chairman of the board	Princeton, Stanford, Dartmouth, Pennsylvania, Purdue

Data from *Standard and Poor's Industrial Index* and *Who's Who in America.*

Of Lockheed's eighteen directors, ten are college trustees, while United California's thirty directors include fifteen college trustees![21] The universities these corporate magnates control are no less important and powerful than their own institutions: they include the University of Chicago, Stanford, MIT, Brandeis, the University of Southern California, the University of California, Columbia, and Harvard. Yet the question again arises: are these corporations typical or atypical, exceptional or run-of-the-mill for their concern with higher education?

An examination of the university affiliations of the directors of five of America's leading corporations is enough to provide us with persuasive evidence that Lockheed and United California Bank, far from being exceptional, are in fact typical of corporations of their caliber.

It becomes patently clear that in their own corporate circles John Canaday and Edward Carter are far from unique as trustees of a major university, and that the big businesses they serve have extensive and important connections with America's major universities. For as G. William Domhoff has commented,

"Control of America's leading universities by members of the American business aristocracy is more direct than with any other institution which they control. . . . Upper-class control of major universities is achieved through such financial support as family endowments (e.g. Duke, Stanford, Vanderbilt), personal gifts, foundation gifts, corporate gifts, and through service on the boards of trustees. These mechanisms give the upper class control of the broad framework, the long-run goals, and the general atmosphere of the university."[22]

Notes

1. Cited in Joseph Frazier Wall's definitive biography, *Andrew Carnegie* (New York: Oxford University Press, 1970), p. 834.

2. Hubert Park Beck, *Men Who Control Our Universities* (New York: King's Crown Press, 1947).

3. Scott Nearing, "Who's Who Among College Trustees," *School and Society* 6 (September 8, 1917); Evans Clark, unpublished Ph.D. thesis referred to in Upton Sinclair, *The Goose Step* (Pasadena, Calif.: published by the author, 1923), and in Jerome Davis, *Capitalism and Its Culture* (New York: Farrar & Strauss, 1941); J. A. Leighton, chairman, "Report of Committee T on Place and Function of Faculties in University Government and Administration," *Bulletin of the American Association of University Professors* 6 (March 1920).

4. Nearing, op. cit., p. 297, cited in Beck, op. cit., pp. 8-9.

5. Clark, op. cit., unpublished manuscript, cited in Beck, p. 10.

6. Leighton, op. cit., p. 20, cited in Beck, p. 11.

7. Data in this section from Beck, chapter 6.

8. Eduard Lindeman, *Wealth and Culture* (New York: Harcourt & Brace, 1936), p. 41. G. William Domhoff confirms this observation in *Who Rules America?* (Englewood Cliffs, N.J.: Prentice-Hall, 1967). He says (p. 29) that "Protestants, who usually became Episcopalians or Presbyterians, very much controlled the industrial revolution" in the United States and consequently comprised the heart of "the old upper class" which established its dominance a century ago and has yet to relinquish power. E. Digby Baltzell traces the historical emergence of these tendencies in his admirably succinct "Religion and the Class Structure," in *Sociology and History: Methods,* ed. Seymour Martin Lipset and Richard Hofstadter (New York: Basic Books, 1968).

9. Troy Duster, "The Aims of Higher Learning and the Control of the Universities," University of California, Berkeley, booklet (n.d.), p. 11.

10. Data in this section from Beck, chapter 7.

11. George S. Counts, *The Social Composition of Boards of Education* (Chicago: University of Chicago Press, 1927); Earl J. McGrath, "The Control of Higher Education in America," *Educational Record* 17 (April 1936), pp. 259-72.

12. McGrath, op. cit., p. 266.

13. A formulation in striking contrast to capitalist economic theory, which denies that housewives are in any sense workers. For a more detailed discussion of this theme, see chapter 10 of this work or *The Power of Women and the Subversion of the Community*, by Mariarosa Dalla Costa and Selma James, published as a pamphlet in 1972 by Falling Wall Press.

14. Data in this section from Beck, chapter 9.

15. Adolf Berle and Gardiner Means, *The Modern Corporation and Private Property* (New York: MacMillan, 1932).

16. V. I. Lenin, *Imperialism: The Highest Stage of Capitalism* (New York: International Publishers, 1967; originally published in 1916), p. 17.

17. See, for example, the data presented by Regent Frederick G. Dutton, *Changing Sources of Power* (New York: McGraw Hill, 1971).

18. Andrew Carnegie, "Wealth," first published in *North American Review*, June 1889.

19. Duster, op. cit. Further quotations from this booklet will not be individually footnoted.

20. Morton A. Rauh, *The Trusteeship of Colleges and Universities* (New York: McGraw Hill, 1969), published in collaboration with the Educational Testing Service. Further quotations from this book will not be individually footnoted.

21. Information derived from *Who's Who in America* and *Who's Who in the West*.

22. Domhoff, op. cit., p. 77.

Part II
The Genesis of Ruling-Class Control

3
The Genesis of Ruling-Class Control

The developing American ruling class of industrial capitalists and bankers first asserted haphazard control over the universities during the latter half of the nineteenth century. In the subsequent ten decades, as capitalism in the United States underwent a succession of developmental changes, finally ripening into mature monopoly capitalism, the nature of ruling-class control of the universities underwent a parallel development and transformation.

Three stages in this process can be distinguished and analyzed. The first consists of the rough-and-tumble early period of competitive capitalism following the bloody conclusion of the Civil War. In this period, while the American wilderness was tamed and the last of the Native American tribes were forced onto reservations, the robber barons of early capitalism were amassing huge fortunes east of the Mississippi. Men like Andrew Carnegie, Jim Hill, Jay Gould, John D. Rockefeller, Diamond Jim Fisk, and Commodore Vanderbilt were growing wealthy in the steel, oil, and railroad industries at the expense of their half-starved workers and broken competitors. Recognizing an increasingly urgent need to develop new kinds of administrative and technical skills for their industries, and hoping to immortalize their names, the robber barons began to reinvest some of their giant profits into higher education, on a small scale at first but in larger and larger amounts as the century drew to a close.

This kind of random and uncoordinated "philanthropy"

was an important stimulus to the growing system of higher education in America, but it produced a chaotic and unbalanced growth, allowing universities to sprout like weeds across the country. Then, around the turn of the century, as the process of industrial concentration and monopoly formation quickened, and as the technological needs of capitalism grew more complex (with, among other things, the emergence of large chemical and electrical industries), two of the most important capitalists—Andrew Carnegie and John D. Rockefeller—established giant foundations designed to impose order on the chaotic universe of American higher education. With the power of vast quantities of money behind them, these two foundations were able to systematically shape and restructure the university system in America in the forty years before World War II. By tailoring the universities to meet the needs of an increasingly powerful but unstable capitalism, Carnegie and Rockefeller transformed higher education into an invaluable instrument of capitalist rule.

The purpose of higher education at this juncture of history was to provide society with an elite of talented investment bankers, lawyers, and government officials. Prior to World War II, the production of an educated stratum of the wage-labor force was only a secondary and small-scale facet of university operations. After World War II, for social and economic reasons which will be explained in chapter 7, capitalism was faced with two primary and imperative needs, both of which had existed prior to the war but on a much smaller scale: (1) the need for an educated labor force capable of coping with the sophisticated administrative and research demands of modern, war-oriented capitalism; and (2) the need for the new technical and social knowledge necessary to keep capitalism expansive, stable, and vital. The universities were the ideal institutions for the fulfillment of these goals.

Thus, beginning with the passage of the first G.I. Bill in 1946, a new era in the history of capitalist control of the universities was ushered in. Acting in concert, the state and the corporations thoroughly altered the direction and focus of the university system. Needing huge numbers of a new kind of worker, the ruling class channeled a large flow of potential blue-collar and traditional service workers through a university system reconstituted to socialize a technical and administrative work force.[1] Requiring a steadily increasing quantity of social and technological knowledge, the ruling class converted the universities into high-powered research and development centers. The state, financing its expenditures with tax money taken from the working class, has been the key agent in this process, but the large corporations have played a significant role as well. The central fact to remember is that throughout this process, the state and the corporations have functioned together as a whole—for this is the period of state monopoly capitalism, still in progress. During this period, the class identity of the bulk of students has been transformed into its opposite, from ruling class to working class, while the nature of higher education has been altered radically in every sphere.[2]

What is important for us to note here is the continuity in the different stages in the evolution of ruling-class control of the universities. For although the methods of control may have grown more subtle and the specific ends may have altered with the changes in capitalism, the general motivation and nature of the control has remained essentially the same: the desire to use the universities to serve the needs of growing capitalism. It is this which differentiates the emergence of capitalist higher education in particular from the emergence of higher education inspired by the needs of industrialism in general—for capitalism, as a system based on production for profit, has worked to build a system of higher education corresponding not to the logic of industrial production per se but to the logic of capital accumulation underlying industrial production in capitalist society.

How has this difference manifested itself? In several ways. First of all, the governing structures of the universities have been dictated in their general outlines by the need of capitalists to exercise their power in matters of university policy through various forms of trusteeship patterned after the board-of-directors model established in business. Second, the needs of capitalist industry have dictated the priorities of instruction (leading, for example, to the emergence of business studies—"business administration" with a profit-making orientation—as a key field of inquiry). Third, business control of the universities has led to the development of social sciences imbued with the ideology and world-view of the oppressing class. And fourth, from the moment the production of an educated stratum of the wage-labor force emerged as one of the key functions of the university system, business control of the universities resulted in the training of workers schooled in all the arts necessary to ensure continued and expanding profits for business itself. The basic class relationship between capitalists and workers, in other words, has become strongly embedded within the system of higher education. *Businessmen* are training *workers* to produce *profits.* Viewed in this light, the specifically capitalist character of the contemporary university system becomes glaringly evident. For a system of higher education flexibly adapted to the needs of industrial production is unquestionably necessary and desirable; but such a system can take many forms, of which the capitalist model is only one.

Notes

1. This development was anticipated in a partial way as early as 1872 by a member of the California Board of Regents. In a precisely correct but antique mode of expression, he said that "the University is

founded primarily on that essential principle of free Republican government which affirms that the state is bound to furnish the citizen with the means of discharging the duties it imposes on him: if the state imposes duties that require intelligence, it is the office of the state to furnish the means of intelligence." Cited in Frederick Rudolph, *The American College and University: A History* (New York: Alfred Knopf, 1967), p. 278.

2. Before going further, I should explain that I have used the expressions "higher education" and "the universities" almost interchangeably in this work. I have not devoted special attention to the stratification of the higher education system itself, nor have I included a study of the rise of junior colleges, state colleges, etc. Although these subjects are immensely important for a complete understanding of the nature of higher education in the United States, they are also subjects which would have required Herculean labors of further study for sufficient exposition, without materially altering the thrust of my argument. For it is my belief that the universities are representative of higher education as a whole: their subordination to business is the archetypal model of such subordination, and the services they render to business are representative of the services rendered by higher education to business in general. Specifically, and most importantly, all levels of the higher education system produce college-educated workers (if, by and large, the universities produce more highly trained workers for higher status firms than less prestigious schools do, the difference is a matter of degree and emphasis—not function). Only with respect to the research function is there a major divergence between the universities and other levels of the higher education system, for here only the universities play a significant role. Nevertheless, since this is one of the key functions performed by "higher education" as a whole, it deserves special study—and how could it be studied better than through a study of the universities? A sufficient study of the stratification of higher education, in other words, must come from another source.

4
The Robber Barons

The quickened life in the United States during the period from the Civil War to the turn of the nineteenth century wrought drastic economic and intellectual changes which, in turn, profoundly affected education from its lowest to its highest levels. . . . Along with the amazing growth of machine technology and large-scale industry, the exploitation of the West proceeded more rapidly than ever; and the dominance of the business and manufacturing classes in American life was assured.[1]

R. Freeman Butts
The College Charts Its Course

In the early mercantile period of American history, before the middle of the nineteenth century, institutions of higher education in America were few and far between. Their central concerns were of a literary and philosophical nature, and were guided by the established religions which founded most (if not all) of the colleges and academies of the day. With few exceptions, the students were children of wealthy merchants or landowners preparing themselves for positions of power and prestige. The society, until the middle of the century, remained primarily mercantilist in nature, fueled by extensive, globe-encircling trade and by the intensive production of cotton in the slave-owning South.

Beginning in the 1840s, however, with the development of a Northern-based textile industry, competitive capitalism began to take root in American soil. By the end of the Civil War, the last major obstacles in the path of capitalist growth had been forcibly removed and Northern industrial capitalism had achieved final sway over the economic life of the country.[2] As a corollary development, the nature and dimensions of the system of higher education underwent a series of rapid and profound changes. Colleges began springing up everywhere, their focus shifting from an intellectual, "impractical" classical education to an education designed to meet the practical needs of industry. In the words of two leading students of the subject, Merle Curti and Roderick Nash, "At the same time that colleges and universities were springing up at practically every crossroads, a reorientation of their purpose gradually took place under the impact of demands for a more practical higher education. . . . With the force of big money behind them, scientific, technological, and commercial instruction chipped substantial niches in the standard course of study."[3] What forces provided this impetus for change? Curti and Nash offer a concise explanation: "The pressure for change toward the practical that philanthropy applied to higher education during the nineteenth century depended also on the emergence of a new elite in American society. . . . Increasingly, the men of means were businessmen who built railroads, extended commercial networks, and directed the operation of factories. . . . Instead of patronizing the classical colleges run by and for the old elite, many nineteenth-century entrepreneurs sought to transform existing institutions or to found new ones that would be more responsive to current demands as *they* defined them. The great fortunes of the members of the new elite gave them the opportunity, through philanthropy, to implement their novel educational ideas."[4]

As a result of the successes of capitalist enterprise, therefore, the new men of wealth were able to restructure the system of higher education in America in line with the social and economic needs of developing capitalism. Ultimately, capitalist "philanthropy" became a vital and determining element in the shaping of American higher education. "Given the large number of colleges and the relative scarcity of money in the young country," Curti and Nash explain, "a struggle for existence was inevitable. The fittest in this competition were the institutions that were successful at raising money. In this situation philanthropy assumed crucial importance in the selection of survivors."[5] Colleges and universities which were able to adapt themselves to the changing needs of newly capitalist society survived; those which proved incapable of satisfactory adaptation or tried to swim against the current of industrial change were ultimately jettisoned, relegated to the flotsam of historical failures.

The primary fact to understand is that a new ruling class had come into power, and, as a consequence, new demands were placed on the system of higher education which were to lead to its ultimate transformation. From 1838 to 1869, during the final period of traditional aristocratic ascendancy, nationwide college enrollments had steadily declined in proportional terms. As Richard Hofstadter comments, it was clear that "a crisis had come. But what the momentarily static condition of the older colleges foreshadowed was not a continued decline, much less a collapse; but a revolutionary turning point in the history of American higher education. The age of the college had passed, and the age of the university was dawning."[6]

The colleges and academies which capitalism inherited from the past were distinguished by their small size, their religious flavor, their time-encrusted traditions, and their emphasis on the classical disciplines: Greek, Latin, etc. The universities which were to be fashioned from the clay of the old colleges differed from them in every respect. Religious domination was abruptly displaced, business interests came to the fore, departments were formed, bureaucracies arose, and the curriculum exploded in size as science and business disciplines were introduced into higher learning. Specialization and research were encouraged; graduate schools emerged. For the first time, a multifaceted and complex university system was in the process of formation. Although its growth during this period was uncoordinated, in the midst of apparent confusion a definite order was being established. The structural foundations of the universities were to crystallize during this period.

The demands placed on higher education by the new ruling class of capitalists and financiers constituted a decisive rupture with the educational practice of the past. In the following pages, we will explore the ways in which the *content* of the changes demanded by the robber barons—the emphasis on technological and business disciplines—were to be slowly but surely translated into far-reaching changes in the *form* of education. From colleges serving a mercantile and slave-owning aristocracy came universities serving a capitalist ruling class. The transformation was epoch-making in its significance for higher education.

Power Changes Hands

> *The remark is not infrequently made that college and university education are not merely agitated by reforms; they are rather convulsed by a revolution. . . .*[7]
>
> Noah Porter, President of Yale, 1871

When Harvard College was founded in 1637, the Pilgrims who had chosen to settle on the rocky shores of North America explained their involvement with higher education in the following manner: We do not want, they said, "an illiterate ministry . . . when our present ministers shall lie in dust."[8]

By the middle of the nineteenth century, this vision of the purpose of higher education had finally exhausted itself, after two hundred years of uninterrupted ascendancy. The mercantile interests of the North, in uneasy alliance with the slave interests of the South, had dominated higher education for most of this early period, but now Northern industrial capitalism was beginning to emerge and powerful forces were coming into conflict with one another. The antagonistic forces underlying Northern capitalism and Southern slave production were beginning to contend with one another in the early stages of the contest for political power which would reach fruition in the Civil War. It was not surprising, therefore, that in an era which witnessed monumental struggles and far-reaching changes, the quiescence and infertility of the old-style colleges became increasingly evident. Andrew White, the first president of Cornell University, declared that the old-fashioned colleges were "as stagnant as a Spanish convent and as self-satisfied as a Bourbon duchy."[9] Sweeping changes were taking place in the industrial and political life of the nation, yet colleges remained apparently unaffected by the ferment going on all around them.

Francis Wayland of Brown University was the first to point to the storm signals on the horizon and to call for reforms in higher education. As early as 1850, in an influential report which shattered the academic calm, he noted that the United States had 120 colleges, 47 law schools, 42 theological seminaries—but not a single institution "designed to furnish the agriculturist, the manufacturer, the mechanic, or the merchant with the education that will prepare him for the profession to which his life is to be devoted."[10] He appealed, therefore, "for a course of study that would be 'for the benefit of all classes,' but especially for the rising middle class."[11] This meant practical education in disciplines directly relevant to commerce and industry—for Wayland was convinced that "if the college did not provide the training desired by mercantile and industrial interests . . . businessmen would set up competing schools."[12]

In the decade before the Civil War, Wayland remained little more than a prophet in the wilderness. While his proposals prefigured the spirit of change which was to revolutionize higher education in the later years of the century, he was incapable of initiating those changes in the absence of a concerted movement supporting him. The clash of social systems which occurred during the Civil War, and the resultant triumph of Northern capitalism, proved ultimately to be the necessary precondition for the decisive break with the past which Wayland advocated.

The Civil War has been accurately characterized by the educational historian R. L. Duffus as the "struggle of a free labor system against a slave labor system."[13] The slaveholding South, although dependent on the merchants of the North for the sale of their cotton, had managed to hold uneasy sway over the political destinies of the nation since the 1830s. Now, for the first time, the hegemony of the Southern slavelords was being challenged by a new and vigorous class, the Northern industrial bourgeoisie. Youthful and energetic, the bourgeoisie aligned itself with the free farmers of the West to form the Republican party, and together, in 1860, they captured state power. The South, however, was unwilling to relinquish power without a struggle. The cataclysm of the Civil War was the earthshaking result of their effort to preserve aristocratic class rule on the basis of slave production. With the conclusion of the war in 1865, however, the failure of this effort was complete: for a revolutionary transfer of power had unalterably taken place and a new ruling class had emerged in virtually undisputed control of the critical institutions of society.[14] Within a generation, most of these key institutions were to be wholly transformed.

The impulse which led most directly to the radical restructuring of higher education was the desire expressed by the newly powerful robber barons to integrate science and business disciplines into the curriculum. The tempo of technological change was accelerating and business organization was becoming increasingly complex: to cope with the baffling new problems of the capitalist era, it became necessary for the robber barons to focus their attention on expanding and reshaping higher education. As Curti and Nash point out, "Their common experience in the world of business and industry impressed upon them the need for technical talent. They were well aware that the graduates coming from the campuses of the classical colleges were totally unprepared to meet the problems involved in building a bridge, operating a bank, or designing a machine."[15] It was the determination of significant members of the new ruling class, therefore, to forge an educational system which would equip capitalism to deal with these problems. Their desire, to borrow a phrase of Benjamin Franklin's, was to reduce the relative importance of the "ornamental" disciplines in favor of the "useful" disciplines;[16] and those useful disciplines were clearly in the realm of technology and business administration.

Ultimately, the robber barons' success was ensured by their wealth and power, for as Laurence Veysey points out, "Earlier efforts at innovation in the field of American college education had proved abortive in large part simply because there had not been money to sustain them. American colleges and universities have always been basically dependent upon philanthropy. . . . In the post–Civil War years, the university could not have developed without the Cornells, Hopkinses, and Rockefellers . . ."[17]

The impact of business on education was experienced almost immediately after the Civil War and proved, ultimately, to be decisive in determining its nature. In 1867, Ezra Cornell founded Cornell University, an institution which was to lead many of the campaigns for reform which developed during these decades. In the same year, Ralph Waldo Emerson expressed his awareness of the coming transformation when he commented: "A cleavage is occurring in the hitherto granite of the past and a new era is nearly arrived."[18]

A rough estimate of the magnitude of the changes occurring in this period can be gained from an understanding of the size of the investment made by the robber barons in higher education. Business gifts were by far the single largest source of income for the colleges during this period (from 1872 to 1905).[19] Between 1878 and 1898 alone, $140 million was plowed into the institutions which were to emerge as universities, and the effects of these gifts were truly impressive.[20] In the century from 1750 to 1850, only 174 colleges were formed, but in the fifty years from 1850 to 1900, 453 colleges were founded, fully 63 percent of the total.[21] In 1870, only 67,350 students were enrolled in institutions of higher learning; by 1890 this figure had more than doubled, reaching a total of 156,756 students, and by 1910 it had quintupled, reaching a total of 355,215.[22]

The depth and intensity of the assault on traditional higher education waged by the science- and business-minded robber barons resulted not only in the rapid growth of the institutions themselves but in far-reaching changes in the structure of the colleges. The emergence of the elective system of undergraduate study was the first fruit of this radical restructuring. Allowing students to choose from a broadened spectrum of classes instead of following a rigidly structured program of requirements, the system of "free election" signaled the emergence of a greatly expanded curriculum emphasizing technical and administrative fields of learning in addition to the traditional humanities.

The intensified division of labor nurtured by the elective system resulted in a complex series of developments. Specialization on the part of students was the first immediate result, followed by the formation of departments organized around subdivisions of the expanding subject matter. In-depth research and a network of graduate schools grew from the specialization of academic work, and a system of administrative bureaucracy eventually crystallized as a necessary step for the coordination of the multifarious activities and expanding physical plant of the newly forged universities. No longer could they be considered colleges; that era had passed. As Veysey comments, "The American university of 1900 was all but unrecognizable in comparison with the college of 1860. Judged by almost any index, the very nature of higher learning in the United States had been transformed."[23]

The Elective System

With the introduction of science and business administration into the curriculum, "the ancient tree of learning," in Charles Eliot's words, became "top-heavy with numerous new branches."[24] The elective system, elastic and uncomplicated in its conception, was the structural device which enabled the growing colleges to cope with the proliferation of disciplines and courses which took place. By allowing students to choose their own courses of study, it opened the door to specialization, departmentalization, and the blossoming of graduate study.

As an agency of revolutionary change, however, the elective system did not prevail without strong opposition. In fact, "the central educational battle of nineteenth-century America was fought over the elective system. This is the question which aroused the greatest amount of controversy in the academic world, inflamed passions as no other educational issue was able to do, and most clearly reflected the impact of modern technology upon the traditional college."[25] For thirty years a stubborn resistance was waged against the elective system in the name of more conservative conceptions of education. When this resistance weakened and finally disappeared in the first decade of the twentieth century, it did so only because its futility had become painfully apparent.

The chemist Charles Eliot, inaugurated president of Harvard in 1869, was among the first to demonstrate the potential of the elective system, beginning with a set of experimental programs in the early 1870s. According to R. F. Butts, "Eliot saw clearly the direction in which the winds of public opinion and industrial activity were blowing, so he opened the doors of Harvard to meet the demands of democracy and industry for more specialized and professional training. He took advantage of the tremendous financial resources available to him as a result of the vast fortunes created under the new industrial capitalism and so built up the foundations of Harvard."[26]

Inspired by the success of Eliot's program, Columbia, under the leadership of Frederick Barnard, emulated Harvard's program of elective studies and thus laid the groundwork for the creation of a genuine university. Other important institutions to follow in Columbia's footsteps were Cornell (under Andrew White), Johns Hopkins (under Daniel Coit Gilman), Stanford (under David Starr Jordan), the University of Chicago (under William Rainey Harper), and countless others. "These institutions, along with Harvard, Brown, and Michigan, represented the outstanding leaders in the growing movement to convert colleges into universities."[27] Additionally, David Starr Jordan was the first to initiate a system of "major" and "minor" studies. Experimenting with this idea first at the University of Indiana in 1885, he transferred his conception to Stanford when he became its first president in 1890. Before long, the success of Stanford's example had captured the imagination of university administrators across the nation and the "major/minor" system had become a fundamental element of higher education throughout the United States.[28]

Thus, slowly but surely, the elective system became the leading form of undergraduate study in the nation. When in 1901 E. D. Phillips of the University of Denver made an exhaustive study of the progress of the elective system, he arrived at the confident conclusion that "the elective system is a fixture as far as our colleges are concerned. The tendency is more and more towards free election."[29] Why was this the case? John Brubacher and Willis Rudy offer a succinct explanation: "The elective system flourished from 1870 to 1910," they say, "because it met the needs of the American culture of that period. A rural society was being transformed into a great industrialized nation."[30] In other words, capitalism and the robber barons needed new kinds of knowledge and new forms of instruction in order to revolutionize production and facilitate competition. As both the battering ram and the result of their search for a new mode of education, the elective system was thus fully integrated into the structure of American higher education.

Structural Revolution

The triumph of the elective system had two major results: first, it led to the direct integration of science and business into the university curriculum; and second—structurally—it led to the emergence of departments, graduate schools, and administrative hierarchies. In this section, before coming to a discussion of the rise of science and business, we will glance briefly at the structural ramifications of the changes taking place in higher education and consider their meaning.

For the system as a whole, the importance of the elective system was that it broke the stranglehold of the humanities on higher education. Through the elimination of rigid programs of required classical studies it made room for the expansion of the college curriculum desired by the business interests now dominant in higher learning.

For the student, the importance of the elective system was twofold: on the one hand, it allowed greater freedom of choice in courses of study appropriate for graduation, and, on the other hand, it encouraged intensified specialization in narrower and narrower fields of study. This second point was structurally the more important one, for as Laurence Veysey points out, "in his freedom the student was supposed to become a trained expert in some field."[31] Since expertise in fields important to business was the end product desired by the wealthy friends of education, specialization increasingly came to be the reality of university studies. As Richard Hofstadter comments, "The elective system seemed like an academic transcription of liberal capitalist thinking [for] it added to the total efficiency of society by conforming to the principle of division of intellectual labor."[32]

The division of labor which took place during this period led naturally to the formation of coherent and unified disciplinary departments. Veysey echoes this point when he comments that "From the very first the elective system fostered an organization according to precise subject of study. The pursuit of research made the crystallized department seem even more desirable."[33] Departmental formation occurred primarily during the early years of the 1890s, after the elective system had been in operation long enough to prepare the ground for such administrative development. It was in this period, too, that graduate schools emerged as the vertical extensions of the research and specialization tendencies inherent in the elective system.[34]

The first approximation of a graduate school came into existence at Yale in 1847. In 1861, Yale then became the first college to confer the Doctor of Philosophy degree, and in 1876 it began conferring the Master of Arts. Harvard established what was known as a "graduate department" as early as 1872, but it wasn't until the 1890s that this department gained any real strength. Johns Hopkins, founded by a Baltimore businessman in 1876, was the first explicitly research-oriented school: ". . . here scholarly investigation on a large scale was first encouraged. The influence diffused by this institution, both through its example and through the attainments of the scholars whom it trained, was most salutary in promoting the development of graduate study and research in American universities."[35] By the turn of the century, no fewer than fifteen major graduate schools were in operation in America.[36]

As late as 1850, only eight graduate students had existed. By 1871, after only a few years of capitalist rule, the total had crept up to 198. Then a period of rapid growth began. By 1890, the number had soared to 2,382, and by 1900 it had risen to 5,668.[37] Describing graduate enrollments as "a measure of the growth of the universities," Hofstadter comments that it expanded during this period "with astonishing speed."[38] As an index of the changes taking place in industrial methods and technology, the emergence of graduate studies thus constitutes a significant milestone in the process of transformation engulfing the universities in this period.

As the universities mushroomed in size and complexity, it became necessary for administrative structures to grow correspondingly. Veysey has identified two key stages in this growth of administrative power: the first, highlighted by the regimes of men like White, Eliot, and Angell, consisted of one-man rule during a period of significant growth;[39] the second, occurring primarily during the 1890s, consisted of the flowering of full-scale bureaucracy. "The trend of the nineties," as Veysey observes, "was much more widespread than could be accounted for by one or two commanding personalities. Deans became important figures at Harvard during this period; typewriters appeared and typists began flooding the correspondence files at nearly every prominent institution. By 1900 it could be said that administration had developed something like its full measure of force in American higher education."[40]

The rise of bureaucratic forms of administration marks a very real point of departure in the growth of the universities.

Just as in the realm of industrial capitalism per se, an era dominated by colorful personalities was coming to a close. For the robber barons themselves, having laid the foundations for monopoly capitalism, had thus placed themselves on the brink of obscurity and disappearance. No longer could single, commanding figures dominate an environment increasingly composed of monopoly corporations and faceless boards of directors. Although the luster of robber capitalists of the stature of Carnegie and Rockefeller would continue to shine for many years, the rough-and-tumble era which had enabled them to rise to power was coming to an end. Much the same was true for the universities. The dynamic leaders who had brought the universities to the level of complexity and relative maturity achieved by the turn of the century were slowly on their way out. They were to be replaced by massive administrative hierarchies deriving strength from the power of the representatives of capitalism now dominant among the trustees of the universities.

On another and more subtle level, a Stanford chemist captured the spirit of the changes taking place in administration when he contrasted the informality of the earlier colleges to the more highly disciplined workings of the later universities. The colleges, he said, functioned as "a republic of letters, or perhaps an oligarchy of learning." The emerging universities, on the other hand, considered all questions "from the standpoint of the efficiency of the university organism."[41] The vast gulf between these two positions is clearly tangible.

The Rise of Science

In its earliest stages, technical education was inspired primarily by military needs. West Point, founded in 1802, was the first school to introduce technical studies into its curriculum, and its focus was principally on engineering.[42] The second school of technical studies, Rensselaer Polytechnic

Institute, was not opened until 1824, and the third, Annapolis Naval Academy, 1844.[43] Technical instruction was barely born, therefore, when the whirlwind of the Civil War led to the reordering of the forces and needs of the nation.

Capitalism and the robber barons had been dominant for only a short period before science began its steep climb upward in the college curriculum. As early as the decade of the 1860s, more than twenty-five colleges opened science departments, indicating the beginning of a trend which was to gather force as time passed.[44] Part of the cause for this rapid advance can be located in the vast panoply of needs generated by the war effort; for as Walter Lunden points out, "The Civil War created new demands for technical knowledge and skill which included all phases of life, from transportation to refrigeration."[45] The second major stimulus for this advance, however, must be located in the science needs experienced by the leading figures of competitive capitalism; for as Richard Hofstadter notes, in the post-Civil War era, "industry created an almost insatiable demand for technicians, which the older educational system was unable to produce in sufficient numbers. It called not simply for the preservation and transmission of knowledge but for research to enlarge it."[46]

In addition to the formation of science departments on numerous campuses, many technical and scientific schools designed solely for industrial research purposes were founded during this period (by the turn of the century more than forty were in operation).[47] Among the more famous of these was the Illinois Institute of Technology, which profited greatly from the $20 million bestowed upon it by photography millionaire George Eastman.[48]

The essential motivation underlying the robber barons' creation of technically oriented universities and institutes is clear-cut and simple. "Their purpose in founding technical institutions was to provide the type of education needed in a society whose forte was economic expansion and technological advancement. In their own business experience, the businessmen philanthropists found that higher education did not supply either the skilled technicians or the inventive scientists with an eye to the application of their discoveries required by industrial progress."[49] By directing their almost limitless funds into channels appropriate to their business needs, the robber barons soon reversed this situation. Science became a central part of the curriculum and a direct link between the industry and the university. In the years since, it has never ceased playing this role.

The Rise of Business Education

Unlike science, business education was not immediately integrated into the college curriculum in the years following the Civil War. Its rise to prominence did not occur until around the turn of the century, because the needs it was intended to fulfill didn't become pressing until capitalist industry had grown complex enough to require systematic organization. As Richard Hofstadter observes, "When the business schools emerged, American industry was undergoing a major transition. Its central concern was no longer the task of erecting a nation's industrial plant and increasing productivity. Industry had reached maturity. Problems of internal personnel management, marketing, salesmanship, research, efficiency engineering, and public relations had pressed to the fore." Moreover, "the emergence of a stable and effective trade union movement made it clear that problems of dealing with the labor force would be more pressing" than in the past.[50] For all these reasons, it became apparent that business administration, the art of management, would have to become a more methodical and sophisticated branch of corporate activity to cope with the constellation of new problems facing it. In order to deal with rising labor militancy and the purely organizational intricacies of monopoly capitalism, bureaucracy thus became internally necessary to industrial enterprise. The emergence of business education in the years after 1890 was one of the cardinal elements in this process.

The first school of what would now be called business administration was set up in 1881, as the result of an initiative undertaken by Joseph Wharton, a wealthy Philadelphia manufacturer of zinc, nickel, and iron. Early in 1881, Wharton wrote a letter to the trustees of the University of Pennsylvania pointing out that a large number of technical and scientific schools had recently been created as a result of "the general conviction that college education does little toward fitting for the actual duties of life any but those who propose to become lawyers, doctors, or clergymen," but that very little had been done to establish comparable schools in the realm of business education.[51] With $100,000 backing up his offer, he proposed that the trustees of the University of Pennsylvania create a school of business administration, the now famous Wharton School of Finance and Commerce.

From the very beginning, Wharton specified exactly what was to be taught in his school, and his demands are illustrative of the social origins and motives of much business philanthrophy. To begin with, as a capitalist, Wharton was adamant that what he perceived to be the necessity of a protective tariff—a central issue which had divided industrial capitalists from the merchants and slave-owners of the old elite as early as 1846—be an article of faith in his classrooms. Second, he expressed a rock-solid determination that "no apologetic or merely defensive style of instruction must be tolerated" about what he called "the right and duty of national self-protection" in the realm of "industrial and financial independence."[52] America was to grow strong as a capitalist nation in competitive battle with the capitalists of the European nations and should not, therefore, shy away from either the battle or the national self-aggrandizement the battle entailed.

Wharton's philosophy accorded well with that of John D. Rockefeller, who in 1898 established the second major school of business administration, the College of Commerce and Administration at the University of Chicago. Later in 1898, a third school of business administration was formed, the College of Commerce at the University of California, and in 1900 four more such colleges were founded.[53] As monopoly formation in the context of the turn of the century corporate merger movement progressed with increasing speed, schools of business administration arose with lightning rapidity. By 1915, forty schools of commerce were in operation, and by 1925 one hundred eighty-three had been organized.[54] In other words, when it became necessary for capitalism to focus its energies on its own internal organization, it was capable of doing so with furious rapidity.

The Rise of High Schools and Teacher Training

According to one leading historian, "The rise of the university was paralleled by a similar development in secondary education—the emergence of the public high school—without which the great expansion of higher education would have been impossible."[55]

Prior to the Civil War, public high schools had been a negligible social force. Later, they emerged as a permanent and growing part of public education. Between 1870 and 1900, the number of high schools multiplied six times, from 1,026 in 1870 to 6,005 in 1900; similarly, the number of high school students multiplied seven times, from 72,158 in 1870 to 519,251 in 1900.[56] "The high school responded to the needs of an expanding technology. It recognized the fact that life was growing less simple, that more skills and understandings were required. It reflected the growing industrialization of America."[57]

Business needs were thus ultimately determining in the

growth of high school education during the latter decades of the nineteenth century, but they were not the sole determinants. A closely related set of goals intertwined with direct production needs were embodied in the desires of leading capitalists for the effective socialization of the work force, i.e., for the pacification of the militant and potentially revolutionary working-class movement which was emerging late in the century. As Merle Curti comments, "Some thought that the extension of the high school would provide the more intelligent son of the worker with an education that would enable him to find an honorable and profitable place within the existing industrial system, and prevent him from becoming an agitator."[58] This desire to put an end to dangerous labor agitation was fully compatible with the specific production and profit needs of the robber barons; in fact, the continual re-creation of bourgeois power and control has always been correctly understood by the bourgeoisie to be an essential precondition to profit-making. Thus, in the particular context of developing monopoly capitalism in which public education first blossomed, it was understood that the twin desires for skilled labor and a passive working class were complementary. They dovetailed in the shaping of secondary education which took place in this era.

One necessary consequence of the rise of high school education was the emergence of an accentuated demand for qualified teachers. Teacher-training thus rose to prominence as an important facet of higher education, and women, as the essential reservoir of teaching talent called upon by the high schools, quickly and for the first time were integrated into higher education.

Before the Civil War, only a handful of colleges had been open to women, almost all of them small, exclusive women's colleges. By 1870, however, the tide had visibly turned and dramatic changes were underway. Eleven thousand women were enrolled in colleges across the nation, comprising one-fifth of all college students,[59] and coeducational institutions were now twenty times as numerous as separate women's institutions.[60] By 1900, 40 percent of all students were women[61] and coeducation had spread to 71.5 percent of all colleges and universities.[62] A rapid and abrupt break in the continuity of the two-hundred-year tradition of men's colleges had thus occurred in the space of a few short years, encountering no major obstacles. The impelling force which produced this sudden change was the widespread and urgent demand for skilled high school teachers which began to express itself in this period. Far and away the largest number of women enrolled in college were being prepared for teaching roles, as Mabel Newcomer makes clear: "Of the 61,000 women enrolled in coeducational schools in 1900, 43,000 were in teacher training courses . . ."[63] Moreover, teaching institutes were increasingly the most important form of non-coeducational women's schools.

Thus, although drawn primarily from middle-income families, the women involved in higher education faced typically few options regarding the nature of their education. Their opportunities were limited by the same vocational needs of capitalism which had provided the impetus for their integration into higher education in the first place.

Conclusion: Capitalism in Power

With rare honesty, Charles William Eliot of Harvard argued in 1908 that "dangerous" class influences played no significant role in determining the shape and direction of the universities in their formative years. This was true, he said, because the privately funded colleges of his day were free from "class influences such as that exerted by farmers as a class, or trade unionists as a class." Who then did exercise control over higher education? According to Eliot, the social grouping which controlled the universities was typified by "the highly educated, public-spirited, business or professional man—a man who has been successful in his own calling."[64] With reference to this statement, Frederick Rudolph wryly comments that "such men were perhaps also capable of exerting class influences, but for President Eliot such influences would not be dangerous. For these men represented the classes whose point of view was increasingly welcome and increasingly dominant in that instrument of power—the college corporation."[65]

As the nineteenth century drew to a close, therefore, business was firmly in control of the emerging universities which constituted the core of the system of higher education in America. Not only had the robber barons succeeded in placing higher education between the hammer and the anvil of capitalist needs and abilities; not only had higher education been melted down and recast in the shape of the robber barons' desires; but the more the universities conformed to the requirements of capitalism, the more thoroughly and directly the capitalist ruling class came to control them. The random philanthropy which had marked the initial impact of the robber barons on higher education proved to be only the first part of a long-term process leading to their institutional integration into the power structure of higher education.

For as Charles and Mary Beard point out, "As the flood of gold rolled into the chests of the various colleges . . . ," grateful college administrators "drafted men of money into the service of collegiate direction until at the end of the century the roster of American trustees of higher learning read like a corporation directory."[66] Frederick Rudolph throws additional light on this situation when he writes that "on the whole, the sound, conservative men of wealth who came to dominate the college governing boards were pillars of the better classes, and while their duties permitted them to perform a social responsibility, their authority also enabled them to keep the colleges true to the interests and prejudices of the classes from which they were drawn."[67] Class rule, in other words, was becoming firmly entrenched.

One of the major consequences of the increasingly direct power exercised by businessmen over the universities was the deformation of the spirit of critical and potentially radical scholarship which had begun to appear in the 1880s and '90s, largely as a corollary to the budding labor movement. From the beginning of the period under consideration, strong pressures, direct and indirect, were placed on faculty members to prevent them from developing radical critiques of bourgeois society and capitalist rule. This process culminated during the 1890s and during the early years of the twentieth century with a strong wave of academic repression directed against instructors who failed to voice ideas compatible with the desires of their employers. As Veysey points out, in a tone of dry understatement, "Among the younger professors in the emerging social sciences a group began to appear who took the injunction to public service a bit more earnestly than had been intended by the university presidents who talked in this vein. Everyone was against corruption; these particular professors believed that corruption could be traced back to the spirit of unchecked private enterprise, at least in its monopolistic form. In consequence nearly all of them found it difficult to retain their academic positions during the 1890s."[68]

A single example will be sufficient to give us a sense of the flavor of the era. Edward Ross, one of America's leading sociologists and a man whose only sin was that in a single public speech he had rebuked business for some of its excesses, found himself summarily dismissed from his post at Stanford on the initiative of Jane Stanford, the widow of robber baron Leland Stanford, who had poured $20 million into the university. Mrs. Stanford defended her position by saying that Ross was guilty of associating himself "with the political demagogues of San Francisco, exciting their evil passions, and drawing distinctions between man and man—all laborers, and equal in the sight of God—and literally plays into the hands of the lowest and vilest elements of socialism. . . . I must confess I am weary of Professor Ross mixing in political affairs, and I think that he ought not to be retained at Stanford University. . . . God forbid that Stanford University should ever favor socialism of any kind."[69]

The special kind of blindness which allowed university presidents to participate in forms of academic repression apparently antithetical to their liberal principles was exemplified best by the contradictory stance taken by Andrew White of Cornell, who maintained that he believed "in freedom from authoritarianism of every kind. This freedom did not, however, extend to Marxists, anarchists, and other radical disturbers of the social order."[70] The position taken by the robber barons themselves on the issue of academic freedom was considerably less complex. With no pretense of "objectivity," they tried "to run the college as if it were an industry, and they were inclined to look upon the faculty as employees whose opinions should coincide with their own."[71] Ultimately, therefore, bourgeois hegemony in the realm of ideology was ensured by the virtually unquestioned sway of big businessmen over higher education, for although pitched battles were fought within the university, the weaponry available to radical faculty members paled by comparison with the might concentrated in the hands of the robber barons. "In trying to resist board and presidential encroachment on their academic freedom, faculties found themselves almost powerless."[72] As Rudolph comments, "The professionalization of the professors had not brought them any new authority in college and university affairs; actually it had only helped to widen the gap between them and the governing board . . ."[73]

Without the necessary strength to resist the invasion of the curriculum undertaken by the robber barons in this period, the faculties increasingly became auxiliaries to business interests in the developing class struggle. "With few exceptions," as Merle Curti points out, educators "not only advanced social ideas thoroughly in keeping with the existing system of profit-making industrialism; they also aided it in its struggles with farmers and workers."[74] As early as 1881, in an address foreshadowing future developments, a speaker at the annual meeting of the National Education Association declared that "men stand aghast at the prophetic rumblings of an unreasoning and relentless communism . . . a more serious thing . . . than many of us dare speak of above our breath."[75] By the conclusion of the century, it could safely be said that the majority of university professors had been enlisted into the struggle against "relentless communism" in order to defend the business interests threatened by the socialist tendencies of the working class. For the universities had been transformed into institutions serving capitalism and the capitalist ruling class on many levels. Science and business disciplines had been forced into the curriculum, the structure of higher education entirely altered, and the political thrust of teaching and learning placed under rigid controls. "Thus from the days following Appomattox, education rendered assistance to industrial and financial capitalism in its struggles with other groups, and helped to promote the spirit of business enterprise which captured America's middle class as well as her captains of industry and finance. Education, in turn, was affected by business methods and purposes . . ."[76] It was, in fact, not only "affected," but revolutionized.

Notes

1. R. Freeman Butts, *The College Charts Its Course* (New York: McGraw Hill, 1939), p. 159.

2. See Louis M. Hacker, *The Triumph of American Capitalism* (New York: McGraw Hill, 1965).

3. Merle Curti and Roderick Nash, *Philanthropy in the Shaping of American Higher Education* (New Brunswick, N.J.: Rutgers University Press, 1965), p. 60.

4. Ibid., p. 61.

5. Ibid., p. 43.

6. Quoted in Richard Hofstadter and C. DeWitt Hardy, *The Development and Scope of Higher Education in the United States* part 1 (New York: Columbia University Press, 1952), pp. 29-30.

7. Cited in Laurence R. Veysey, *The Emergence of the American University, 1865-1910* (Chicago: University of Chicago Press, 1965), p. 1.

8. Cited in Walter Lunden, *The Dynamics of Higher Education* (Pittsburgh, Pa.: The Pittsburgh Printing Co., 1939), p. 188.

9. Cited in R. L. Duffus, *Democracy Enters College* (New York: Scribner & Sons, 1936), p. 36.

10. Cited in John S. Brubacher and Willis Rudy, *Higher Education in Transition: An American History* (New York: Harper, 1958), pp. 62-63.

11. Cited in Frederick Rudolph, *The American College and University: A History* (New York: Alfred Knopf, 1962), p. 239.

12. Hofstadter, op. cit., p. 24.

13. Duffus, op. cit., p. 34. Marx and Engels agreed with this analysis. In an article published November 7, 1861, they declared: "The present struggle between the South and the North is, therefore, nothing but a struggle between two social systems, between the system of slavery and the system of free labor. The struggle has broken out because the two systems can no longer live peacefully side by side on the North American continent. It can only be ended by the victory of one system or the other." From Marx and Engels, *The Civil War in the United States* (Secaucus, N.J.: Citadel Press, 1961).

14. See Hacker, op. cit., and Barrington Moore, *The Social Origins of Dictatorship and Democracy* (Boston: Beacon Press, 1966).

15. Curti and Nash, op. cit., p. 61.

16. Cited in Duffus, op. cit., p. 25.

17. Veysey, op. cit., p. 3.

18. Cited in Rudolph, op. cit., p. 241.

19. Jesse B. Sears, *Philanthropy in American Higher Education* (1922), p. 55.

20. Lunden, op. cit., p. 177.

21. Ibid., p. 175.

22. Hofstadter, op. cit., p. 31.

23. Veysey, op. cit., p. 2.

24. Brubacher and Rudy, op. cit., p. 112.

25. Ibid., p. 96.

26. Butts, op. cit., pp. 182-83.

27. Ibid., pp. 183-84.

28. Ibid., pp. 199-200.

29. Ibid., p. 240.

30. Brubacher and Rudy, op. cit., p. 111.

31. Veysey, op. cit., p. 67.

32. Hofstadter, op. cit., p. 50.

33. Veysey, op. cit., p. 320.

34. Ibid., p. 320.

35. Cited in Elbert Vaughn Wills, *The Growth of American Higher Education* (Philadelphia: Dorrance & Co., 1936), p. 191.

36. Brubacher and Rudy, op. cit., p. 188.

37. Ibid., p. 187.

38. Hofstadter, op. cit., p. 64.

39. Veysey, op. cit., pp. 305-6.

40. Ibid., p. 306.

41. Ibid., p. 309.

42. Wills, op. cit., p. 102.

43. Lunden, op. cit., p. 193.

44. Rudolph, op. cit., p. 233.

45. Lunden, op. cit., pp. 194-95.

46. Hofstadter, op. cit., p. 31.

47. Brubacher and Rudy, op. cit., p. 62.

48. Curti and Nash, op. cit., pp. 78-79. MIT is now the nation's sixty-seventh largest military prime contractor, only four places behind Eastman Kodak on the list of war profiteers.

49. Ibid., p. 78.

50. Hofstadter, op. cit., p. 93.

51. Curti and Nash, op. cit., p. 73.

52. Ibid., pp. 74-75.

53. Wills, op. cit., p. 99.

54. Ibid.

55. Hofstadter, op. cit., p. 31. See also Joel H. Spring, *Education and the Rise of the Corporate State* (Boston: Beacon Press, 1972), and David K. Cohen and Marvin Lazerson, "Education and the Corporate Order," *Socialist Revolution* no. 8 (March-April 1972).

56. Brubacher and Rudy, op. cit., p. 157.

57. Duffus, op. cit., p. 30.

58. Merle Curti, *The Social Ideas of American Educators* (Paterson, N.J.: Pageant Books, 1935), p. 220.

59. Mabel Newcomer, *A Century of Higher Education for American Women* (New York: Harper, 1959), p. 19.

60. Brubacher and Rudy, op. cit., p. 68.

61. Veysey, op. cit., p. 272.

62. Ibid., p. 68.

63. Newcomer, op. cit., p. 91.

64. Cited in Rudolph, op. cit., p. 175.

65. Ibid.

66. Charles and Mary Beard, *The Rise of American Civilization* (New York: MacMillan, 1936), vol. 2, p. 470.

67. Rudolph, op. cit., p. 173.

68. Veysey, op. cit., p. 73.

69. Ibid., p. 402.

70. Brubacher and Rudy, op. cit., p. 159.

71. William C. DeVane, *Higher Education in Twentieth Century America* (Cambridge, Mass.: Harvard University Press, 1965), p. 30.

72. Veysey, op. cit., p. 355.

73. Rudolph, op. cit., p. 427.
74. Curti, op. cit., p. 259.
75. Ibid., p. 220.
76. Ibid., p. 232.

5
Carnegie and Rockefeller

By the turn of the century, capitalism had succeeded in fundamentally altering the nature of American higher education, while leading capitalists had become firmly entrenched in positions of power within the university structure. Nevertheless, it wasn't until Carnegie and Rockefeller launched their respective foundations in the early years of the twentieth century that the shaping of American higher education became systematic and thorough. Only then were the needs of newly corporate capitalism fully reflected in the uniformity imposed upon the anarchy of American higher education by the two leading captains of American industry: Andrew Carnegie and John D. Rockefeller.

In the first three decades of this century, the essence of what Carnegie and Rockefeller achieved can be described as the standardization of American universities and colleges. Confronted by a situation in which hundreds of insitutions fought with each other for survival, Carnegie and Rockefeller decided to work for the systematic transformation of American higher education from an unstructured and disorganized welter of universities loosely serving the robber barons to a tightly knit system of higher education systematically serving corporate capitalism. Their method was simple and effective. From the hundreds of colleges competing for funds, they chose to invest in only a handful, imposing stringent conditions as they did so. The result of this policy was that colleges and universities favored by the foundations thrived, while other, less fortunate institutions either withered on the vine or struggled along in obscurity. "Influencing foundation thinking on this matter was the vast number of colleges, many of inferior grade, bequeathed to modern times by the college boom years. For entrepreneurs used to destroying weaker competitors, a solution to the problem was readily apparent: the weaker colleges had to be eliminated and the survivors made to emerge as institutions of the highest quality."[1] Thus, during the crucial formative years at the beginning of this century, the biggest of the big robber barons were allowed to define and control American higher education.

The Foundations

The foundations were the key mediating institutions through which the needs and desires of increasingly monopolistic capitalism and its corporate representatives were systematically built into the structure of higher education during the early years of the century. Made possible by the vast accumulations of surplus wealth generated during the early stages of competitive Northern capitalism, they were, as Jesse B. Sears comments, "a really new type of philanthropic enterprise in education."[2]

During the course of the nineteenth century, not more than six foundations had been established; in the first decades of the twentieth century, approximately twelve such foundations were created, with Carnegie and Rockefeller playing pivotal roles in this development.[3] In this quicksilver time—the first major period of monopoly formation—the leading capitalists at the head of the corporations "began pouring out their millions in the development of this new *business*, the business of educational philanthropy."[4] The results were far-reaching.

Between 1893 and 1915, gifts to education were by far the

largest single part of overall philanthropy, a total of 43 percent. In the crucial decade from 1898 to 1907, education never received less than 45 percent of all gifts, and once received 79 percent—in 1906, the year in which Carnegie's Foundation for the Advancement of Teaching first moved into action.[5] From 1902 to 1938, beginning with the formation of Rockefeller's General Education Board in 1902, the leading foundations spent a total of roughly $680 million on higher education.[6] "With these resources," as Frederick Rudolph remarks, "the philanthropic foundations became an apparent or a hidden presence on every American campus."[7]

As "children of the same parents," the universities and the foundations served burgeoning capitalism in different but closely related ways. While the universities provided direct services for business, the foundations regulated and systematized those services. As Ernest Hollis observes, "The leading foundations entertained the idea of bringing a group of institutions under their influence and thus promoting a 'comprehensive system of higher education.' . . . For almost two decades the grants of the General Education Board and the Carnegie Foundation were based on such a program."[8]

One of the paradoxes of business philanthropy, however, was that it acted to shape higher education in indirect ways. The reason for this, as Hollis points out, is that "the unfavorable public estimate of the elder John D. Rockefeller and Andrew Carnegie made it inexpedient, in 1905, for their newly created philanthropic foundations to attempt any direct reforms in higher education. . . . there could be no objection, however, to colleges receiving grants from these sources for such general and noncontroversial purposes as endowment, buildings, and professors' pensions. Nearly all foundation grants during the first two decades of the century were made for such purposes as these." Nevertheless, as Hollis concludes, "Far-reaching college reform was carefully embedded in many of these noncontroversial grants."[9] In the following pages we will explore this process.

Carnegie

Andrew Carnegie grew rich as the founder and owner of Carnegie Steel, later the major enterprise that went into the formation of U.S. Steel. For thirty years before he retired and became a "philanthropist" in 1901, he was best known to the public as a ruthless competitor and a brutal employer. The incident which most clearly defined him in the public consciousness was his role in leading the bloody suppression of the Homestead Steel Strike of 1892, one of the most fiercely fought labor struggles in the history of the United States. The strike began when Carnegie, as the owner of Carnegie Steel, outlawed unionization and lowered wages 22 percent. In outraged response, eight thousand workers at the Homestead, Pennsylvania, plant walked off the job. The Amalgamated Association of Iron and Steel Workers, spearheading the strike, immediately formed a defense committee to prevent Carnegie (along with Henry Clay Frick) from bringing in scab labor to end the strike.

After a few unsuccessful efforts at importing scabs into Homestead, Carnegie sent in a riverboat armada of three hundred armed Pinkerton detectives, hoping to catch the strikers by surprise and overwhelm them by force of arms. When the strikers met fire with fire, however, and several lives were lost on both sides, the Pinkertons surrendered. Furious, Carnegie convinced the Governor of Pennsylvania to send in the National Guard to crush the strike; again the strikers resisted, with surprising success. General Snowden, head of the National Guard, was incredulous: "Philadelphians can hardly appreciate the actual communism of these people," he said. "They believe the works are theirs quite as much as Carnegie's." In three words, Snowden characterized the situation at Homestead: "revolution, treason, and anarchy."[10]

Unable to defeat the strikers militarily, Carnegie and Snowden agreed on a new tactic: a war of attrition. By November, the workers had run out of food and their shoes were wearing thin; to make matters worse, the weather had turned freezing cold with the chill of approaching winter. Finally, incapable of further resistance and on the verge of starvation, the strikers gave in. The National Guard occupied the town and the Amalgamated Association of Iron and Steel Workers was forcibly disbanded. Carnegie had won. Many lives had been lost and much suffering endured—but the Steel King, with the help of the military might of the state, was able to get what he wanted.[11]

In 1901, when Carnegie sold Carnegie Steel to J. P. Morgan for $300 million, Morgan congratulated him on being "the richest man in the world." Soon afterwards, the former Steel King began a new career in philanthropy. He began by founding the Carnegie Institute and several other philanthropic funds.[12] These occupied his attention until a fateful summer day in 1904 when he met Henry Pritchett at one of Theodore Roosevelt's White House luncheons. Pritchett, then president of the Massachusetts Institute of Technology, was bursting with ideas about the organization of higher education in America, and proposed, to begin with, that Carnegie finance a program of pensions for professors. Carnegie, impressed by Pritchett's arguments, agreed to give the matter serious consideration. "Fortunately for Pritchett, Carnegie . . . put higher education at the head of his list of worthwhile charities . . . In his theory of social progress through philanthropy, education was the Key."[13] At the beginning of 1905, Carnegie established the Carnegie Foundation for the Advancement of Teaching (CFAT) with a grant of $10 million, and named Henry Pritchett the Foundation's first president.

Pritchett, resigning from the presidency of MIT, began work immediately.

Thinking over the possibilities inherent in the program, Pritchett's imagination began to take fire. "I am persuaded," he wrote on May 10, 1905, to Carnegie at the millionaire's castle in Skibo, Scotland, "that nothing you could have done would in the end be so far-reaching in educational matters."[14] Later that year, in November of 1905, Pritchett wrote to Carnegie again, in a similar vein, saying ". . . the more I have seen of the work . . . the more clearly I understand that this Foundation is to become one of the great educational influences in our country, because it is going to deal, necessarily, not alone with the payment of retirement pensions to deserving teachers, but as well with the most far-reaching educational questions and with the most important problems of educational policy . . ."[15]

Near the end of 1905, following Pritchett's advice, "Carnegie . . . included in his board of trustees the heads of the wealthiest eastern schools." According to Joseph Wall, Carnegie's major biographer, it was the millionaire's strength of will and tactical flexibility which "enabled probably the ablest group of college administrators that could have been selected at that time to set standards for higher education. Setting such standards had never before been done on a national basis, and it was to have consequences reaching far beyond Carnegie's and even Pritchett's original intentions."[16]

The effects of Carnegie's gift on the educational community were immediate and devastating. Galvanized by pressing financial needs, American colleges and universities began an intense scramble for the money. In Wall's words, "There were emergency sessions of boards of trustees throughout the country, and charters that had been considered inviolate were in many places quickly changed."[17]

Working in conjunction with his talented administrators, Pritchett launched an in-depth study of the institutions of higher education in America in an effort to narrow the scope of possible donors to a few dozen of the leading schools. On March 10, 1906, while Pritchett's study was still in progress, the bill incorporating the CFAT "became law over the signature of President Theodore Roosevelt, a mutual friend of both Carnegie and Pritchett."[18] Then, in July of 1906, it was announced that the list of possible recipients of Carnegie money had been narrowed down to a total of forty-eight institutions.

Carnegie and Pritchett advanced a systematic structural definition of higher education which came to be accepted as the general model for colleges and universities throughout the nation. In capsule form, the key structural ideas they advanced were expressed in the 1905 report of the CFAT, which decreed that "An institution to be ranked as a college must have at least six professors giving their entire time to college and university work, a course of four full years in the liberal arts and sciences, and should require for admission not less than the usual four years of academic or high school preparation or its equivalent."[19] These demands collided with the previous disorganization of higher education with stunning impact. By 1910, higher and secondary education had moved far toward conforming to these principles. No longer would higher education remain a chaotic ensemble of varying requirements, forms, and outlooks; for the first time, system was being introduced into higher education.

When the Foundation finally began handing money out, one of its primary stipulations was that "if its professors were to receive pensions, a college must confine its admissions only to those students with four complete years of secondary education. So that this requirement would not be misunderstood, the Foundation sponsored a conference in 1908 that devised the 'Carnegie Unit' as a measurement device. Fifteen units of work were demanded of those desiring to matriculate at a bona fide college or university,"[20] and a unit was defined as "any one of four courses carried for five days a week during the secondary school year."

Characterized by Frederick Rudolph as "in some ways the ultimate in organization, the epitome of academic accountancy, and the symbol of the search for standards,"[21] the Carnegie unit was the first rigorous definition of secondary education to be taken seriously and put into practice. As Ernest Hollis points out, "The unit method of college admission . . . performed the indispensable function of bringing order and quantitative meaning to the four years of high school work underlying the college curriculum."[22]

Also put forward by Carnegie and Pritchett were the Ph.D. requirements for professorship and the definition of a college in terms of the number of professors employed. The Carnegie requirement of six professors for a college "usually meant a college with six or eight distinct departments," and the requirement of the Ph.D. degree for professors led to the expansion and standardization of graduate education.[23] Even more important, Carnegie had a potent and lasting effect on education through his decisive role in determining which institutions would survive and which would sink. By giving money to some institutions and not others, he had inestimable power concentrated in his hands. His handling of the state universities is a case in point. "Pritchett had long entertained the idea that a state university properly belonged organically at the apex of the state's entire school system. Now, having a grip on the state institutions, he determined to use the weapon of withholding pensions from them until he was satisfied that they conformed to his conception of their position and role."[24] This kind of pressure was applied to the educational system in Ohio, a state with three major universities. Under Pritchett's influence, the Carnegie Foundation pressed hard for the welding of these three universities into a single institution as part of a plan to build a "comprehensive and consistent educational system."[25] In keeping with this plan, the Foundation refused to give money to any of the three schools in the state until they finally succumbed and agreed to merge.

An even more arresting aspect of the power wielded by the CFAT is demonstrated by its decision not to give money to denominational colleges, a decision which caused the eventual demise of the Christian denominationalism which had hitherto honeycombed American higher education. Many small colleges died a slow death during this period from lack of funds and many more ended their histories of formal denominational control in order to become eligible for Carnegie money.[26] In some senses, therefore, the actions of the Carnegie Foundation represented the final victory of business over the religious interests which had formerly dominated higher education.

As Elbert Vaughn Wills concludes, the "service of the [Carnegie] Foundation as an instrumentality for the standardization of American colleges and universities has proven the most important phase of its work in its influence upon American higher education. Its formulation of a definition of the 'unit' of preparatory training, and the fixing of a clear line of demarcation between preparatory and collegiate departments in colleges produced noteworthy results in the standardization of entrance requirements and in defining more clearly the work of the college level."[27]

Cognizance of the critically important role played by the Foundation was widespread. In 1909, *The New York Independent* summed up the half-awed feelings of Carnegie's contemporaries in the following manner: "Who anticipated," they asked, "that in less than five years it would effect profound changes in the constitution and management of our colleges, severing venerable denominational ties, tightening up requirements for admission, differentiating the college from the university, systematizing finances, raising salaries, and in more subtle ways modifying the life and work of thousands of educators?"[28]

Public response to Carnegie's gift-horse, however, was more varied. Although in some sectors of society "Carnegie's reputation as a shrewd and generous philanthropist had replaced his earlier image as a brutal industrialist,"[29] in other sectors considerable hostility was generated toward his "generosity." While university presidents praised him to the skies, representatives of the working class took him to task. The editor of the *Railroad Trainmen's Journal,* for example, wrote that "Carnegie, who has reduced wages to a point of starvation, who has caused the sacrifice of life in his endeavor to acquire greater riches [is a] canting hypocrite . . . and all his high sounding talk of morality is simply hypocritical rot."[30] These sentiments were echoed by the editor of the *Cigar Maker's Official Journal,* who declared that, when "the Carnegies, Rockefellers, and that ilk" give money to higher education, they are giving for the benefit of the rich, and the rich alone.[31] At the same time, when Colorado State Legislator Alma Lafferty accusingly declared that "every dollar that Carnegie owns came from the life blood of the people at Homestead, and now he is trying to buy with his tainted millions a semblance of respectability," President Hadley of Yale was able to laugh and say, "Bring on your tainted money! We will purify it with the Yale spirit."[32]

But issues more significant than hypocrisy or tainted money were raised in connection with Carnegie's gifts. The astute editor of the *Oakland* (California) *Inquirer,* for example, said that he did "not believe that Mr. Carnegie in this is actuated entirely from principles of philanthropy"; on the contrary, he maintained that "the canny Scot sees in these subsidy schemes a shrewd method of entrenching the system of special privileges through which he has extorted millions of dollars from the wage earners and consumers of this country."[33] This charge is essentially accurate. For much of the antagonism expressed against the "generosity" of the robber capitalists was rooted in a correct perception of their exploitation of the American worker through low wages and high prices. It was understood by many that capitalists' contributions to higher education were not separate from their class interests, but were consciously intended to "entrench the system of special privileges" which had enabled them to rise to wealth and power. Their goal in "giving" to the colleges was, as I. S. Bygland of Nebraska charged, to entrench "the rule of property."[34] How? By going to the structural roots of the universities and, "veiled in benevolence," rearranging them on the basis of gifts given to them—gifts with enough strings attached to make the universities dance like puppets whenever Carnegie called the tune—which he did frequently.

Rockefeller

What was true of Andrew Carnegie was equally true of John D. Rockefeller. Rockefeller's philanthropy had begun in a big way as early as the 1880s, but it wasn't until 1902 that he established a foundation—the General Education Board (GEB)—to coordinate his philanthropy and give it more purpose and direction. In 1905, Rockefeller effectively launched the GEB with a grant of $10 million designed "to promote a comprehensive system of higher education in the United States."[35] Frederick T. Gates, a white-haired Baptist ex-minister, was the architect of Rockefeller's system-building, just as Pritchett was the architect for Carnegie's programs; and he shared Rockefeller's ambitious goals. "The cardinal point, Gates pointed out, was a word appearing in the last sentence of the letter of gift: The word was *system.* The purpose of the ten million dollar contribution, Rockefeller's advisor explained, 'is not merely to encourage higher education in the United States, but is mainly to contribute, as far as may be, toward reducing our higher education to something like an orderly and comprehensive *system*, to discourage unnecessary duplication and waste, and to encourage economy and efficiency. Mr. Rockefeller desires the fund all the time to be working toward this great end.' "[36] The board of trustees Rockefeller chose for his foundation included most of the leading lights of American higher education at the time: Charles W. Eliot of Harvard, Daniel Coit Gilman of Johns Hopkins, William Rainey Harper of Chicago, David Starr Jordan of Stanford, and Woodrow Wilson of Princeton, among others.

One of the first acts of the trustees was to conduct an extensive survey of American colleges and universities to enable them to separate the academic wheat from the educational chaff. In its consequences this study was very similar to the one initiated by Henry Pritchett at approximately the same time. And, as with Pritchett, "to choose among the applications which arrived in every mail, once the ten million dollar gift had become known, was a staggering labor."[37] All the colleges, as Gates had predicted, wanted money, and there were far too many of them. Gates believed that "about a fourth of the entire number of American colleges and universities could be formed by careful selection into a system of higher education, and this sytem, carefully nourished, would prove adequate."[38]

In the sixteen years following his initial $10 million plunge, Rockefeller added $118 million to the GEB fund. For this reason, ". . . with their millions, the trustees had within their power the ability . . . to determine whether or not an institution would continue to exist. Coercion may not have been overt, but in making grants the board naturally selected those institutions whose policies and programs they approved. As a result these practices became unofficial standards for many other colleges."[39] The trustees, operating on the principle that some institutions were worthy of support and should be strengthened, felt that others, in the words of Frederick Gates, "must perish and ought to do so."[40]

Rockefeller's goals were, for all intents and purposes, virtually identical to Carnegie's, and each was successful in achieving his goals. In 1924, the GEB invested a record $60 million in the field of higher education.[41] Then, in its annual report for 1925-1926, the Board made this statement: "The General Education Board considers its activities in respect to the increase of general college endowments as practically concluded . . ."[42] The trustees of the GEB did not go so far as to discontinue their philanthropic activities but they did feel that, after twenty-one years of concentrated effort, the urgency underlying their program of expenditures had been relaxed and that much of consequence had been achieved. Higher education, in other words, had shaped up to Rockefeller's expectations.

Results

The foundations concentrated the bulk of their philanthropy on a handful of elite schools. According to Ernest Hollis, from 1902 to 1934 only twenty institutions received more than 73 percent of the funds disbursed by the leading foundations. Curti and Nash observe that "in the interwar period, foundation philanthropy to higher education continued to be dominated by the creations of John D. Rockefeller and Andrew Carnegie. Also continuing was the policy of selecting the strongest and most promising centers of learning as recipients. Between 1923 and 1929, for example, of the $103,000,000 that the five largest foundations gave to private institutions, $88,500,000—or about 86 percent—went to only thirty-six colleges and universities. Out of a total of more than a thousand institutions in the United States, this was indeed concentrated giving. In the following six-year period, fifteen institutions received about three-quarters of foundation allotments."[43]

The conclusion we can draw from these statistics is that the trustees of the foundations were living up to their many words. By focusing their attentions on a small circle of schools, they ensured that the cream of the crop would both survive and thrive—but *only on terms set by the foundations themselves;* and those terms were dictated by the interests of the class which had created the foundations in the first place.

It is not enough to say that the desires of capitalists for the accumulation of capital and the expansion of profits were the primary motive forces leading to the standardization of higher education in this period, for these twin desires are intrinsic to capitalism at every stage of its development. What interests us here is our attempt to discern the *special* nature of this particular era. What special role was played by the universities at this time? What unique historical conditions determined the form and content of the changes occurring in higher education?

The answer to these questions is threefold. We should remember, first, that the consolidation and systematization of ruling-class power over the universities paralleled the movement toward business consolidation and monopoly formation occurring in the economy as a whole. It makes sense for us to conclude that in a period when the representatives of monopoly capital were asserting control over the economic life of the country as a whole, a parallel effort should be made to exert control over the additional major spheres of social activity, and, hence, over the other major institutions of society, ranging from the federal government[44] to the system of higher education. As William DeVane comments, "The tightly organized university of these years corresponded surely to the industrialized society that supported it. Both had expanded in size and grown in complexity. Corporate bureaucracies had developed as a means of governing universities as well as large industrial plants."[45] A smaller and smaller circle of businessmen now controlled the universities as well as the monopoly and oligopoly corporations, demonstrating the tendency toward monopoly formation in each field.

Second, the universities at this time were elite institutions allowing only children of the rich, and unusually capable poorer students, to attend. University students were expected to be the standard-bearers and leaders of the rising empire. It was essential, therefore, that they be adequately prepared to perform their tasks—a consideration not qualitatively different from the desires of the unorganized robber barons of the preceding generation, but one which required new levels of efficiency and planning; Gates was therefore entirely serious when he said that the achievement of maximum educational efficiency was one of Rockefeller's primary objectives in his philanthropy.

Third, and more directly related to current problems, capitalism was growing increasingly complex on a technological level. The technical and scientific needs of capitalist industry were leaping ahead; not only were the chemical and electrical industries beginning to emerge, but the steel and oil industries were becoming more and more sophisticated. Developing monopoly capitalism had a growing need for technicians and techniques, engineers, scientists, accountants, and the applications of scientific method to industrial problems. Universities were important in this process because they were both the necessary training grounds for the new technicians and the research centers for the fulfillment of the new technical needs of industry.

Who were the foundation trustees making the important decisions during this period? Not surprisingly, they were men very similar in their social and economic backgrounds to the men Beck studied as the trustees of the major universities. According to Eduard Lindeman, who reported the findings of a study of four hundred foundation trustees in his book *Wealth and Culture*, "... a typical trustee of an American foundation is a man well past middle age; he is more often than not a man of considerable affluence, or one whose economic security ranks high; his social position in the community is that of a person who belongs to the 'best' clubs and churches, and he associates with men of prestige, power, and affluence.... He receives income primarily from profits and fees. In short, he is a member of that successful and conservative class which came into prominence during the latter part of the nineteenth and early twentieth century, the class whose status is based primarily on pecuniary success."[46]

It is no wonder, then, that these men should have acted to shape the system of American higher education to mesh with their own class interests. What would truly have been a wonder would have been their not doing so.

Notes

1. Merle Curti and Roderick Nash, *Philanthropy in the Shaping of American Higher Education* (New Brunswick, N.J.: Rutgers University Press, 1965), p. 8.
2. Jesse B. Sears, *Philanthropy in American Higher Education* (1922), p. 81.
3. Ernest V. Hollis, *Philanthropic Foundations and Higher Education* (New York: Columbia University Press, 1938), p. 4.
4. Sears, op. cit., p. 81.
5. Ibid., p. 60.
6. Hollis, op. cit., p. 283.
7. Frederick Rudolph, *The American College and University: A History* (New York: Alfred Knopf, 1962), p. 431.
8. Hollis, op. cit., pp. 35-36.
9. Ibid., p. 127.

10. Philip Foner, *History of the Labor Movement in the United States* (New York: International Publishers, n.d.), vol. 2, p. 212.

11. As an example of the pro-capitalist orientation of American educators in this period, it is worth noting that, according to Nicholas M. Butler, later president of Columbia University, the following resolution was "adopted by unanimous vote with tremendous enthusiasm by the National Education Association at Asbury Park in 1894," shortly after the workers' defeat at Homestead: "At such time," the men of learning pontificated, "we deem it our highest duty to pronounce enthusiastically, and with unanimous voice, for the supremacy of law and the maintenance of social and political order. Before grievances of individuals or organizations can be considered or redressed, violence, riot, and insurrection must be repelled and overcome." As Merle Curti points out, "In no instance, apparently, did the Association take cognizance of the causes of the strikes or suggest other realistic means for the solution of grievances. It appears that violence in strikes was not condemned when used by owners of factories or railroads or by the government." Merle Curti, *The Social Ideas of American Educators* (1935), pp. 215, 219.

12. For detailed information on Carnegie and his various foundations, see Joseph Frazier Wall, *Andrew Carnegie* (New York: Oxford University Press, 1970).

13. Theron Schlabach, *Pensions for Professors* (Madison, Wis.: University of Wisconsin Press, 1963), pp. 6-7.

14. Cited in Raymond Fosdick and Henry Pringle, *Adventure in Giving* (New York: Harper & Row, 1962), p. 42.

15. Schlabach, op. cit., pp. 22-23.

16. Wall, op. cit., p. 873.

17. Ibid., p. 874.

18. Schlabach, op. cit., p. 28.

19. Cited in John S. Brubacher and Willis Rudy, *Higher Education in Transition: An American History* (New York: Harper, 1958), p. 343.

20. Curti and Nash, op. cit., p. 220.

21. Rudolph, op. cit., p. 432.

22. Hollis, op. cit., p. 136.

23. Ibid., p. 136.

24. Schlabach, op. cit., pp. 83-84.

25. Ibid., p. 8.

26. Sears, op. cit., p. 98.

27. Elbert V. Wills, *The Growth of American Higher Education* (Philadelphia: Dorrance & Co., 1936), p. 156.

28. Cited in Hollis, op. cit., p. 52.

29. Schlabach, op. cit., p. 6.

30. Ibid., p. 8.

31. Ibid.

32. Ibid., p. 79.

33. Fosdick and Pringle, op. cit., p. 51.

34. Schlabach, op. cit., p. 74.

35. Fosdick and Pringle, op. cit., p. 127.

36. Ibid., p. 129. An insight into Gates's bombastic character can be gleaned from the following passage from his farewell speech to the Rockefeller Foundation: "Shaking his fist at a somewhat startled but respectfully attentive Board, he vociferated: 'When you die and come to approach the judgment of Almighty God, what do you think he will demand of you? Do you for an instant presume to believe that he will inquire into your petty failures or your trivial virtues? No! He will ask just one question: What did you do as a Trustee of the Rockefeller Foundation?' " (Fosdick and Pringle, p. 208).

37. Ibid., p. 131.

38. Ibid.

39. Curti and Nash, op. cit., pp. 216-17.

40. Ibid., p. 217. Also Fosdick and Pringle, op. cit., p. 130.

41. Fosdick and Pringle, op. cit., p. 135.

42. Ibid., p. 204.

43. Curti and Nash, op. cit., p. 222.

44. See James Weinstein, *The Corporate Ideal and the Liberal State* (Boston: Beacon Press, 1968), and Gabriel Kolko, *The Triumph of Conservatism* (Chicago: Quadrangle Books, 1963).

45. William C. DeVane, *Higher Education in Twentieth Century America* (Cambridge, Mass.: Harvard University Press, 1965), p. 77.

46. Eduard Lindeman, *Wealth and Culture* (New York: Harcourt & Brace, 1936), p. 46.

6
The State and College-Educated Labor

In the years following World War II, the United States assumed a new role in a world pregnant with revolutionary possibilities. As the new and virtually undisputed leader of the imperialist bloc, fragmented until recently by six years of global war, the United States became one of the chief actors in the worldwide polarization of forces in which anti-imperialist and socialist forces engaged in a struggle with the armed might and financial strength of European and American capitalism.

In Vietnam, the French became entangled with the socialist Vietminh in a long-term struggle which was to have explosive repercussions for the stability of imperialism in general. In Greece, communist insurgents tottered briefly on the brink of achieving power before being finally annihilated in 1948, defeated by a coalition of forces supported by Stalin as well as by the United States. In China, the Communist party swept to power in 1949 on the crest of an earthshaking revolutionary upsurge which shook the international balance of power and gave new hope to revolutionaries throughout the Third World. In Africa, new nations arose by the handful as old-fashioned colonialism gave way to neocolonialism, exploitation based not on direct political control but on indirect economic relations of unequal exchange. In Korea, war broke out between communist liberation fighters and the United States itself.[1]

As the leader of the imperialist forces, the United States

played a pivotal role in the conflicts which developed on the basis of this global polarization of forces. New needs and new capabilities began to come to the fore as the American capitalist class shouldered the burdens of empire for the first time. These new needs and capabilities were to lead, before long, to the radical transformation of numerous aspects of American life.

The institutions of higher education were among the key elements of American society most profoundly affected by the new situation. While previously they had catered to the children of the ruling class as an agency for the direct transmission of class privileges, in the new era they became the primary training grounds for the children of the working class now being called upon to perform the varied technical and administrative tasks newly important to capitalism. While previously the universities had been small schools for the instruction of an elite, in the new era they became multiversities, vast crucibles for the socialization and training of a broad and widening stratum of the wage-labor force.[2]

The state played the key organizational role in this process. Although never unimportant, the state for the first time during this period played the *major* role in solving the social dilemmas once left to the invisible hand of the market for unraveling.

Two major branches have grown from the root of state involvement with higher education: (1) a sizable and rapidly widening college-educated sector of the work force, and (2) an expanding array of scientific and social knowledge. The historical processes which led to the development and fruition of these elements of contemporary production will be the primary focus of attention in this chapter. Each of the separate strands of ruling-class involvement in this process—corporate, foundation, and above all state, "giving"—will be examined, but what will emerge will not be an image of isolated and distinct forces operating *apart* from each other but a complex interweaving of motives, methods, and personnel, all springing from a common source: the continuously developing needs of American capitalism.

Early Corporate Giving

The first instances of corporate giving to support education were spontaneous and unrehearsed. In 1882, five years after the Great Rail Strike of 1877, the Pennsylvania Railroad created a trust fund to educate the daughters of deceased employees. A short while later, the Oliver Mining Company—a subsidiary of Carnegie Steel—set up an educational program for foreign-born employees working in the Mesabi iron range in Minnesota. These early corporate efforts were for the most part small-scale and innocuous. Thus, it wasn't until the turn of the century that corporate giving (as distinct from individual philanthropy) grew large enough to be noticeable on the map of educational spending.

The essential stimulus for corporate giving in this period was the increasing technical complexity and sophistication of industry. "In the youthful electrical industry, for example, art and science and adaptation were leaping ahead so rapidly in the 1890s from arc lighting and transformers and streetcars to Edison's incandescent lamps and his bipolar dynamos ('long-waisted Mary Anns') that formal engineering education institutions often lagged behind industry's application . . ."[3] To rectify matters, leading corporations in the rising chemical, electrical, and petroleum industries tentatively initiated university programs designed, on the one hand, to advance the levels of industrial knowledge in these three fields, and, on the other, to prepare students more adequately for careers with firms like General Electric, Shell Petroleum, or du Pont.

These three rising new industries—the chemical, electrical,

and petroleum industries—relied heavily on the work of the university community. Thus, Eells and Patrick argue that "General Electric—and the same was true of Westinghouse—could not have come into being, and certainly could not have survived, without a vital relationship with the educational community."[4]

One of the earliest corporate contributors to higher education was the Shell International Petroleum Company. Shell's first major grant was awarded to Cambridge University in 1912 for a Readership in Physical Chemistry. In 1919, Shell gave Cambridge a further grant of £50,000, explaining its action in these words: "The oil industry depends essentially upon science and technology, and, while it is well able to train recruits in the application of these branches of knowledge to the business, it can only do so if they arrive equipped with the necessary background of secondary and higher education."[5] Shell later went on to vastly broaden its schedule of giving, in the United States as well as the United Kingdom. During the period 1953 to 1962, when corporate giving as a whole rose rapidly, Shell gave "every university and every college of science and technology in the United Kingdom . . . some financial assistance."[6] In the words of a company statement released in 1963: "What we have had to do . . . is to assess our future manpower requirements and . . . remove difficulties in the way of University Departments attracting and training the necessary specialists in sufficient numbers."[7] In other words, the wisdom of the company's ripe old age of experience turns out to be fully consonant with its practice from 1912 onwards.

Du Pont, a chemicals firm, initiated a program of careful educational investments in 1918 when it "foresaw an increasing need for scientists in industry."[8] At about the same time, General Electric substantially accelerated its giving, for the same reasons. Other companies especially important in this early period included Standard Oil of New Jersey and American Cyanamid, another chemicals firm. In 1929, General Motors began its first cautious program of planned educational investment, wading slowly at first into the muddy waters of "philanthropy" and growing bolder only after a decade of experience.

"These beginnings," as Curti and Nash point out, "were confined to supporting technical training or subsidizing ad hoc research projects clearly related to the limited conception of improving production and distribution of the product."[9] These hesitant beginnings were reinforced by the more intensive efforts of Allied Chemicals and Sears Roebuck in the early thirties, with the result that by 1936, according to the U.S. Treasury Department, corporate spending on higher education had risen to an annual sum of $30 million.[10] Following the 1935 passage of a bill giving corporations a major tax exemption for contributions to higher education, contributions began to flood in. Thus, by 1945, corporate giving had soared to the impressive total of $266 million per year.[11]

The passage of the 1935 tax-exemption bill constitutes one important example of the power of the capitalist class. For as the social environment continued to change and as the corporations developed new needs (specifically, a need for enhanced technology), it became clear that the laws had to be adjusted in order to accommodate the new desires of the capitalist class, which, as a *ruling* class, directly or indirectly exerted major control over the principal organs of the federal government, including Congress and the courts. "Before 1936, corporations could not deduct charitable contributions from taxable income. In the Revenue Code of 1935, Congress inserted a provision that permitted corporations to deduct up to five percent of their new taxable income for contributions to charitable institutions and causes."[12] This code, which was enacted only after leading capitalists applied considerable pressure on Congress, had significant consequences for higher education insofar as it removed one of the major obstacles blocking the path of corporate philanthropy.

The Ford Foundation

The second major surge in foundation giving began in 1936 with the establishment of the Ford Foundation. This development in many ways paralleled the early leap in corporate spending which also occurred during the late thirties; not only did it occur at approximately the same time, it also had its roots in the changing structure of the law. As Curti and Nash point out, "Disinterested benevolence did not figure as a primary motive when Henry Ford and his son Edsel established their philanthropic agency on January 15, 1936."[13] What prodded them into action was the passage of a new tax law threatening traditional family control over the Ford Motor Company. The creation of an ostensibly "charitable" foundation appeared to them to be the only way out of the legal trap facing them. In 1947, after the death of both Fords, the Ford Foundation received about 90 percent of all Ford Motor Company stock, with an estimated value of more than $2 billion. It began its major programs soon afterward.

One of the first things the Foundation did was establish a committee to study the problem of spending the money. The conclusions reached by this committee echoed the conclusions of Rockefeller and Carnegie fifty years earlier. Education was to be the primary focus of expenditures.

In 1951, the Foundation set up the Fund for the Advancement of Education (the FAE) to provide a vehicle for the management of its spending on educational matters, which before the decade was out had reached truly prodigious levels. During the 1950s, the Ford Foundation spent $744 million on educational affairs, including $260 million at one stroke. At the same time, although on a somewhat smaller scale, the Sloan and Rockefeller foundations continued their programs, while "the Carnegie Corporation maintained a program of vigorous philanthropy," with Devereaux Josephs as its president then and Clark Kerr as its president now.[14] The primary focus of foundation giving during this period was on educational and technological innovations.

During the course of the fifties, with the rise of state spending and the end of the overwhelming significance of giant foundations like the GEB and the Carnegie Foundation, the "philanthropy" of foundations and newly conscious corporations came very close to merging. The Ford Foundation's Fund for the Advancement of Education helped subsidize the initial corporate studies which explored and tested the profitability of investment in higher education and human capital. As always, the various branches of capitalist spending on higher education had a single, overriding purpose beneath their veneer of "social responsibility": to retain ruling-class control over the enormous surpluses produced in the economy, enabling the capitalist class to use the wealth and power derived from those surpluses to affect and control the direction of society.

Corporate Giving Comes of Age

The corporations became newly conscious of the potential profitability of investment in higher education in the years following World War II. According to Curti and Nash, "The combined efforts of corporations and their philanthropic agencies grew phenomenally during and after World War II, quickly becoming a major source of revenue for American colleges and universities."[15] This resulted, according to Eells and Patrick, because in the contemporary period "the problems of the American economy have become more sharply defined than ever before in terms of the resources of higher education—new knowledge, better-educated manpower, and the environmental influences . . . upon economic, social and political stability. For a company these are the determinants first of survival and then of progress, and they necessarily engage the first attention of the business executive."[16] Requiring new kinds of workers and special technological knowledge which only the universities could provide, the corporations began to move slowly but massively toward organized support for higher education.

Before corporate support for higher education could emerge on a large scale, however, one major barrier had to be overcome: a law existing in many states, notably New Jersey, made it illegal for corporations (as opposed to individual businessmen) to give money to universities and colleges. In 1951, the chairman of the board of Standard Oil of New Jersey, Frank Abrams, came out publicly in opposition to the law. Shortly thereafter, the A. P. Smith Manufacturing Company, a small New Jersey firm, consciously violated the problematic law and awarded Princeton University a token sum "in what may have been a maneuver planned by the New Jersey corporations themselves [i.e., Standard Oil] to provoke a test case."[17]

In their initial decision to contribute to the welfare of Princeton University, the directors of the A. P. Smith Company declared: "It appears that in order to maintain, over a period of time, the conditions under which corporations in general and this corporation in particular can exist and do business for a profit, it is necessary that understanding of the benefits to the nation flowing from private enterprise and corporate organization be continued and if possible broadened and strengthened."[18] Later, the president of the company, Hubert O'Brien, explained the action further in these revealing words: "It seems to me that if we as a corporation have a right, as I clearly feel we have, to invest funds in the training of personnel who operate our machines and our various productive processes in the plant, that we have an equal right, certainly, to assure the continuation of the institutions of higher learning who supply us with the trained manpower to man the technical posts, the management posts, without which modern industry cannot effectively continue."[19] The reasoning which led the universities to be integrated into the industrial fabric of the economy during the next two decades was becoming apparent. Echoes of this reasoning were to be heard innumerable times in the coming years.

When the A. P. Smith Manufacturing Company was brought to trial later in 1951, on hand to testify for the defense were Abrams of Standard Oil and Irving S. Olds, chairman of U.S. Steel. Both men focused their statements on the importance of educated labor to big business, echoing O'Brien. According to Abrams, ". . . in the protection of the huge investment of corporation stockholders, management must have power to make the relatively small expenditures necessary to ensure the continued availability of these vital and irreplaceable sources of supply of effective men and women."[20] Olds's testimony was equally to the point: "If it is necessary," he declared, "for us to spend millions of dollars to beneficiate the ore which goes into our blast furnaces and to process the coal which goes into our coke ovens, then why is it not equally our business to develop and improve the quality of the greatest natural resource of all, the human mind?"[21]

When delivering the verdict which simultaneously acquitted the A. P. Smith Company and overturned the law prohibiting corporate contributions to higher education, Superior Court Judge Alfred Stein made several revealing comments indicating his respect for the logic of the arguments advanced by Abrams, Olds, and O'Brien. First, he declared that "as industrial conditions change, business methods must change with them and acts become permissible which at an earlier period would not have been considered to be within corporate power."[22] Specifically, Stein thought that it had become important to legalize corporate contributions to higher education because it was now necessary for the health of the economy to assure industry of a "friendly reservoir" of technically and administratively skilled workers from which the corporations might periodically replenish the highly skilled sector of their work force. Before many years were to pass, as the logic of this position became inescapable for the capitalist class as a whole, higher education found itself increasingly integrated into the expanding process of production.

The responsibility for pushing the powerful American business community in the direction of large-scale investment in higher education belongs in this early period to a relatively small vanguard of far-sighted corporate executives. Frank Sparks, co-founder and treasurer of Noblitt-Sparks, Inc., and president of Wabash College in Indiana, was among the first of these men and represented a fusion of business and educational interests characteristic of most of them. In 1948, Sparks and Thomas Elisha Jones, president of Fordham College, formed the Associated Colleges of Indiana for the purpose of enticing businessmen to support higher education.[23] Touring Indiana, they focused on "appeals that were to become commonplace in soliciting American business: liberal arts colleges preserve freedom; they produce many essential scientists and business executives; tax laws make it inexpensive to give," and so on.[24] Sparks and Jones were well rewarded for their efforts, and similar associations soon emerged in many other states.

In 1952, shortly after the Stein decision in the A. P. Smith case, Rockefeller's General Education Board, the Sloan Foundation, the Carnegie Corporation, and the Ford Foundation cooperated to build what swiftly emerged as the leading corporate fund-raising and research organization for higher education, the Council for Financial Aid to Education. The first president of the CFAE, which had a board of directors composed of sixteen leading capitalists and twelve university presidents, was Wilson Compton, who, like Frank Sparks, was not only the former president of a university (Washington State) but also a leading businessman as chairman of the board of the Cameron Machine Company and the former secretary and general manager of the National Lumber Manufacturers Association and former vice-president of the American Forest Products Industry. Frank Abrams, chairman of the board of the Standard Oil Company of New Jersey, became the first chairman of the executive committee of the CFAE; as a trustee of Syracuse University, the Ford Foundation, and the Sloan Foundation, he was as deeply enmeshed in the fusion of business and education as any other member of the capitalist class.

The four other principal leaders of the CFAE were Alfred Sloan himself, founder of the Sloan Foundation, former chairman of the board of General Motors, and a trustee of the MIT Corporation; Irving S. Olds, chairman of the council of directors of the CFAE, former chairman of the board of U.S. Steel, and a fellow of the Yale Corporation; Walter Paepcke, chairman of the board of the Container Corporation of America and a trustee of the University of Chicago; and Henning W. Prentis, Jr., chairman of the board of the Armstrong Cork Company, former president of the National Association of Manufacturers, and president of the trustees at Wilson College in Pennsylvania, while simultaneously serving as a trustee at Franklin and Marshall College.[25]

These men stood at the heights of both the corporate and educational hierarchies in the United States, representing the highest offices in the nation's largest corporations and sitting on the boards of some of the most prestigious universities. They were capable, thus, of comprising a corporate vanguard dedicated to channeling much of corporate investment into higher education.

Following the formation of the CFAE, and partly as a result of its extensive campaign in favor of business giving to higher education, corporate philanthropy began to grow with great speed. By 1956, enough corporations were contributing to higher education to enable the CFAE to publish a booklet entitled *Aid-to-Education Programs of Some Leading Business Concerns,* containing the facts and figures of business support for higher education. The book contained brief statements from each of the contributing firms explaining the motivations underlying their aid-to-education programs. This book—and each of its successor volumes—constitutes a gold mine of revealing insights into the sound profit-making rationale for business "aid to education."

The key reasons for supporting higher education, according to the CFAE, were identified by the "top management" of General Electric in 1956. According to GE, business gets: "(1) *new knowledge* through research and competent teaching; (2) an adequate supply of *educated manpower;* [and] (3) an *economic, social and political climate* in which companies like GE can survive and continue to progress." According to the CFAE, "What business gets out of institutions of higher education is summarized in those three carefully considered points."[26]

The explanations put forward by the bulk of the other companies involved in aid-to-education programs tended to mirror the ideas expressed by GE, sometimes amplifying or modifying them but rarely disregarding them. Bethlehem Steel, for example, gave almost $600,000 "in recognition of the fact that . . . his education makes the college graduate a valuable asset in the conduct of Bethlehem's business."[27] Similarly, Socony-Mobil stated that "contributing to higher education . . . will help assure to business for many years a supply of competent people capable of handling the problems of an ever more complex society." Eastman Kodak contributed $650,000 in 1956 because "the training and ability of college graduates who have come to the company have contributed greatly to Kodak's progress." The Bankers Trust Company of New York said that it hoped "to attract well-trained college and business school graduates, seeking a banking career, to Bankers Trust Company," while Armstrong Cork declared that "we feel we have a responsibility to help support our American colleges and universities, many of which supply us year after year with new, well-trained personnel." The directors of Burlington Industries stated that "expenditure for education yields a high return for business. A well educated person produces and consumes more." Lockheed said that "we wish not only to help worthy young men and women obtain advanced training but to encourage them to choose careers in private industry, especially the aircraft and missile industry." Time, Inc., announced that it considered its giving "an investment in improving the educational level of the country and in the Company's development of its present and future manpower," while U.S. Steel contributed over $1 million in 1956 without commenting on that fact.

In 1958, the biggest multinational corporations (such as those which participated in the creation of the CFAE), spent huge sums of money on higher education but, like U.S. Steel, made no comment. Their actions spoke eloquently, however. General Motors gave in excess of $5 million, while Ford Motors spent $3 million. Du Pont spend $1,300,000, Standard Oil of Indiana $800,000. Hughes Aircraft explained its own $900,000 contribution by saying that "industry depends upon education to supply creative people and new ideas," while Boeing maintained that its considerable gifts were motivated by a desire to keep up with "the increasing need for technical and professional employees." IBM justified its

$500,000 expenditure by saying that "no part of the American economy is more dependent on education than industry." And finally, ITT analyzed "educated manpower" as "one of this nation's most precious commodities."

In 1964, the CFAE summarized the rapid growth of business spending on higher education during the previous decade and offered a cogent analysis of its motivational roots. Corporate spending, they showed, had continued to rise steadily during the eight years since the boom in corporate spending had begun to even out in 1956. One core group of 171 leading corporations studied by the CFAE was found to have contributed "127.1 percent more in 1964 than they had eight years earlier." In addition, the size of the average contributions of the leading firms in this period had risen from $171,615 in 1960 to $258,118 in 1964. In 1962, a total of $82 million had been spent by the 701 firms studied by the CFAE, while in 1964, 993 companies spent $118 million. Further, in 1964 there were more than 16 companies spending in excess of $1 million annually on higher education, and more than 207 companies spent over $100,000. The magnitude of giving had become truly impressive.

Moreover, corporate spending, like the foundation philanthropy of an earlier era, was highly concentrated. One hundred forty-five mammoth corporations were found to contribute 27 percent of all business giving to higher education, while 24 of those firms accounted for fully 20 percent of *all* giving and 80 percent of the giving of the leading 145 firms. The motives underlying this highly concentrated giving were summed up by the CFAE: "Company contributions have now been tested by experience over a long enough span of time to be proved a sound investment. They are *not* philanthropy. Guided by reason and a clear purpose, they *are* an aspect of good management in the conduct of business." The cardinal concluding points included the following: "The men who led the business aid-to-education movement in its early stages were quite clear about its main purpose: insuring a steady and adequate flow of *educated manpower* into business and industry. . . . All of business-industry today depends in one way or another on *research,* out of which comes new knowledge and new products. . . . Equally, leading companies know that vital to their interests is the pure *research* carried on almost alone in the major colleges and universities of the country. Their research teams make many of the basic discoveries which are the true life blood of an industrial nation . . ."

Although many of the statements of the leading corporations in recent and more sophisticated years have been couched in a cloudy rhetoric of "human welfare" and "national interest," "What is in the national interest to many a businessman," as Eells and Patrick point out, "is a healthy, driving, profit-oriented economy, and this is a lot of nuts and bolts and steel mills and smokestacks."[28] Educated labor and new knowledge, in the context of the achievement of a loosely defined social stability, are the products of higher education most desired by the corporations—and, as we shall see, they are also the essential products most desired by the state in its vast program of giving.

The State

> *Since World War II, it has been evident that if society is to meet its responsibilities—responsibility for survival as well as progress—it must, through government action, call on colleges and universities for those things which they alone in our society produce: highly trained manpower and new knowledge.*[29]
>
> Bureau of Labor Statistics
> *Tomorrow's Manpower Needs*

When the torrent of state spending on higher education began in the early 1940s, with the advent of World War II, it fell on fields not previously irrigated by federal spending. Before 1940, the state had never been more than peripherally involved in higher education. Federally funded agricultural research programs dating back to the period of the Morrill Land Grant Act of 1862 and intensified during the first and third decades of the twentieth century had been the sum total of the state's involvement with higher education in America. Then, with the beginning of World War II and the consequent introduction of a set of new demands on the economy, the second major transformation of the universities was begun. Carnegie, Rockefeller, and the earlier robber barons had succeeded in shaping the university system into a rough diamond to be cut and polished for use by the ruling class. The state—during World War II—began to cut that rough diamond and put it to work as the cutting edge of a new expansion in military research and development which would soon lead to the overall transformation of the basic purposes and functions of American higher education.

World War II saw a great leap forward in research and development work, centered in the major universities and vital to the success of the war effort. For the first time, the federal government established high-ranking governmental agencies not only intended to promote the dynamic growth of research and development centers but directed by scientists. The noted scientist Vannevar Bush served as the chief of the two successive war-science agencies created during World War II which greatly expanded America's war technology at a total expenditure of $3 billion.

By the end of the war, the universities had been converted largely into weapons development centers. In the almost thirty years since the end of the war, this aspect of the state's involvement with the university system has become more and more pronounced, augmented especially by the wars in Korea and Indochina and by the pressures of the Cold War. In addition, a new dimension of state involvement arose, beginning with the passage of the GI Bill in 1946. For the first time, the state began to concern itself with the task of providing opportunities for otherwise ineligible people to go to advanced schools, thus taking pressure off the economy in terms of employment problems while preparing thousands of workers for technically sophisticated jobs.

The two key questions and needs underlying the passage of the first GI Bill were correctly identified by Alice Rivlin in 1960: "Would men," she asked, "whose education had been interrupted by four or more years of military service return to schools and colleges for the training needed for jobs in the postwar economy? *And if they did not, would the economy be able to absorb several million new workers, who would flood the labor market even before reconversion was complete?*" Out of the discussion of these issues, she commented, "came the educational provisions of the GI Bill."[30]

The GI Bill guaranteed forty-eight months of free schooling to all veterans of World War II, and by 1947 over a million were enrolled. They were being prepared to fill newly important positions in the economy as technically and administratively educated workers (a development to be analyzed in detail in the next chapter). They were also being diverted from the blue-collar labor force in an effort—coordinated by the state—to avoid the massive postwar unemployment and depression predicted for the American economy by both leftists and capitalist officials. By solving these problems, the GI Bill fulfilled its mission and contributed greatly to the growth and stability of the economy and society as a whole. In terms of the vast state spending which was to follow, however, it constituted at most an important beginning.

Immediately after the conclusion of World War II, recognizing the new importance of the universities as instruments for the achievement of social stability, President Harry Truman appointed a Commission on Higher Education (under the active leadership of George Zook) to conduct an intensive examination of the university system. Probing deeply into many of the problems and possibilities confronting the state in the realm of higher education, the Zook Commission found itself frustrated when it tried to bring about the implementation of its proposals. Congress—splintered politically, conservative, and uncertain of the significance of many problems—refused to pay the price necessary to translate the Zook Commission proposals into reality. Nevertheless, it did act to pass a number of bills significantly advancing America's effort to cope with its changing structural needs. One of these bills was the Housing Act of 1950, which provided for the housing of the army of new university students. "The immediate impact on the colleges of returning veterans of World War II was tremendous. . . . Instructors, classrooms, and housing had to be found for this influx almost overnight."[31]

Research and development expenditures, which doubled during the Korean War, were increasingly channeled during this period through the newly created National Science Foundation, founded in 1950 for the purpose of developing and encouraging "the pursuit of a national policy for the promotion of basic research and education in the sciences."[32] Moreover, the creation of an educated labor force was further advanced by the passage in 1952 of the Korean GI Bill. This second GI Bill, which continued and expanded the first, had effects similar to those of its important predecessor. Combined, the two bills sent over ten million veterans to school.[33]

The corporations, too, began to make significant and systematic efforts to develop new knowledge and an educated sector of the labor force in the early and mid-1950s. Combined, state and corporate spending financed the education of millions of workers. Thus, despite the absence during the fifties of an *official* federal strategy for the expansion of education, education was greatly expanded. And further, despite the absence of a clearly articulated strategy for the transformation of the universities, the universities were nevertheless transformed. In the closing years of the decade, several developments took place which culminated in the belated emergence of a national policy for higher education which contributed to its transformation.

In 1956, President Eisenhower appointed a second Commission on Higher Education, directed by Devereaux Josephs of the New York Equitable Life Insurance Company and the Carnegie Corporation. Whether the far-reaching proposals of the Josephs Commission would have been ignored like those of the Zook Commission if larger events had not intervened is unknown; what is known is that when the Soviet Union launched its Sputnik satellite in 1958, dramatic national action was immediately undertaken and the proposals of the Josephs Commission were thoroughly studied.

The first and most important legislative enactment passed in response to America's dawning awareness of the Soviet Union's technological prowess was the National Defense Education Act of 1958, which for the first time placed the state's relationship to higher education on a consciously formalized basis. "To meet the present educational emergency," declared the authors of the bill, "requires additional effort at all levels of government. It is therefore the purpose of this Act to provide substantial assistance in various forms to individuals, and to states and their subdivisions, in order to insure trained manpower of sufficient quality and quantity to meet the national defense needs of the United States."[34] With the flight of the Soviet satellite, a cold fear suddenly gripped American legislators that the United States had fallen behind the Soviet Union in technological development. In order to strengthen the United States militarily and to further strengthen the economy, significant steps were taken in the context of the NDEA to open the doors of higher education to hundreds of thousands of young people who otherwise would have been unable to attend college. The basic purpose of the massive NDEA scholarship and assistance programs—which have been revised, extended, and expanded numerous times since 1958—was to assure the scientific and engineering predominance of the United States in global affairs. Through the NDEA and subsequent bills, tens of billions of dollars have been poured into this effort.

When public attention was focused on higher education following the passage of the NDEA, the new concern was greeted by the publication of a profusion of books and articles on higher education and the state. The essential idea to be learned from these books was expressed by Alice Rivlin: "The most important reason for reconsidering the role of the federal government in financing higher education is the now widespread, yet comparatively recent, realization of how important higher education is to national economic and military strength. Both our military capacity and the economic growth on which it partially depends have become vitally linked to rapid advances in research, and the availability of highly trained manpower to carry out the research and to utilize the results."[35]

Acting on the basis of their new commitment to the *systematic* transformation of American higher education to meet the research and manpower needs of developing capitalism, America's legislators passed a "torrent of education bills"[36] during the 1960s. President Kennedy explained the rationale for the state's concern with higher education in his Education Message of January 29, 1963: "This nation," he said, "is committed to greater investment in economic growth; and recent research has shown that one of the most beneficial of all such investments is education, accounting for some 40 percent of the nation's growth and productivity in recent years. It is an investment which yields a substantial return in the higher wages and purchasing power of trained workers, in the new products and techniques which come from skilled minds and in the constant expansion of this nation's storehouse of useful knowledge."[37]

The first important bill to be passed in the 1960s dealing with educational matters was the Manpower Development and Training Act of 1962, intended primarily (1) to combat unemployment and (2) to swell the ranks of highly skilled workers. The passage of this bill was followed by the formulation by members of the Kennedy Administration of an ambitious "omnibus bill" covering the major areas of educational concern. Although this bill was ultimately defeated, three fragments survived as bills in their own right and were passed in late 1963, shortly after Kennedy's death. The $3.3 billion allocated for their implementation is a measure of the government's concern about higher education.[38]

An especially momentous bill, according to President Johnson, was the Higher Education Facilities Act of 1963. This bill was passed, according to Johnson, "to assist the nation's institutions of higher education to construct needed classrooms, laboratories, and libraries in order to accommodate mounting student enrollments and to meet demands for skilled technicians and for advanced graduate education."[39] A total of $1.2 billion was allocated for this bill, which in many ways paralleled the Housing Act passed a decade earlier.[40]

During the rest of the decade, numerous bills and laws were passed extending and deepening the commitment of the state to higher education. These bills, which included the extremely important Higher Education Act of 1965 and the Elementary and Secondary Act of 1965, generally mirrored the concerns and ideas expressed by the authors of earlier bills.

As before, educated labor and new knowledge were stressed as the primary products of the universities, desirable for their stabilizing effects on the economy, their military value, and their profitability. As before, in each case, the state gave lavishly to ensure that what the National Science Foundation called "the available supply of well-trained technicians" would not fall short of the "demand for these workers."[41] At the end of the decade, Grayson Kirk, president of Columbia University during the 1968 uprising, was able to declare in tones of almost biblical enthusiasm that the 1960s were a "watershed in our educational history . . . It was a time when the federal government assumed new degrees of financial responsibility for the support of American education. It was a time when the research activity of American higher education began to receive levels of federal and state investment that would have been unthinkable a few short years before."[42] It was a time, in other words, when the universities were transformed by the force of state involvement into a new kind of institution designed to serve a ruling class confronted with the necessity of performing a delicate social, political, and economic balancing act as the inheritor of the burdens of world empire in a time of instability and revolution.[43]

Notes

1. See Gabriel and Joyce Kolko, *The Limits of Power* (New York: Harper & Row, 1972), for an exhaustive account of America's new role in international affairs.

2. The specific terminology employed in this passage derives originally from Carl Davidson's pioneering pamphlet, "The Multiversity: Crucible of the New Working Class," published by Students for a Democratic Society in 1967.

3. Richard Eells and Kenneth Patrick, *Education and the Business Dollar* (New York: MacMillan, 1969), p. 27.

4. Ibid., p. 30.

5. Ibid., p. 32.

6. Ibid.

7. Ibid., pp. 32-33.

8. Ibid., p. 34.

9. Merle Curti and Roderick Nash, *Philanthropy in the Shaping of American Higher Education* (New Brunswick, N.J.: Rutgers University Press, 1965), p. 240.

10. Ibid.

11. Ibid.

12. Ibid., p. 241.

13. Ibid., p. 246.

14. As an indication of Kerr's class consciousness (and as an entertaining story), it's worth noting that the inscription in Kerr's personal copy of Alfred Sloan's *My Years with General Motors* reads as follows: "To President Clark Kerr [of the University of California], who is doing for higher education what Alfred Sloan achieved for GM in the fight of corporate management. Xmas greetings, Bill Henley." I am indebted to Ilene Phillipson for this invaluable item of historical knowledge.

15. Curti and Nash, op. cit., p. 238.

16. Eells and Patrick, op. cit., p. 19.

17. Curti and Nash, op. cit., pp. 242-43.

18. Thomas H. Devine, *Corporate Support for Education* (Washington, D.C.: Catholic University of America Press, 1956), p. 78.

19. Ibid., p. 80.

20. Ibid., p. 82.

21. Ibid.

22. Ibid., p. 113.

23. See Eells and Patrick, op. cit., and Curti and Nash, op. cit.

24. Curti and Nash, op. cit., p. 245.

25. All this information comes primarily from Curti and Nash, op. cit., and Eells and Patrick, op. cit.

26. The Council for Aid to Education, *Aid-to-Education Programs* (1956), p. 1.

27. This quote and its successors, citing business motivations for educational "philanthropy," were drawn from the literally numberless pages of the various CFAE books, unless otherwise noted.

28. Eells and Patrick, op. cit., p. 21.

29. Homer Babbidge and Robert Rosenzweig, *The Federal Interest in Higher Education* (New York: McGraw Hill, 1962), p. 28.

30. Alice M. Rivlin, *The Role of the Federal Government in Financing Higher Education* (Washington, D.C.: Brookings Institute, 1961), p. 65.

31. Ibid., p. 69.

32. Babbidge and Rosenzweig, op. cit., p. 35.

33. Rivlin, op. cit., p. 67.

34. Babbidge and Rosenzweig, op. cit., pp. 50-51.

35. Rivlin, op. cit., p. 8.

36. James D. Koerner, *Who Controls American Education?* (Boston: Beacon Press, 1968), p. 5.

37. Sidney Tiedt, *The Role of the Federal Government in Education* (New York: Oxford University Press, 1966), p. 180.

38. Hsien Lu, *Federal Role in Education* (New York: Lawrence Letter Service Corporation, 1965), p. 187.

39. Ibid., p. 156.

40. Ibid., p. 192.

41. Tiedt, op. cit., p. 64.

42. Eells and Patrick, op. cit., p. 230.

43. See David Horowitz, *Empire and Revolution* (New York: Random House, 1967), for a superb analysis of the growth and development of imperialism in the context of world revolutionary movements (and vice versa).

Part III
The Meaning of Ruling-Class Control

7
Capitalism and the Universities

The Nature of Ruling-Class Control

As the capitalist process of production and exchange grows more complex, ruling-class power evolves correspondingly. In the last four chapters, we have traced the evolution of capitalist control of a single institution, the university. From a distance, and through a lens focused primarily on the universities, we have glanced briefly at the changing nature of the problems facing capitalism which have forced the ruling class to exercise power in new and different ways during the past century.

We have seen that in the earliest period of competitive capitalism, power was exercised on an anarchic and individualistic level. In this period, the random and disjointed philanthropy of the robber barons impelled development of the universities, leading to a bewildering and uneven growth. Later, with the rise of monopoly corporations, Carnegie and Rockefeller acted to *organize* and *systematize* the universities for the first time. This transmutation of ruling-class power over the universities reflected larger changes in the class relations of society as a whole, changes signaled by the emergence of monopoly corporations as the primary vehicles of bourgeois rule.

Under the influence of the monopoly corporations, the political and economic structure of society was organized in a newly efficient fashion in this period. The systematic organization of the universities thus mirrored and contributed to the systematic organization of capitalism itself taking place during this era. As the training ground for the elite of business administrators charged with organizing the economy along monopolistic lines, the universities found themselves deeply integrated into developing monopoly capitalism.

These early changes represented important stages in the growth of the universities. The most striking and significant break with the past, however, in terms of the nature of capitalist control of the universities, has occurred within the last thirty years. Now, the universities and their primary social products (college-educated labor and new knowledge) are important to the system as instruments of the ruling-class effort to achieve the continued stability and progress of capitalism in a new situation. As Bogdan Denitch comments, "This change in the role of the universities reflects new needs of the economy: needs for increasing numbers of salaried people with technical and bureaucratic skills who will be dependent on institutions in which they hold no power."[1]

Capitalism now is threatened on a global scale by the eruption (or potential eruption) of a wide variety of class antagonisms and international crises, ranging from socialist wars of national liberation to domestic unemployment. Fearing both the loss of its worldwide ascendancy and the profits which result from that ascendancy, the American ruling class has been doing everything in its power to make sure that its international strength remains unshaken in the coming decades.

Further, impressed by the magnitude and severity of the Great Depression of the thirties, the ruling class has become painfully aware of the fundamental instability of unregulated capitalism. Faced with the critical dangers posed by the anarchy of unregulated production, the ruling class thus made the choice, during the crucial years of the Roosevelt administration, to transform the state into the central agency of a broad program of political and economic stabilization policies. State intervention in the affairs of the economy, through the medium of fiscal and monetary policies originating in Washington, before long became essential to the stability and vitality of capitalism. Moreover, as an instrument for the political and military protection of the interests of the capitalist class in several spheres, the state has come to perform multiple services of inestimable value to capitalism.

Historically, bourgeois rule stems directly from bourgeois control over the essential productive and financial units of the economy (the industrial corporations and the banks and other financial institutions). In the present era, however, the institutions of the state have become the essential social and political media of bourgeois rule. Without the state as an agency of economic stabilization, capitalism would be perpetually unstable. Without the state as an agency of political stabilization, the ruling class would be perpetually vulnerable to attack from its class enemies. Recognizing this, the leading corporations and the principal organs of the state—under bourgeois rule—have worked together hand in glove in the pursuit of ruling-class goals since the New Deal.

The fundamental structural importance of this fact is that the state has become not just an agency of capitalist control but *an integral part of the process of production itself,* for in the contemporary era, the functioning of the state has become vital to the functioning of the economy as a whole. Production now is critically dependent on the activity of the state, and the society in general is influenced by it in myriad ways.

In classical Marxist terms, this development can be best described as the interpenetration of the economic and political spheres of social life. While in the past the political superstructure of society has always been closely related to the economic base, in the present the two have come together in a dramatic confluence of shared goals and mutual activity.

While formerly the state was almost entirely a vehicle for the political expression of ruling-class desires, currently it functions as a necessary part of the process of production itself. In other words, it has been drawn into the orbit of the economy, where its chief function is to make continued production and exchange not only possible but profitable.

The universities, like the government in general and under the influence of state spending, have played an important part in fulfilling the changing needs of capitalism in the contemporary era. Working to produce new scientific knowledge and a college-educated stratum of the working class capable of putting that knowledge into practice, the universities (like the state) have thus become organically linked to the process of production and critically important to its functioning.

What is politically significant is that, while higher education has played an increasing role in revolutionizing the contemporary capitalist mode of production, it has not done so in a humane and nonexploitative manner; instead, it has done so in a manner distorted by the special needs of capitalism as a system of exploitation. As science, for example, has more and more come to provide the basis for contemporary production (with the universities as the focal point of scientific research), the *uses* of science have increasingly come to be defined not by the real needs of working people but by the warfare and sales needs of the ruling class. Moreover, as an educated stratum of the work force has more and more come to be a precondition for the scientific and organizational work central to production, higher education in both its authoritarian form and ideological content has increasingly become a mirror image of the profit-oriented goals and interests animating the ruling class. Shaped and limited by the needs of capitalism, higher education has thus been remade in the image of the social system it serves.

The Needs of Capitalism and the Ruling Class

The universities have been important to the ruling class at different points in history for different reasons. Their importance at any given time can be gauged by the importance of the needs they fulfill and by the uniqueness of the qualities which enable the universities, rather than some other institution, to fulfill those needs. When the development of early industrial methods and the training of a ruling-class elite were the essential functions of higher education, the universities were definitely important, but on a scale much more modest than in the present. For in the current period, with college-educated workers and new knowledge as their principal products, the universities are *vital.* This is true because the needs they satisfy are among the crucial needs of capitalism.

What are the crucial needs of capitalism which have necessitated the transformation of the university system? Briefly, we can summarize these needs as follows: (1) the need to absorb surplus production; (2) the need to absorb surplus labor; and (3) the need to organize and defend the illusory rationality of capitalist interests. In the following pages, I will explain the general significance and meaning of these needs, and then show specifically how the universities work to satisfy them.

1. The Need to Absorb Surplus Production. The need to absorb surplus production—i.e., the need to prevent overproduction—has been a need intrinsic to capitalism at all stages of its growth. Capitalists have always been confronted with the dangerous possibility of a crisis of overproduction, leading first to a fall in prices, then to a fall in employment, and ultimately to depression. The numerous depressions occurring in capitalist countries between 1830 and 1930 had their roots in severe, cyclical crises of overproduction, as both bourgeois and Marxist economists agree. After the catastrophic crisis of overproduction which precipitated the Great Depression of the thirties, it became apparent to leading organs of the state and to many significant economists (notably Keynes, Kalecki, and Robinson) that systematic state intervention in the affairs of the economy would be necessary to prevent future crises of overproduction.[2] Recognizing that overproduction results when corporations are unable to sell the full measure of their production—either because workers are unemployed or because they are too poorly paid to buy back the goods they produce—government and industry began in the 1930s to make far-ranging efforts (1) to prevent domestic unemployment and its dangerous social consequences; (2) to capture markets in Europe, Asia, Africa, and Latin America and thus increase sales; and (3) to ensure continuing high levels of corporate sales and profits through governmental expenditures (primarily for military goods) financed by steadily rising levels of taxation which hit lower- and middle-income people harder than anyone else.

The essence of capitalism as a social system is the fact that capitalists *exploit* their employees by paying them less than the full value of the goods and services they produce. Workers, through their labor, produce the material wealth of society, but capitalists, through their class strength (rooted in their ownership of capital) *appropriate* large parts of that wealth. Marx called this process the extraction of surplus value and explained it in the following manner.

According to Marx, the value of any commodity is the quantity of labor required to produce or reproduce it. The value of the labor power which the worker sells to the capitalist is a *special* commodity in this sense because it requires less labor for its own reproduction than it is capable of performing itself. For example: if the worker produces enough value in four hours of labor to assure the physical and social survival of that worker for a day, then the remaining hours of labor expended each day create a surplus of value beyond the worker's socially defined subsistence needs. Another way of expressing this is to say that the value of the worker's daily labor is greater than the value of the labor required to assure the worker's survival. The *surplus value* produced is appropriated by the capitalist, who uses this surplus value as the essential source of all profit and all capital for capital accumulation. The *value* of the worker (as socially defined) is customarily measured by the payment of wages; the actual money surplus accruing to the capitalist is thus the difference between the money value of the goods and services sold and the money value of the wages paid for the *production* of those goods and services; this difference is called *profit.*[3]

From Marx's standpoint, the extraction of surplus value is the essential form of exploitation in capitalist society, comprising at one and the same time (a) the crux of capitalism, insofar as it is necessary to the process of capital accumulation, and (b) the essential springboard for class struggle in the epoch of capitalism.

Without class exploitation in the form of the extraction of surplus value, capitalists would be unable to accumulate either capital or profits and would thus be unable to function as capitalists. If capitalists were to pay their workers the full exchange value of the goods and services they produce, no capital accumulation could take place and capitalism would effectively cease to exist.

On the other hand, the fact that class exploitation occurs makes class struggle both possible and necessary. The exploitation of the proletariat by the bourgeoisie makes the proletariat a potentially revolutionary class, with definite long-run interests in the overthrow of the bourgeoisie and in the revolutionary transformation of capitalist social relations. Class struggle is necessary, therefore, as long as men and women refuse to abandon their desires for a better life.

As far as surplus production goes, however, other dilemmas confront capitalism in addition to the threat of revolution. Workers, paid less than the value of the product of their labor, find themselves incapable, therefore, of buying back the full measure of social production. As a consequence, in order to avoid overproduction crises in which surplus goods go unsold and profit rates fall, capitalists must seek out and find additional markets in which to sell their wares (frequently in foreign countries). The expansion of capitalism beyond national boundaries as part of this process leads to competition for markets between the capitalists of different countries, one of the vital elements of what Lenin called imperialist rivalry. Ensuring that the profitable disposal of the surpluses accumulated by the capitalists of the various nations is blocked by the intense competition between those nations, imperialist rivalry works to intensify the problems of overproduction and instability experienced by each of those nations.[4] For overproduction crises are fundamentally rooted in the periodic and recurring inability of the capitalist class to dispose of the surplus it appropriates from the working class.

Another fact which should be noted is that both the extraction of surplus value and the absorption of surplus product can take different forms in different periods. In the present period, a large proportion of the total surplus extracted from the working class is appropriated indirectly by the ruling class, through state taxation, and then redistributed to the corporations in the form of generous contract and subsidy allocations. At the same time, and as part of the same process, the absorption of surplus product occurs through state spending (made possible by high levels of taxation). This is so because the government is a market limited in its potential elasticity only by the will of the people governed. A massive upsurge of popular anger over issues of excessive taxation or the misuse of state funds represents the only possible obstacle to state taxation and spending policies—yet such an upsurge would be truly potent in its consequences and vastly important in its implications for the developing class struggle.

Although the state's intervention in the affairs of the economy serves as a powerful stabilizing influence on monopoly capitalism, destabilizing countertendencies also exist. Strong tendencies toward inflation and recession, though intrinsic to capitalism at all stages of its development, have nevertheless been significantly magnified in volume and intensity during the monopoly phase of capitalism. The reason the monopoly phase of capitalism has been more profoundly endangered by the recurring threat of severe inflation and unemployment than earlier phases—and here again both Marxist and bourgeois economists agree—is due to the fact that, when monopolies or oligopolies dominate an industry, the levels of both pricing and productivity cease to be directly determined by market pressures. In the early, competitive phase of capitalism, pricing and productivity levels were determined by the competitive struggle between different firms. While prices were held down by the intense competition which characterized the era, productivity levels tended to fluctuate, making pendulum swings from periods of oversupply to periods of undersupply. In this era, no single firm was able to determine what the market price or quantity of a commodity would be.

With the advent of monopoly, all this was changed. Pricing in the monopoly phase of capitalism—largely freed from the restraints of competition—tended to move upward in an inflationary spiral, making it more difficult for working people to buy back the commodities they produced. Monopoly corporations, recognizing that maximum profits could be achieved at relatively high prices, set their price levels high, with inflation as the result. In the same way, monopoly corporations recognized that maximum profits could be achieved at relatively low levels of productivity, which led them to the underutilization of the work force as well as the rest of the productive apparatus. Unemployment was the result.

In an ironic manner, then, we find that the search for profits, which originally spurred the vast process of capital accumulation and productivity growth which characterized early capitalism, has since become a barrier to the continued growth of the productive forces of society. Production for profit instead of production for need has, in other words, become a deadly obstacle to the continued growth of production itself, and has resulted in a growing and continual underemployment of our productive capacity (human as well as mechanical). The United States has been operating far below full productive capacity for many years now and has come to officially define full employment as 4 percent *un*employment (recently, former Treasury Secretary John Connally suggested that 6 percent unemployment might be a more realistic estimate of what "full employment" means in the U.S.).

2. The Need to Absorb Surplus Labor. When people are out of work, they can't buy many commodities. It is at this point that the problem of overproduction—the disposal of surplus production—becomes most clearly linked to the second principal need of modern capitalism, the need to absorb surplus labor and prevent unemployment.

During the past century, capitalism has developed a crippling and increasing inability to provide jobs for workers in the directly productive processes of industry. Prodded onward by the necessity of accumulating profits, businessmen have increasingly substituted machinery for human labor and have attempted to keep productivity low in accordance with profit maximization. As a consequence, the corporations have found themselves incapable of providing blue-collar work for the entire working class, a fact which has thrown up the specter and the likelihood of mass unemployment. Fearful of the dangerous consequences of large-scale unemployment—social unrest and a serious decline in consumption demand which would be likely to lead to depression and more social unrest—the corporations and the state have made every effort to create new white-collar and technical jobs to absorb the labor surplus and thus tenuously preserve what General Electric has called "an economic, social, and political climate in which companies like GE can survive and continue to progress."[5] Although the white-collar and technical jobs which have been created are clearly necessary to capitalism purely from the standpoint of the functions they fulfill, their simultaneous role in the absorption of the surplus cannot therefore be denied. These jobs—and the workers who fill them—are important for both reasons.

3. **The Need to Defend Capitalist Interests.** The third and major need of capitalism in the present epoch I have defined as the "organization and defense of the illusory rationality" of the system itself. This is not an entirely new category since in some respects it overlaps the first two, but it is nevertheless important enough and unique enough for us to view it as a distinct entity with its own coherence and meaning.

In order to survive in the context of the contemporary class struggle and struggle between nations, the capitalist class in the United States must structure a defense of its interests on several levels. First, as an imperialist power, the United States must be prepared (1) to engage in tariff, trade, and financial wars on the level of the international monetary system; (2) to participate in direct wars of counterinsurgency against revolutionary peoples (such as those in Korea and Vietnam); and (3) to build programs of support for political regimes friendly to the interests of American capital (e.g., Greece, South Africa, Brazil, the Philippines, etc.).

Second, as an embattled ruling class at home, the capitalist class must be prepared to protect its fragile and exploitative property interests from radical insurgency among all sectors of the working class by an elaborate system of socialization and social-control institutions (such as schools, prisons, the military). A self-seeking, cynical attitude must be nurtured among the people as one of the key weapons in defense of ruling-class interests; for as long as working people are convinced that human nature is fundamentally capitalist and antisocial in nature, and that meaningful change is therefore not possible, no change is likely to occur. Through the media, and through such institutions of socialization as the schools, the ruling class skillfully attempts to convey the impression that capitalism is strong and inevitable, leading people to an illusory awareness of their own powerlessness and thus making them cynical about the possibilities of change. At the same time, while the possibility of a satisfying life in the realm of work and social relations is implicitly denied, a false salvation is offered in the realm of consumption. Color, creativity, and noncompetitive social relations are denied us in our everyday lives, so the capitalist offers to sell them back to us in the guise of commodities—the very same commodities which we ourselves have been exploited to produce!

Finally, while the instruments of socialization and pacification are employed overtime to convey the impression of capitalist rationality to working people, corporate and government administrators are working equally hard to give that impression reality by perpetuating the system itself, through programs of governmental spending, welfare distribution, etc. Faced with multiple problems, the capitalist class increasingly needs large numbers of skillful social and economic technicians to organize the irrationality of capitalism and give it a lasting lease on life, harmonizing minor problems and attempting to reduce the possibilities of revolution, depression, and significant class struggle inherent in unregulated capitalism.

Scientific and Technological Advances

Capitalism in the United States has been altered in many ways since World War II. One of the most fundamental alterations has occurred in the relationship between science and production. Until the middle of the century, as Roger Garaudy shows, "The demands of technology and production were generally the chief motivational factor in scientific progress."[6] For the most part, the practical problems of production determined the directions in which science would go. The laws of thermodynamics, for example, were developed almost accidentally as a result of the search for an optimally efficient steam engine. Thus, although science was important to industry in this period, it was not among the driving forces at the base of production.

In recent times, however, what some theorists call a "third industrial revolution" has occurred. Science has now become central to production, and its relationship with problems of practical technology has largely been inverted. "That is," as Bettina Aptheker points out, "scientific progress now *precedes* technology instead of following at its heels."[7] In Garaudy's words, "Scientific progress becomes a motivational factor in the development of production, which it precedes and leads on instead of following. Einstein's theories anticipated the utilization of nuclear energy and the deployment of atomic technology. Cybernetics saw the light of day before computers came into use."[8]

In the United States today, expenditures on research are the largest single form of investment, exceeding $20 billion annually. Science has thus become a direct productive force of inestimable importance to both industry and the state.[9]

The universities, as the essential laboratories for the production of new scientific knowledge, thus find themselves tightly woven into the production process, which, as Bettina Aptheker comments, "is no longer *enclosed* in the factory per se. . . . For as scientific progress precedes technological capability and as science emerges as a direct productive force, the systematic, interdisciplinary research . . . which is most effectively organized within the university, becomes the essential prerequisite for technological development. It is this fact which increasingly renders the university, as an institution, a *constituent part* of the productive process . . . (and) the emergence of the university as a constituent part of the productive process is the *material* base for a qualitative change in the class position of the intelligentsia. That is, it is becoming a constituent part of the working class."[10]

The Role of Educated Labor

> *If business and industry could not draw upon a large reservoir of educated manpower, they would be handicapped in every phase of their operations. American education does a job for business and industry.*[11]
>
> Frank Abrams
> Chairman, General Motors

> *The corporation today is the major beneficiary of the product that the college or university manufactures—the trained mind.*[12]
>
> Louis Lundborg
> Chairman, Bank of America

As Gareth Stedman Jones points out, "Advanced industrial societies have an imperative need for large numbers of highly trained professional and technical cadres. Industry, government, communications and education now have a rapidly expanding demand for intellectually skilled manpower. The rapid rate of technical and scientific advance in the last two decades has created for the first time in history the beginnings of mass intellectual labor."[13]

From 1950 to 1970, the category of workers to grow the most rapidly has been the stratum of "professional and technical" workers, made up for the most part of teachers, engineers, accountants, and nurses (these four occupations have accounted for more than 50 percent of the category since at least 1950). At the present moment, professional and technical personnel comprise 14.4 percent of the labor force, considerably more than in 1950, when they represented 8.6 percent of a smaller labor force. Moreover, as Jay Mandle points out, "a high proportion of this category–88 percent according to the most recent census data–are wage earners and thus should qualify for inclusion in the Marxian definition of the working class."[14] For, as Kim Moody argues, "Much of the growth in technical and professional employment represents a process of proletarianization of previously independent or academic fields. Unlike the professionals of past decades, the post-war professional and technical worker sells his or her labor to an industrial capitalist, under conditions set by the capitalist."[15]

Leaving out the 1.2 million independent, self-employed professionals who otherwise would be included in this category, we are left with a total of 10.1 million professional and technical workers, comprising 12.9 percent of the labor force. This figure represents a single but significant milestone in a process of rapid growth which has yet to come to an end.

Since 1940, the *percentage* of wage-earning professional and technical workers has more than doubled, rising from 6.4 percent to 12.9 percent of the labor force, while the *absolute number* of such workers has more than tripled, going from 3,310,000 to 10,100,000. As Martin Oppenheimer shows, using 1971 employment figures as the basis for his conclusions, professional and technical workers now constitute the third largest category of employed workers, following clerical workers and semi-skilled blue-collar operatives.[16] Professional and technical workers are now 37 percent as numerous as the entire blue-collar proletariat, and expanding rapidly. This does not mean that the blue-collar sector of the working class is disappearing, or about to be superseded by a completely "new" working class composed of technocrats and bureaucrats, as some theorists have suggested.[17] In fact, although blue-collar workers have significantly declined as a percentage of the working class since 1950 (declining from 41.1 percent to 34.9 percent of the labor force), their numbers have continued to grow in absolute terms during this period (rising from 24,266,000 to 27,452,000). This absolute growth has resulted principally from the demands placed on the economy by military spending in connection with the war in Vietnam and by the rise of blue-collar service work. For, as Mandle observes, "The dominant trend in the working class in the post-war era has been the growth of service producing as compared to [goods] producing workers."[18]

The rapidly changing composition of the working class, of which the emergence of college-educated labor is the most important *structural* aspect, has occurred largely in the context of the growth of service, as opposed to goods-producing, industries. Service industries involving both blue- and white-collar workers have been growing swiftly in recent decades. According to the *Monthly Labor Review*, "The most dramatic change in industry employment in recent years has been the employment shift towards service-producing industries. Shortly after the turn of this century, only three in every ten workers were in service industries. By 1950, the weight had shifted to just over every five in ten; by 1968, the proportion had inched to six in every ten. In 1980, close to seven in every ten workers—or 68 million—are projected to be in service industries."[19] In other words, at present more than 50 percent of all workers are employed in service industries.

Part of the explanation for this "dramatic shift" in employment has to do with capitalism's need to absorb surplus labor and prevent unemployment. As smaller and smaller proportional quantities of manual blue-collar labor have become necessary to the functioning of the economy, larger and larger numbers of white-collar jobs have been created, partly to sponge up the potential labor surplus. A full explanation of this process, however, goes far deeper than a surplus labor argument would lead us to believe, for the technical and supervisory jobs which have emerged in recent decades serve tangible and important needs. Paraphrasing Robert Carson, we can say that during the course of this century (most notably since World War II), it has become both necessary and possible for the ruling class to create new kinds of jobs and workers to satisfy new but deeply felt needs that could not otherwise have been fully satisfied, at the same time that "it became necessary, from the point of view of maintaining the social and economic order, to reorder the labor force so as to eliminate the historic capitalist tendency toward chronic unemployment."[20] What this means is that several of the primary needs of developing capitalism have dovetailed in the process of being fulfilled. Educated workers are needed primarily for their specialized skills and abilities, but also because capitalism has little room for them in the blue-collar sector of the working class. When we speak about college-educated workers, therefore, we are not speaking about a one-dimensional category with a single social function but about a complex and many-faceted stratum of the working class with a wide variety of social roles.

One of the principal functions of the large numbers of white-collar sales and professional workers in industry is to make the absorption of surplus production as efficient and profitable as possible. Although no market is eternally elastic, capitalism must, in order to survive, eventually open up and saturate every potentially available market. Since the beginning of the monopoly phase of capitalism at the turn of the century, the problems of production confronting capitalists have largely been displaced by problems of consumption. In order to ensure continuing high levels of sales, profits, and employment, continued consumption must be facilitated by the creation of growing numbers of "market researchers, media planners, entertainment specialists, fashion designers, and advertising copywriters." In Jones's words, "These are the technicians of *consumption* who form the indispensable complement of the technicians of *production.*"[21] Working to streamline sales techniques and create new "needs" through advertising and innovations in product design, these sales and media workers help to stretch the market to its plastic outer limits. They are aided in this task by the rapidly expanding pool of technical and scientific workers also employed by the corporations.

College-educated workers are necessary not only for the development of the increasingly complex machinery of communication and transportation basic to our society but also for the development of new kinds of goods. Such product diversification has become an increasingly important part of the corporate effort to sell larger and larger quantities of commodities on nearly saturated markets. Additionally, big corporations with bleak prospects for expansion in their primary fields frequently move in on small or competitive industries in an effort to use their surplus capital profitably. This also entails product diversification, on a multi-industry level, which requires vast numbers of competent technical and scientific workers as well as the discovery, development, and use of a rainbow variety of new scientific techniques and knowledge.

In light of the above, we can see that product diversification reflects a genuine need of capitalist industry and is not simply an exercise in organized gimmickry. This is confirmed by Peter Kraushar, a leading market development consultant in Great Britain, when he says, "In the early 1950s, many companies did not think that new products were necessary to them. Their growth had been based often on one or two products . . . and it did not seem to make sense that a satisfactory profit position should be jeopardized by going in for new things, often in fields in which the company would have little or no experience. Since then, however, the situation has changed completely. In the late 1950s and early 1960s the importance of new products became recognized to such an extent that it is never challenged today. . . . Companies now realize that they must innovate not only to increase their profits but even to maintain them."[22] Or, in the words of James R. Killian, president of MIT, "The vigor of the American economy has resulted in part from the new industries, new processes, and new products generated in the scientific laboratories of the nation."[23]

A study conducted in the United States in 1960 showed that over 47 percent of the fastest-selling consumer goods on the market had been launched at some time in the ten-year interval from 1950 to 1960. In 1965, American research and development expenditures equaled more than 3 percent of the gross national product—more than twice as much as in 1957. Since then, the rise of diversification expenditures has continued to be steep and inexorable. This has been true not only in the United States but in Western Europe and Japan as well, for product diversification and innovation have proven themselves indispensable to the corporate sales effort.

So far, we have spoken only of the labor performed by technical workers and the "technicians of consumption" employed by capital to reduce the dangers of overproduction. On a different level, however, state workers, responsible for the implementation of increasingly complex organizational tasks, have also grown swiftly in numbers. According to the *Monthly Labor Review,* in fact, "Employment has grown faster in government than in any other sector in the economy. From 1960-1968, employment grew at the rate of 4.5 percent a year, nearly 2½ times the rate for total employment."[24]

Not all public-sector jobs require a high degree of education, but a great many do. In order to organize the economy and, above all, the social services, the labor of an army of skilled administrators and project workers is required; as the state bureaucracy has grown, the number of people employed as bureaucrats has also grown.

A similar phenomenon has taken place within the realm of business. Administrators, charged with organizing the increasingly complex and stratified process of production, have come to occupy a larger and larger place within the labor process. As Michael Reich shows, while total output rose 79 percent in manufacturing industries between 1950 and 1965, the number of production workers employed increased by only 7 percent while "white-collar non-production employment increased by 70 percent"; in the field of mining during the same period, output increased by 38 percent while production employment fell 40 percent and white-collar nonproduction employment rose 60 percent.[25] The trend is unmistakable.

In general, the educational levels of the working class have grown with as much speed and diversity as the class itself. All sectors of the working population are becoming more educated and an increasingly large percentage of the population has had at least minimal college experience. "In contrast to 1950 when only 15 percent of the labor force had achieved at least one year of college education, this percentage in 1968 stood at almost 25 percent."[26] By 1970, "in the western region of the United States, 42.8 percent of all white males from 25 to 44 had at least one year of college. The national average for all white males was 33.8 percent and for all males was 32.0 percent."[27]

According to the Bureau of Labor Statistics, "Workers in the United States acquire the education and training necessary to perform their jobs through a variety of methods. Of those holding white collar jobs, professional, technical, and kindred workers generally acquire their occupational training in a four year college or university."[28] Currently, more than ten million people are considered professional, technical, and "kindred" workers. These workers generally require extensive education and training. According to the Bureau, "Professional workers usually acquire their specialized knowledge in a college or university; most of them need a bachelor's degree to enter their occupations." Moreover, "Clerical workers, the largest of the white collar occupational groups, generally complete high school business courses, or post secondary training in business schools and in junior colleges. Sales workers who sell complex products such as scientific instruments or industrial machinery may acquire their training in a college or university, supplemented by specialized training given by their employers."[29] In its effort to prepare young workers for new kinds of jobs, it is clear that the system of higher education in America has undertaken a task of the first magnitude.

An understanding of this point leads us to agree with Marxist economist James O'Connor when he writes that "The most expensive economic needs of corporate capital as a whole are the costs of research, development of new products, new production processes . . . and, above all, the costs of training and retraining the labor force, in particular technical, administrative and non-manual workers." Because, as O'Connor goes on to comment, "No one industrial-finance interest can afford to train its own labor force or channel profits into the requisite amount of research and development," the state has been forced, in the three decades following World War II, to shoulder the primary financial burden for the transformation of the universities.[30] This development is vitally important on the level of exploitation because the state, by undertaking the financial support of the universities, has thus *socialized* the costs of education. What this means is that the general population now bears the brunt of the costs of training a labor force to serve the ruling class. This situation came about in the following manner, O'Connor says, confirming the analysis in the last chapter: "The first step was the introduction of the GI Bill, which socialized the costs of training (including the living expenses of labor trainees) and eventually helped to create a labor force which could exploit the stockpile of technology created during the war. The second step was the creation of a vast system of lower and higher technical education at the local and State level, the transformation of private universities into Federal universities through research grants, and the creation of a system to exploit technology in a systematic, organized way. . . . This reorganization of the labor process and, in particular, the free availability of masses of technical-scientific workers, made possible the rapid acceleration of technology."[31]

Clark Kerr, then president of the University of California, declared in 1963 that "the university has become a prime instrument of national purpose. This is new. This is the essence of the transformation now engulfing our universities."[32] For the university has come not only to provide monopoly capitalism with much of its most important technical and scientific knowledge, but also with a new and important stratum of the working class without which capitalism would be incapable of coping with some of its most important problems.

The State, Defense, and Higher Education

In the arena of defense spending, the state, business, and the universities have come together in a fusion of interests and shared responsibilities which makes any argument about their "independence" from one another clearly untenable. In the final pages of this chapter, we will explore the ramifications of this complex interrelationship.

In terms of the absorption of surplus production, the structural significance of defense spending is that it allows the government to buy vast quantities of technically advanced products that otherwise would remain unsold. According to Baran and Sweezy, "The military plays the role of an ideal customer for private business, spending billions of dollars annually on terms that are most favorable to the sellers."[33] Defense spending thus enables the government to prevent overproduction by artificially keeping consumption demand at high enough levels to avert disastrous declines in profits and employment. Intense government demand for advanced military goods thus enables sales and profit levels to remain high enough to sustain a continual demand for large quantities of labor, both college-educated and less-educated. According to government statistics, for every job created in the defense industry, four additional jobs come into existence in defense-related industries.[34]

The rapid rise in government spending has served most importantly to stifle the latent tendencies toward overproduction and unemployment inherent in monopoly capitalism. As one example of the dampening and stabilizing effects fiscal spending can have on the economy, Sweezy and Magdoff have shown that 22.3 million workers—"a staggering 25.1 percent of the total labor force"—are currently either unemployed (8.1 million) or employed by the Defense Department or by firms producing defense goods (14.2

million!).[35] The unemployment crisis, in other words, muted by military spending, would clearly be magnified greatly if such spending ceased. Spending by the government is thus crucial to business insofar as it keeps the economy on an even keel and ensures the vitality of the leading corporations. As the essence of what is sometimes called "the Keynesian revolution," the central function of government spending is to police the economy and arrest destabilizing developments before they ripen into full-blown crises.[36]

Additionally, defense spending has a further dimension of importance which goes beyond its role in stabilizing the economy: the defense of the empire. Since the end of World War II, the United States has been the leading imperialist power in the world. In 1945, with Europe ravaged by war and the Japanese defeated amid the ruins of Hiroshima and Nagasaki, the United States was able to seize an unprecedented opportunity to establish American political and economic hegemony over most of the world, supplanting the influence of America's recently defeated imperialist rivals in the Third World and simultaneously beginning an intensive economic invasion of Europe itself. "This alone," in Baran and Sweezy's words, "would be enough to explain why United States military needs, enormously inflated during the two wars, remained huge by any peacetime standards after the second war. The undisputed leader must maintain a clear military superiority either through its own armed forces or through the manipulation of alliances, or both. The United States chose both. At the same time, as the old colonial empires increasingly broke up—for a complex of reasons which we cannot analyze here—the United States used its military and financial power to attract large segments of them into its own neo-colonial empire. In this fashion, a vast worldwide American empire has come into being, the control and policing of which have added greatly to United States military needs."[37]

The necessity of protecting its fragile neocolonial empire has led the ruling class to mobilize for wars of counter-insurgency on a massive scale under the auspices of a policy of "containing communism." Whenever the oppressed peoples of an Asian, African, or Latin American nation rebel against imperialist domination and declare their right to control their own lives, the United States or another imperialist power moves in militarily to protect its neocolonial interests. This has occurred openly in Vietnam, Korea, Algeria, and the Dominican Republic, and covertly in Greece, Guatemala, Laos, Bolivia, and dozens of other countries. These interventions, combined with the spirit of Cold War militarism engendered in the United States by the media and institutions of the ruling class, have led military expenditures during the past decades to materialize as the principal form of government spending confronting (1) the problems of an economy faced with the permanent threat of overproduction and (2) the problems of an imperialist power confronted with the need to buttress and preserve its tenuous international position of power.

For all these reasons, defense spending remains vital to American capitalism. One major result of the unending stream of state defense monies flowing into industry has been what Charles Nathanson calls the *militarization* of the economy. Now, according to Nathanson, "The producer goods industries are spending almost as much on defense area research and development as they are on products in their own field." Moreover, "The scope of the movement towards military diversification can be seen from the fact that 93 major firms whose traditional manufacturing base is outside the defense sector are now producing within it." More than two hundred of the five hundred leading corporations are now deeply immersed in military research or production, including seventy of the one hundred leading corporations. In light of these facts, Nathanson concludes that there virtually "is no non-defense industry."[38]

The militarization of the economy has involved a massive increase in the size of the educated labor force. This labor force, called forth by defense needs, has consisted primarily of scientists and technicians, since the problems raised by war production fall principally within the realm of scientific research and development. As one House investigating committee pointed out, "Any demand on the economy, public or private, of the size of federal spending on research and development is also a demand for manpower on a large scale."[39]

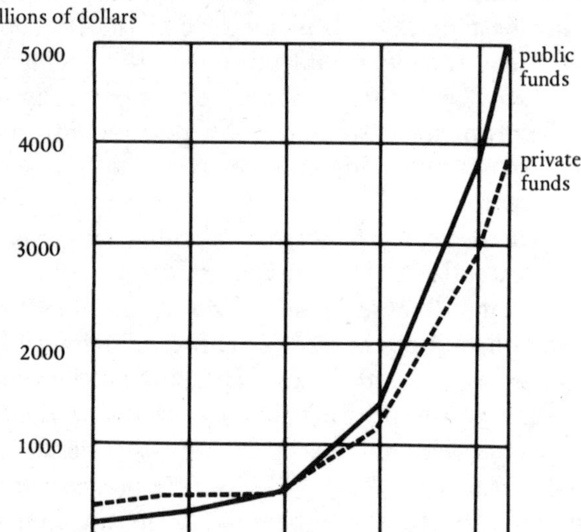

Table in Bettina Aptheker, *The Academic Rebellion in the United States* (Secaucus, N.J.: Citadel Press, 1972), p. 100. From Sidney W. Tiedt, *The Role of the Federal Government in Education* (New York: Oxford University Press, 1966), p. 7.

The thrust of the demand for technical and scientific labor expressed by the government is mirrored by the extensive war-related research interests of private industry. As Charles Nathanson points out, "It is clear that every major sector of American manufacturing has become deeply militarized."[40] Industry, then, in its involvement with military research and development, also exerts "a demand for manpower on a large scale." Since the universities are the major source of educated labor, it was natural that on this level the defense needs of the state would invite cooperation with higher education.

In general, thus, the state has played an important role in shaping the contours of the American system of higher education. The outlines of this role become especially visible when we examine the links connecting state and university research and development programs.

Since 1950, the level of state spending on research and development has grown at an extremely rapid rate, in the neighborhood of 20 percent per year. Currently, more than two-thirds of all research and development programs are sponsored by the government, and the bulk of state expenditures for research and development is concentrated in fields related to war, nuclear energy, and space exploration. Most basic research is done in the university, and much of that work is directly related to defense. The corporations maintain their own labs for applied research because they want the directly useful results of such research under their immediate control. They tend to neglect basic research, on the other hand, even while recognizing its long-run value, because they would prefer not to bear the costs of projects which may not mature into saleable commodities. Centering basic research in the universities, therefore, represents an excellent way for business to socialize the costs involved in such research. While the costs are thus socially borne, the fruits, as always, are reaped only by the capitalist class.

Expenditures for Research and Development in the U.S.: 1940–1969

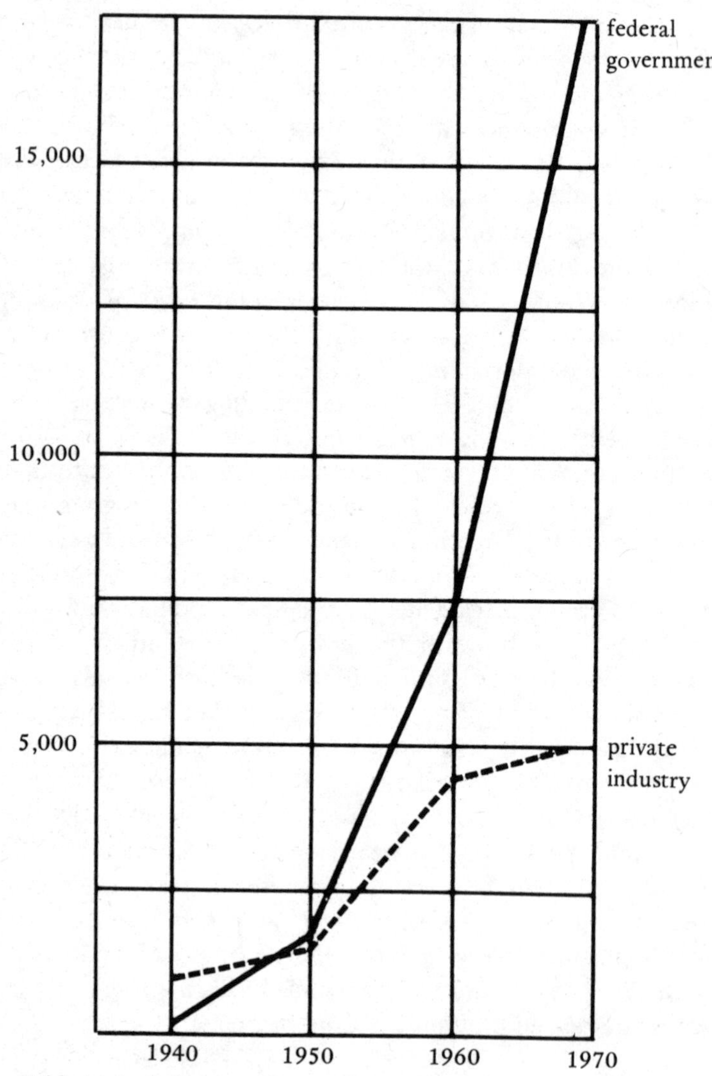

Table in Aptheker, op. cit., p. 98.

Defense, again, is the key to much of the state-funded research which takes place in the universities. In the words of a report prepared by the Stanford Research Institute, "The University is a major performer of defense research and development; a supplier of advisers and consultants to defense research and development agencies; a producer of the technical professional work force that is the prime production factor in the many government, non-profit, industrial, and academic laboratories that produce defense research and development; and a provider of continuing, updating education to the defense research and development work force."[41] The University of California alone—as the principal arsenal of atomic weaponry in the United States—received $288 million in state research and development funds in 1968.

A fuller understanding of the current magnitude of state research and development spending can be gained from Charles B. McCoy, president of the du Pont Chemicals Company: "In 1940, the total federal budget for research and development in the United States was about $74 million. Today, a few of the largest universities individually report research budgets of that order of magnitude."[42] And some, such as the University of California, go considerably beyond that sum.

Gerard Piel, editor of *Scientific American,* explains the historical roots of the current research establishment: "During World War II, the universities transformed themselves into vast weapons development centers. . . . MIT and Harvard undertook to create the strategy and tactics of radar and counter-radar; from Johns Hopkins came the proximity fuse that brought the conventional high-explosive artillery shell to its peak of lethality, and Columbia, Chicago, and California joined in the successful engineering and manufacture of the most fateful weapon of all."[43]

According to Lyle Spencer, president of Science Research Associates and a trustee of three universities, "This process of demand and response has multiplied and remultiplied since World War II. The government has come to dominate the university's research time and facilities. As the demands of the beast have grown, the universities have fed it, apparently with more and more willingness."[44] In fact, the ties between the government and the universities have become exceedingly close. Numerous high-level scientists and administrators from the universities sit on governmental advisory and policy-making boards, while agencies such as the Atomic Energy Commission, NASA, and the Defense Science Board are legendary for their intimate ties with the universities.

As a 1969 statement by the Harvard *Crimson* points out, "The government to a large degree has created its own need for itself among the universities. It is not merely a case of the universities needing money and the government providing it; the government has built up large-scale scientific research as an almost totally new function for universities, a function that only the federal government can finance."[45] In other words, the universities have come to be deeply dependent on the state. But is the reverse true? How fundamentally dependent on the universities is the state?

In terms of the production of college-educated labor, it is clear that the universities—and the rest of the American system of higher education—perform an indispensable function for capitalism. No other institution would be able to train and indoctrinate millions of young workers at the expense of the working class, and no other institution would be able to achieve the social status accorded the American system of higher education.

In terms of the performance of basic research and development, much the same story is true. Although at first it might appear that the important role played by the leading university research centers in the production of necessary scientific knowledge could be transferred to private business, the likelihood of this occurring is very small, since the capitalist class would greatly prefer to let the state continue financing basic research rather than shoulder the burden itself. In this very real sense, therefore, the research function performed by the universities is indispensable to business. As the leading source of both new scientific knowledge and college-educated labor, the universities thus are vital to contemporary capitalism and deeply integrated into its process of production.

Notes

1. Bogdan Denitch, "Is There a 'New Working Class'?" in *Workers' Control,* ed. Garson, Hunnius, and Case (New York: Random House, 1973), p. 431.

2. The New Deal, through which the Roosevelt Administration attempted to raise employment, consumption, and profit levels by direct governmental action, represented the first and epoch-making application of this principle. The subsequent and far-reaching usage of Keynesian policies involving massive state spending in most of the advanced capitalist countries of the West has served to further cement the state's important role in regulating the economy.

3. For a searching exploration of these themes and their historical genesis, see Paul M. Sweezy, *The Theory of Capitalist Development* (New York: Monthly Review Press, 1956), or Ernest Mandel, *The Formation of the Economic Thought of Karl Marx* (New York: Monthly Review Press, 1971).

4. For contemporary analyses of imperialism, see Harry Magdoff, *The Age of Imperialism* (New York: Monthly Review Press, 1969), and Felix Greene, *The Enemy* (New York: Random House, 1970).

5. Council for Financial Aid to Education, *Aid-to-Education Programs of Some Leading Business Concerns.*

6. Roger Garaudy, *The Crisis in Communism* (New York: Grove Press, 1970), p. 23.

7. Bettina Aptheker, *The Academic Rebellion in the United States* (Secaucus, N.J.: Citadel Press, 1972), p. 48.

8. Garaudy, op. cit., p. 23.

9. Although, as Paul Lafargue comments, "It would be insulting capitalism to attribute to it a disinterested love of science, which from its point of view has but one reason for existence, that of utilizing natural forces to the enhancement of its wealth. It cares nothing for pure speculation, and it is by way of self-defense that it allows its scientists to devote their mental energy to theoretical researches instead of exhausting it on practical applications." From "Socialism and the Intellectuals," a speech circa 1900 (reprinted by *New York Labor News,* 1967, p. 10). Lafargue, Marx's son-in-law, was a distinguished leader of the early socialist movement in France.

10. Aptheker, op. cit., p. 61.

11. Cited in Paul Woodring, *Investment in Innovation* (Boston: Little, Brown, 1970), p. 44.

12. Cited in Thomas Devine, *Corporate Support for Higher Education* (Washington, D.C.: Catholic University of America Press, 1956), p. 81.

13. Gareth Stedman Jones, "The Meaning of the Student Revolt," in *Student Power,* ed. Robin Blackburn and Alexander Cockburn (Baltimore: Penguin, 1969), p. 30.

14. Jay Mandle, "Some Notes on the American Working Class," *Review of Radical Political Economy* 2, no. 1 (Spring 1970), p. 48.

15. Kim Moody, "The American Working Class in Transition," *International Socialism,* October-November 1969, p. 10.

16. Martin Oppenheimer, "What Is the New Working Class?" *New Politics* 10, no. 1 (Fall 1972), p. 32.

17. As suggested by Serge Mallet, *La nouvelle classe ouvrière* (Paris: 1963); Herb Gintis, "Revoutionary Youth and the New Working Class," *Socialist Revolution,* no. 3, May-June 1970; etc.

18. Mandle, op. cit., p. 58.

19. "The U.S. Economy in 1980," *Monthly Labor Review,* April 1970, pp. 14-15.

20. Robert Carson, "Youthful Labor Surplus in Disaccumulationist Capitalism," *Socialist Revolution* no. 3, p. 22. Although it isn't apparent in the context of this quotation, I have a real disagreement with Carson about the surplus labor question. Briefly (to oversimplify his argument), he clearly implies that the primary function of the universities is to serve as a holding ground for the "youthful labor surplus,"

which otherwise would flood the job market and destabilize capitalism. I argue, on the other hand, that while this is partially true, historically speaking the primary function of the universities is to train and socialize a labor force which is essential to capitalism for the tasks it performs and for the social relations it reinforces. The universities, therefore, must be viewed primarily as a training ground, not as a holding ground.

21. Jones, op. cit., p. 31.

22. Peter M. Kraushar, *New Products and Diversification* (Princeton, N.J.: Brandon/Systems Press, 1970), p. 24.

23. James R. Killian, "University Research," in *The Corporation and the Campus,* ed. Robert H. Connery (Washington, D.C.: Praeger Publishers, 1970), p. 39.

24. "The U.S. Economy in 1980," op. cit., p. 17.

25. Michael Reich, "The Evolution of the United States Labor Force," in *The Capitalist System,* ed. Richard Edwards, Michael Reich, and Thomas Weisskopf (Englewood Cliffs, N.J.: Prentice-Hall, 1972), pp. 178-79.

26. Mandle, op. cit., p. 63.

27. Albert Szymanski, "Trends in the American Class Structure," *Socialist Revolution,* no. 10, July-August 1972, p. 117.

28. Bureau of Labor Statistics, *Tomorrow's Manpower Needs,* vol. 3, p. 4.

29. Ibid., p. 6.

30. James O'Connor, "The Fiscal Crisis of the State: Part 1," *Socialist Revolution,* no. 1, January-February 1970, pp. 49, 51.

31. Ibid., p. 52.

32. Clark Kerr, *The Uses of the University* (New York: Oxford University Press, 1963), p. 87.

33. Paul Baran and Paul M. Sweezy, *Monopoly Capital* (New York: Monthly Review Press, 1966), p. 207.

34. Cited in Frederick G. Dutton, *Changing Sources of Power* (New York: McGraw Hill, 1971), p. 180.

35. Paul Sweezy and Harry Magdoff, "Economic Stagnation and the Stagnation of Economics," *Monthly Review* 22, no. 11 (April 1971), pp. 8-9.

36. See especially James O'Connor, *The Fiscal Crisis of the State* (New York: St. Martin's Press, 1973).

37. Baran and Sweezy, op. cit., p. 182.

38. Charles E. Nathanson, "The Militarization of the American Economy," in *The Corporations and the Cold War*, ed. David Horowitz (New York: Monthly Review Press, 1969), pp. 222-23.

39. U.S. House of Representatives, Committee on Government Operations, *Conflicts Between the Federal Research Programs and the Nation's Goals for Higher Education,* Report, 89th Congress, 1st session, 1965, p. 1, cited in Michael Klare, "The University-Military Research Network," in *The University-Military-Police Complex,* published by the North American Congress on Latin America (NACLA), 1970, p. 7.

40. Nathanson, op. cit., p. 232.

41. Shapero, Moll, Hemmes, and Howell, *The Role of the University in Defense R&D* (Menlo Park, Calif.: Stanford Research Institute, 1966), cited in Klare, op. cit., pp. 10-11.

42. Charles B. McCoy, "Criteria for Corporate Aid," in *The Corporation and the Campus,* op. cit., p. 167.

43. Cited in the U.S. House of Representatives Report, op. cit., p. 362; also in Klare, op. cit., p. 2.

44. Lyle M. Spencer, "The Research Function and the Advancement of Knowledge," in *Who Goes Where to College,* ed. Alexander Astin (Chicago: Science Research Associates, 1965), p. 56.

45. Cited in Klare, op. cit., p. 9.

8
The Myth of the Middle Class

So far, I have presented an analysis of the class structure of American society which flatly contradicts the logic of the most widely held principle of popular sociology, the belief that the majority of Americans are members of a middle class. In a nutshell, my argument has been that the dual processes of class formation and polarization have continued to take place in contemporary capitalist society, but in new forms and new contexts. While bourgeois theorists have argued that both the capitalist and working classes are dissolving into a single "middle class,"[1] my argument, on the contrary, is that the changes in class structure described by the theory of the middle class are in fact changes occurring within the working class. As the problems of capitalism have grown more complex, the structure of the working class has grown correspondingly complex. Rising levels of income and the proliferation of new and different forms of wage labor thus reflect not the growth of a diffuse middle class but the stratification and diversification of a working class which has expanded in recent years to include technical and supervisory workers in addition to the classic industrial proletariat.

This stratification of the working class has vast implications for political analysis, aspects of which will be explored in the final chapters. First, however, we must arrive at a satisfactory definition of class, since such a definition necessarily precedes an understanding of the differentiations occurring within and between classes. Before we can finally say, in other words, whether or not the middle class is a reality or a fiction, we must know what we mean by the concept of class, both generally and specifically.

The word "class" is an abstraction. Its purpose is to enable us to identify—*classify*—the major groupings in society on the basis of their social roles and possibilities. This is founded on the premise that history is made by the masses of people who make up societies, and that therefore, if we are to make an effort to understand the past and influence the future of society, we must understand the social configurations and classes within society. Without social knowledge, we are likely to find ourselves socially powerless.

Marx defined classes by their relationships to one another in the context of differing modes of production. Class relationships—and the identity of a class is nothing more than the sum total of its evolving relationships—are historically specific and mutable, changing in small ways within every social formation and changing qualitatively in every transition from one form of society to another.

From Marx's standpoint, the defining characteristic of a social formation (e.g., capitalism, feudalism, etc.) is the way in which it organizes the production and reproduction of life. All other forms of social and political organization are ultimately dependent upon the mode of production *defining* the society: they may alter and affect the labor process, but it is the labor process which is ultimately primary in determining the forward motion of society.

If we recognize, therefore, that the labor process at the base of any given society defines both its nature and its forward motion, then it follows that the chief forms of social relations to be found in that society will be located in what Marx called the production relations of society. Historically, class relationships have been the key form of production relations, since it is class relationships which determine who directs production, who labors, and how the product of labor is distributed. Class relationships thus determine not only the nature of the society but the material and social conditions of life for the majority of its members.

In their pure form, class relationships are essentially relationships of alienation and exploitation in the realm of the labor process. "Alienation" Marx defined as the loss of control by the members of a class of laborers over the purposes and results of their labor; it is an objective condition signifying class rule, not, as it is used in the language of daily life, a subjective feeling of estrangement, emptiness, etc. Moreover, as an objective condition, alienation must be understood as the necessary precondition for all forms of exploitative class relationships, since these relationships necessarily presuppose relations of class dominance and subordination—in other words, alienation. "Exploitation" Marx defined as the extraction of a surplus from the labor of one class by another class. Slave owners, for example, extracted a surplus from the labor of their slaves; feudal lords extracted a surplus from their serfs; and capitalists extract a surplus from their workers. In each case, the exploited class produces more useful goods or services than necessary for its own survival; in each case, the surplus is appropriated by the exploiting class. The forms of exploitation have differed widely in the different forms of class society, but in each society they have denoted antagonistic class relationships.*

The special problem at the heart of this study is not, however, the definition of class in general, but the definition of the working class in particular. How is the working class to be defined?

Marx defined the working class as the class of laborers who

* The struggle between classes, moreover, is an integral part of the process of change which leads to the overthrow of one form of society and the creation of another. As Marx and Engels wrote in the *Communist Manifesto*, "The history of all hitherto existing society is the history of class struggles."[2] In an important sense this is true, since no social formation comes into existence without a class of

on the one hand alienate their labor—i.e., sell their ability to work to an "alien" power, a capitalist—and on the other hand produce a surplus which is appropriated by members of the capitalist class. Thus, the condition of being proletarian is simultaneously a condition of alienation and exploitation.[3] Since proletarian labor is, moreover, the only source of capital for capital accumulation (because capital is a part of the surplus extracted from the working class), proletarian labor is thus literally the motor of development in capitalist society. In this fundamental structural sense, the identity of the proletariat has not changed since Marx's time. The working class remains the motor of development in capitalist society, the sole source of capital and material wealth.

This is not to say that the proletariat has not changed in a multitude of ways since the nineteenth century. My basic contention, in fact, is precisely that the proletariat *has* changed—but not, I will argue, in structural terms. Working-class culture, income, schooling, and attitudes have all changed. The forms of work, the specific purposes of work, and numerous secondary forms of social relations have also changed—but the essential role of the proletariat as the collective producer of capital has remained intact. Structurally, the proletariat today is basically the same as the proletariat of a hundred years ago. Capitalism remains capitalism. We are not living in a classless society.

Ernest Mandel has much of value to say on this subject. In a brilliant article entitled "Workers Under Neo-Capitalism" published in 1968, he made the following excellent statement:

"In the history of class society, the situation of each social class is a unique combination of stability and change. The

---

people breaking out of the mold of the old society and leading the way into the new, identifying itself in a structural sense as the decision-making force in the new mode of production and working to subordinate all other classes to its will, however temporarily. Socialism, if it is achieved, will be the first society in history in which class exploitation does not reappear "after the revolution."

structure remains the same; conjunctural features are often profoundly modified.

"There is a tremendous difference both in standard of living and in social environment between the slave on the patriarchal Greek farms of the sixth century B.C., the slave on Sicilian plantations in the first century B.C., and a clerical or handicraft slave in Rome or the South of France in the fourth century A.D. Nonetheless, all three of these were slaves, and the identity of their social status is undeniable. A nobleman living at the court of Louis XV did not have very much in common with a lord of the manor in Normandy or Burgundy seven centuries earlier—except that both lived on surplus labor extracted from the peasantry through feudal or semi-feudal institutions.

"When we look at the history of the modern proletariat . . . we notice the same combination of structural stability and conjunctural change. The proletarian condition is, in a nutshell, the lack of access to means of production or means of subsistence which, in a society of generalized commodity production, forces the proletarian to sell his labor power. In exchange for this labor power he receives a wage which then enables him to acquire the means of consumption necessary for satisfying his own needs and those of his family.

"This is the structural definition of the wage earner, the proletarian. From it necessarily flows a certain relationship to his work, to the products of his work, and to his overall situation in society . . . But there does not follow from this structural definition any necessary conclusions as to the level of his consumption, the price he receives for his labor power, the extent of his needs or the degree to which he can satisfy them. The only basic interrelationship between structural stability of status and conjunctural fluctuations of income and consumption is a very simple one: Does the wage, whether high or low, whether in miserable Calcutta slums or in the much publicized comfortable suburbs of the American megalopolis, enable the proletarian to free himself from the social and economic obligations to sell his labor power? Does it enable him to go into business on his own account?

"Occupational statistics testify that this is no more open to him today than a hundred years ago. Nay, they confirm that the part of the active population in today's United States which is forced to sell its labor power is much higher than it was in Britain when Karl Marx wrote *Das Kapital,* not to speak of the United States on the eve of the American Civil War."[4]

If we are interested, for example, in understanding and applying the abstract concept "matter," then it is necessary for us to penetrate beneath the surface appearances of different objects and realize that, as different *forms* of matter, they are all material substances made up of an intricate structure of molecules, atoms, protons, and electrons. If we can agree on this basic definition, then we can see past the fact that the objects surrounding us are made up of earth, air, fire, and water—for they are also matter. It is important for us to recognize that there are differences between different objects, but it is essential, also, that we recognize that they are all *material* objects.

In much the same way, while it is vitally important for us to recognize the differences between different kinds of workers, if we can agree that the proletariat consists of all those who sell their labor power for a wage and are exploited, then for this level of analysis it doesn't matter that on the surface a Parisian artisan in the 1840s has little in common with a contemporary secretary, or that a turn-of-the-century steel worker has little in common with a contemporary research scientist. If each sells his or her labor power for a wage and contributes to the production of a surplus appropriated by a member of the capitalist class, then each is a member of the working class. While the changes in the working class may have been immense, in structural terms—as the motor of social development—the proletariat continues to play its vital role.

Marx offered a concise explanation of the tendencies in capitalism leading to the perpetually changing conjunctural character of the working class when he wrote, in the first volume of *Capital,* that "Modern industry never looks upon and treats the existing form of a process as final. The technical basis of that industry is therefore revolutionary while all earlier modes of production were essentially conservative. By means of machinery, chemical processes and other methods, it is continually causing changes not only in the technical basis of production, but also in the functions of the laborer and in the social combination of the labor process."[5]

As the process of production evolves, in other words, the working class evolves along with it. In an important article, Kim Moody develops this theme further: "Since the technique, products, and circulation mechanisms of the capitalist mode of production are always in flux, the structure of the working class must change accordingly. Both the perimeter and the internal lines of division of the working class are always in a state of transition. In the past twenty-five years in particular, the structure of the American working class has gone through important changes."[6]

This, then, is my thesis. Rapid, colorful, and significant changes have occurred in the structure and composition of the American working class, in a process not yet understood by the majority of the people involved in that process. It is the purpose of this book to make those changes clear to as many people as possible.

What remains to be said about the widespread myth of the middle class?

The arguments put forward that the opposing classes in American society have dissolved into a broad, amorphous middle class rest on several key ideas, ideas which are particularly important because they are accepted by a large percentage of working people.

Most importantly, it is argued that the contemporary middle class is more privileged than the working class. Privilege is said to be made up of a combination of higher levels of income, higher levels of education, less oppressive job conditions, and the absorption of a set of "middle-class values." This is the essence of an argument advanced in one form or another by bourgeois theorists, the mass media, and some "orthodox" Old Left Marxists.[7] It is a false argument because it fails to provide a sufficient alternative to the Marxist definition of class, which it abandons, and because it misinterprets a reality it sees clearly in its immediate features.

Although all are related, the most important element of privilege is the high levels of income enjoyed by members of the middle class. High levels of income make possible an ethic of consumerism and are in that sense central to the conception of "middle-class values" as well. But what does it mean to say that high levels of income identify people as members of a middle class? If class is definable *in structural terms* as the relationship people have to the process of production, then it is immaterial for our analysis whether the income received by workers is relatively higher or lower. Their identity as alienated labor, exploited for the surplus they produce, is primary. The level of their wages, although crucial to their material well-being, defines neither the essence of their social role nor the forward motion of the system, while their function as wage labor does both. For the kinds of labor they perform determine not only their levels of income and conditions of life but the direction of capitalism itself in a structural sense.

Levels of income, moreover, are transitory and fluctuating, rising and falling with every tremor in the market. A major recession or depression would bring them crashing down—and with them the "middle class." An analysis of income is thus not a sufficient criterion for a definition of class. It tells us nothing fundamental about the nature of the mode of production, the direction of capitalism, or the key forms of social relationships at the base of society. The Marxist definition of class, on the other hand, does all these things well, and thus accurately reflects the structural reality and motion of capitalism.

What about the other elements of "middle-class privilege"? Does their existence alter the essence of our class analysis? I think not. Higher levels of education, for example, reflect little more than the desires of the working class for education and the desires of the ruling class for a college-educated stratum of the work force, as explained earlier. "Middle-class values" themselves, centering around the ethic of consumerism, are largely the result of the higher levels of working-class income made possible by the successes of imperialism and by the intense need expressed by corporations for new and expanded markets. We own many commodities because the capitalist class requires a perpetual market for its products. We do not, however, own the means of production and thus exercise real power over what is produced, how production is organized, or how the distribution of commodities takes place. Our possession of commodities, therefore, in whatever quantity, says nothing real about our class status, which is determined by whether or not we are forced to sell our labor power for a wage smaller in value than the products of our labor.

The question of job conditions is slightly more complex, involving several problems. The theorists of the middle class argue that higher-level wage labor—especially what I have called the technical and supervisory wing of the work force—is allowed to function in more pleasant surroundings and exercise more creativity and judgment than other sectors of the work force. This, they say, in combination with their higher pay, places such higher level workers in the ranks of the vast, amorphous middle class.

The problems with this analysis, however, are the following. First of all, material conditions of work are irrelevant to an analysis of class, for class is determined by the *social* relationships within which work takes place, relationships of alienation and exploitation. As capitalism changes and the forms of work change, the conditions of proletarian labor will necessarily change correspondingly—but such labor will remain proletarian as long as it takes place in the context of alienation and exploitation.

Second, creative judgment exercised in the context of the methodology of the job itself is not the same as the exercise of decision-making power over the purposes and product of the labor. When a "member of the work force" exercises decision-making power over the purpose and product of his own labor or the labor of others, his labor is thus neither exploited nor alienated and he (or she) is clearly not a worker. What the contemporary period has witnessed, however, is not the rise of a new class of people who are neither alienated nor exploited, in this sense, but the rise of large numbers of workers who are being called upon to exercise their creativity in the context of alienation and exploitation, without control over either the profit-motivated uses of their creativity or the end results of their labor. For example, a scientist called upon to design a less expensive combustion engine or a more lethal nerve gas is being exploited for his creativity, since his labor is alienated and contributes to the production of a surplus which he does not control. Similarly, a low-level technical administrator in a manufacturing firm may be allowed a relatively large degree of decision-making in his own sphere, yet he controls neither the goals of production—the accumulation of capital and the expansion of market power—nor the capital itself. His creativity is subordinated to the profit impulses of the capitalist class, just as the creativity of the proletariat has always been subordinated to the interests of the capitalist class, in whatever form it takes shape.

The theorists of the middle class, therefore, have no ground to stand on. They have failed to show that "middle-class privilege" alters either the class status or potential of men and women who sell their labor power for a wage. Thus, while what they describe is important, essential for full-scale political analysis, it does not force us to alter our appraisal of the class nature of capitalist society. It changes the *appearance* of the class structure, but not its *essence.*

Notes

1. This is one of the key premises of modern bourgeois sociology, which bases its class analysis upon an understanding of income levels and status rather than upon an understanding of the nature of the production process. Every college or university with a sociology department offers classes on "stratification" which are based on this premise.

2. Karl Marx and Friedrich Engels, *Manifesto of the Communist Party* (Peking: Foreign Languages Press, 1972), p. 30. A slightly different version of this famous sentence can be found in David Riazanov's classic annotated edition of the *Manifesto,* first published in Russia in 1922 and translated into English in 1928 by Cedar and Eden Paul: "The history of all human society, past and present, has been the history of class struggles."

3. Valuable recent works on this subject include: Istvan Mészáros, *Marx's Theory of Alienation* (London: Merlin Press, 1970), and Bertell Ollman, *Alienation: Marx's Conception of Man in Capitalist Society* (New York: Cambridge University Press, 1972).

4. Ernest Mandel, "Workers Under Neo-Capitalism," a paper delivered at the 1968 Socialist Scholars Conference; first printed in *International Socialist Review,* November-December 1968, pp. 1-16, and re-

printed in *The Revival of American Socialism*, ed. George Fischer (New York: Oxford University Press, 1971), pp. 169-87.

5. Karl Marx, *Capital*, vol. 1 (Chicago: Charles H. Kerr & Co., 1906), pp. 532-33.

6. Kim Moody, "The American Working Class in Transition," *International Socialism*, October-November 1969, p. 11.

7. The media are the main culprits here, since they affect larger numbers of people more directly than other sources of ideas (with the exception of the central social institutions themselves, which *embody* those ideas in their daily functioning).

9
The Changing Composition of the Working Class

Kim Moody makes an essential point when he observes, "In discussing the direction of struggle, it would be misleading to simply discuss the class as a whole unless we understand the roots and nature of the fragmentation, stratification, and differentiation within the class."[1] In this chapter, we will explore the concrete realities of the changing composition of the working class. What does the working class look like in the 1970s?

The Proletarianization of the Labor Force

The first point that should be made is that, as Mandel observed, the percentage of the population which is now functioning as wage labor is higher than it has ever been in the past. "Of all Karl Marx's predictions about the trends in Western capitalism, the one that has most clearly been verified is that the proletariat—workers who do not themselves own their own tools of production, but rather are forced to sell their labor to someone else who then appropriates their labor—would become an ever increasing percentage of the total population."[2]

Since 1940, the percentage of wage and salary workers in the labor force has grown 14.4 percent; from 75.1 percent in

1940 to 89.5 percent in 1969, while the labor force itself has grown by roughly 26.7 million members, from 51.7 million in 1940 to 78.4 million in 1970.[3] Since 89.5 percent of 78.4 million members of the labor force comes out to roughly 70 million workers, with their families these workers thus constitute far and away the majority of the American population. "In short," as Michael Reich comments, "the United States has become a nation of wage and salary employees, who have virtually no access to income from property or control over the production process, and whose economic welfare is determined by the vicissitudes of the labor market. The term 'proletarians' applies to all such employees and not only to assembly-line industrial day laborers."[4]

Independent professionals, artisans, small urban shopkeepers, and independent farmers have declined precipitously as a proportion of the labor force, falling from 18 percent of the labor force in 1950 to 9 percent in 1970, while the percentage of blue-collar workers has fallen slightly and the percentage of white-collar workers has grown rapidly.[5] The sector of the wage-labor force which has grown the most

Table 3

	Wage and Salary Workers	*Self-Employed*	*Ratio*
1940	75.1%	21.6%	3.5
1947	77.5	19.0	4.1
1950	79.6	17.3	4.6
1955	81.9	15.2	5.3
1960	83.7	13.7	6.1
1965	86.3	11.8	7.3
1969	89.5	9.1	9.8

From Albert Szymanski, "Trends in the American Class Structure," *Socialist Revolution*, no. 10, July-August 1972, p. 103.

rapidly (in proportional terms) is the sector of professional and technical workers, which tripled in absolute terms between 1940 and 1970 (rising from 3.3 million in 1940 to 10.1 million in 1970) while doubling as a proportion of the labor force (from 6.4 percent to 12.9 percent). The sector of the labor force which grew the most rapidly in absolute terms during this period was the grouping of white-collar clerical and sales workers. More than doubling in absolute size between 1940 and 1970 (rising from 8.4 million to 18.5 million workers), they rose from 16.3 percent of the labor force in 1940 to 23.6 percent of the labor force in 1970. Manual blue-collar workers also grew in absolute terms during this period, moving from 20.6 million workers in 1940 to 27.4 million workers in 1970, but fell in relative terms from 39.8 percent to 34.9 percent of the work force as a whole.[6]

Finally, it must not be overlooked that, as the proportion of the labor force functioning in the context of specifically capitalist relations of production has expanded, the units of capital employing those workers have become increasingly concentrated and monolithic. As HEW comments, "Out of 3,534,000 industrial units employing 70 percent of the civilian labor force, 2 percent of those units accounted for 50.6 percent of the employees, and more than 27 percent of the employed were accounted for in 0.3 percent of the units."[7] Marx's dual prediction about the parallel concentration of capital and the expansion of wage labor could not be more strikingly confirmed. In his day, these trends were little more than emergent tendencies; in our own, they are largely completed realities.

In order to make use of these statistics and draw conclusions from them, it is important that we examine each of the important strata of the working class separately, attempting to achieve an enhanced awareness of the *motion* and *development* of the class and the linkages connecting the various sectors. Where is the proletariat going? How is it changing?

Table 4

Occupational Groups: Both Sexes

	1900	*1920*	*1940*	*1950*	*1960*	*1970*
Managers, officials, proprietors, farm owners, and managers	7,460 25.6%	9,245 21.9%	9,132 17.7%	9,530 16.1%	10,400 15.5%	9,998 12.7%
Professional and technical	1,234 4.3%	2,283 5.4%	3,879 7.5%	5,081 8.6%	7,475 11.1%	11,322 14.4%
Independent professional and technical	320 1.1%	420 1.0%	570 1.1%	654 1.1%	873 1.3%	1,200 1.5%
Professional and technical workers	910 3.1%	1,860 4.4%	3,310 6.4%	4,427 7.5%	6,602 9.9%	10,100 12.9%
Clerical and sales workers	2,184 7.5%	5,443 12.9%	8,432 16.3%	11,365 19.3%	14,184 21.2%	18,548 23.6%
Service workers	2,626 9.1%	3,313 7.9%	6,069 11.8%	6,180 10.5%	8,349 12.5%	9,724 12.4%
Manual workers	10,401 35.8%	16,974 40.2%	20,597 39.8%	24,266 41.1%	24,211 36.1%	27,452 34.9%
Craftsmen and foremen	3,062 10.5%	5,482 13.0%	6,203 12.0%	8,350 14.2%	8,560 12.8%	10,027 12.8%
Operatives	3,720 12.8%	6,587 15.6%	9,518 18.4%	12,030 20.4%	11,986 17.9%	13,811 17.6%
Non-farm laborers	3,620 12.5%	4,905 11.6%	4,875 9.4%	3,885 6.6%	3,665 5.5%	3,614 4.6%
Farm workers	5,125 17.7%	4,948 11.7%	3,632 7.0%	2,578 4.3%	2,057 3.1%	1,400 1.8%
Total	29,030	42,206	51,742	58,999	66,681	78,408

Sources: *Historical Statistics of the United States*, p. 74. *The Statistical Abstract of the U.S. 1970*, p. 225. *The U.S. Economy in 1980*, Table A-24, p. 57. Table cited in Szymanski, op. cit., p. 107.

Blue-Collar Workers. Although the sector of the working class performing manual labor continues to comprise more than a third of the labor force, it has fallen significantly as a proportion of that labor force. "Taking the working class as a whole," Albert Szymanski points out, "the proportion classified as manual workers increased until 1950 when it stood at an all-time high of 41.1 percent. Since 1950, this percentage has declined significantly to 34.9 percent. The proportion of the labor force classified as 'operatives,' that is, semi-skilled operators of machines of one kind or another, likewise increased to 20.4 percent of the total in 1950, and then declined to 17.6 percent in 1970."[8]

In terms of absolute size, the manual labor force has been growing significantly but irregularly since 1940, growing by four million during the 1940s and by three million during the 1960s, but actually declining slightly during the 1950s.

Since 1950, the absolute size of the blue-collar proletariat as a whole, encompassing both manual and service workers, has been buoyed up principally by the growth of defense spending and by the rise of blue-collar service industries. In the goods-producing sectors of industry, blue-collar workers have declined in absolute numbers as the technology of production has become increasingly powerful. As Michael Reich concludes, "With technical improvements related primarily to mechanization and automation, fewer industrial workers are needed to produce increasing quantities of output."[9]

Marx described this process as "the rising organic composition of capital," saying that any given unit of capital can be spent in one of two ways: either as "variable capital" (for the purchase of labor power) or as "constant capital" (for the purchase of machinery). Marx's prediction was that as capitalism developed, the ratio of machinery to labor power would grow continuously, with labor finding itself a smaller and smaller proportion of the production process. Capitalists, in an effort to defeat their competitors and reduce their costs as much as possible by reducing their expenditures on labor power, would come to rely more and more on the powerful productive apparatus made available to them by the development of technology. As Marx wrote in the *Grundrisse*, "To the degree that large-scale industry develops, the creation of real wealth comes to depend less on labor-time and on the quantity of labor expended, and more on the power of the instruments which are set in motion during labor time, and whose powerful effectiveness itself is not related to the labor-time immediately expended in their production, but depends rather on the general state of science and the progress of technology. . . . Labor no longer appears as an integral element of the productive process; rather, man acts as supervisor and regulator of the productive process itself. . . . He stands at the side of the productive process, rather than being its chief actor."[10] This is, in fact, how capitalism has developed. While the number of blue-collar workers in the goods-producing spheres of industry has tended to decline, the number of service and white-collar workers—trained to perform new functions—has grown rapidly.

This is not to say that blue-collar workers in general or manual laborers in particular are any less significant to capitalism now than they have ever been. Their productive functions remain vital, and their *absolute* size continues to grow. Moreover, if we consider the sexual division of production, we find that the proportion of male workers classified as manual labor has not declined appreciably in modern times. For much of the growth of the white-collar labor force has resulted from the transfer of the center of gravity of "women's work," combined with the dizzying growth of the labor force in general and the decline of agricultural labor and the old middle class. As Albert Szymanski points out, "When we examine the occupational structure for men we see a quite different pattern from that of both sexes together. In 1970, 46.8 percent of the total male work force, a higher percentage than in any census year except 1950, were classified as manual workers. This represented an actual increase during the course of the 1960s."[11] Nevertheless, in historical terms this represents only a minimal change. From 1920 to 1970, manual workers have never comprised less than 44.5 percent of the male work force and never more than 48.3 percent (in 1950). Currently, they comprise 46.8 percent, roughly average for the last fifty years. The percentage of female manual workers, however, has declined precipitously in the same period, from 23.8 percent to 15.7 percent. This decline is especially remarkable when we consider the rapid growth of female participation in the labor force in general during this period, most of which has been concentrated in clerical labor.

Another facet of the continuing importance of blue-collar labor is brought to light by Kim Moody, who comments that "the fastest-growing sector of the work force is state and local government—federal employment has not grown much since 1950. Nearly half of these state and local public workers are blue-collar workers who perform the same tasks, under similar conditions, as their brothers [and sisters] in private industry."[12]

Blue-collar labor thus remains an integral and essential part of the work force, growing as the productive process expands and changing conjuncturally as the focus of production changes. It would be a mistake, however, for us to think that because blue-collar labor has remained vitally important to capitalism, it has remained essentially unchanged by the passage of time. On the contrary, it has changed significantly both as a form of production and in its relationship to other forms of proletarian labor.

In its relationship to the process of production, blue-collar labor has clearly shifted its focus. The rise of blue-collar service work has been the clearest example of this tendency, while the progress of capitalist technology has been the most direct cause of the changes taking place in the nature of blue-collar labor. For as the capitalist technology of production has become increasingly powerful, the focus of blue-collar labor has largely shifted from goods production to the production of services. The *meaning* of "blue-collar labor" has thus proven itself to be as historically specific and mutable as any other category of social life.

One corollary of the changing nature of blue-collar labor has been that the educational level of blue-collar workers has substantially increased in the post–World War II period. Since 1948, for skilled male workers and foremen the average level of schooling completed has risen from 9.7 to 12.1 years, while for semi-skilled operatives the increase has been from 9.1 to 11.3 years, and for unskilled labor from 8.0 to 10.0 years. "Meanwhile, the median year of school completed by all male professional and technical personnel rose from 16.3 to 16.4, virtually no rise at all. Put in other terms, in 1948 professional people had 1.67 times more education than did skilled manual workers, but in 1969, they had only 1.36 times as much, a significant narrowing of the gap in only twenty-one years."[13]

This is just one way in which the relationships between blue-collar labor and other forms of proletarian labor have altered. Other alterations have occurred on numerous levels, including that of "privilege" and its primary element, income. As Michael Reich observes, "Today most white-collar clerical and sales workers earn less than many blue-collar workers. While female clerical and sales workers receive the lowest pay, the average income of male clerical and sales workers alone is below the average income of skilled blue-collar workers."[14] Further, as Albert Szymanski comments, "The wages of the 'new working class' (professional and technical workers) are only slightly greater than those of skilled blue-collar workers. . . . In 1970, the differential between skilled and unskilled blue-collar workers was over three times greater than the differential between skilled and 'new working class' workers."[15] Skilled workers, moreover, are an increasingly large percentage of blue-collar labor, comprising 36.6 percent of all manual workers in 1970. Semi-skilled workers now comprise 50.3 percent of the manual labor force and unskilled workers only 13.1 percent. "In short, many of the old distinctions between blue- and white-collar work are breaking down."[16]

Finally, it should be noted that non-whites are severely underrepresented in white-collar occupations. Black people in particular tend to be heavily concentrated in the blue-collar labor force, especially in the declining goods-producing sectors.[17] Seventy-five percent of all adult black males and 49 percent of all adult black females were listed as members of the work force in 1949, most of them as blue-collar workers.

Thus, although manual and service workers in the blue-collar sector of the economy have been declining, the blue-collar stratum of the working class which they comprise nevertheless remains a vital social force. No serious movement for revolutionary change would be imaginable without the active participation of each of the leading strata of blue-collar labor.

Clerical and Sales Workers. Clerical and sales workers comprise not only the largest single grouping of white-collar labor but also the second largest of all categories within the labor force as a whole, second only to manual labor. Thus, while manual labor comprises 34.9 percent of the labor force, with semi-skilled operatives (17.6 percent) as its largest subcategory, clerical and sales workers constitute 23.6 percent of the labor force, representing almost a quarter of the total work force and comprising roughly 70 percent as many workers as manual labor in general. Moreover, while clerical and sales workers are growing as a proportion of the labor force at a pace eclipsed only by the still more rapid growth of professional and technical labor, manual labor has been declining as a proportion of the work force in recent decades.[18] Clearly, therefore, clerical and sales workers represent a formidable force.

What is most striking about the clerical and sales sector is that it is made up mostly of women. "In 1900, only 8.2 percent of all women in the labor force worked at clerical or sales jobs. In 1970, this had increased to 41.5 percent, a spectacular increase far outmatching any other occupational gains for women." Moreover, "In 1900, only 20 percent of clerical and sales jobs were filled by women; by 1970, this had grown to 66.5 percent."[19] In other words, two-thirds of all clerical and sales work is performed by women. The rapid growth of clerical and sales labor, further, has been almost entirely dependent upon the emergence of large numbers of women as lower-level white-collar workers. Male participation in this sector of the work force has risen only slightly during this century: in 1900, 7.4 percent of male workers functioned as clerical or sales labor; by 1970, 12.8 percent of all male workers were employed in such positions—a 5.4 percent increase in seventy years, compared to the 9.0 percent increase in male blue-collar employment during the same period.[20]

The social and political implications of the rise of female white-collar labor are important and unmistakable. As Martin Oppenheimer observes, "In the context of a changing technology in which ever higher proportions of workers will be in the white-collar strata and in which more of those workers will be women, a radical women's movement confronts unprecedented opportunities to relate to 'the working class.' "[21] In earlier periods, arguments about the "workers" or the "proletarian struggle" conjured up images of male assembly lines, male picket lines, male labor caucuses, and male strike meetings. A new imagery will have to reflect the critical role played by women in the proletarian struggles of the future, not only in the factory but in the office and home as well.

Currently, most female labor is concentrated in a handful of occupations. According to Oppenheimer, "About one-fourth of all women workers are in five occupations: secretary/stenographer, bookkeeper, household service worker, elementary school teacher and waitress. . . . they dominate fields which at least in some ways are extensions of sex-role stereotyped household duties. . . . That is, they take care of people or things."[22] Within the field of clerical and sales labor specifically, six occupations account for more than 50 percent of the total labor force. These six occupations are, in descending order corresponding to their relative size: secretary/stenographer, bookkeeper, cashier, office machine operator, and shipping and receiving clerk.[23]

Szymanski argues that changing occupational trends "reflect the changing requirements of industrial capitalism" but "do not necessarily reflect changes in the class structure."[24] What he means by this is that the significance of the shift to white-collar employment has been largely modified by the fact that much of the white-collar work force consists of women whose husbands remain within the blue-collar stratum of the working class. "Social class," he continues, "as distinct from occupational categories, defines the whole way a family lives, thinks, and relates to people, which is generally determined by the relationship of the head of the family to the means of production. It is generally the occupation of the man of the family that determines a family's social class and concomitant consciousness . . ."[25]

Since 40 percent of all married female clerical and sales workers in 1967 were married to blue-collar workers, it appears reasonable to assume that the class orientation of such female workers is likely to be less radically new and different than might be expected. This argument is furthered by the fact that the percentage of married women workers has risen dramatically in the last three decades. In 1940, only

30.3 percent of all women workers were married, while currently 57.8 percent are married. The percentage of married women currently working has also more than doubled, rising from 16.7 percent in 1940 to 37.8 percent in 1967.[26] For these reasons, therefore, we can agree with the thrust of Szymanski's argument when he maintains that the shifting focus of proletarian labor reflects—at least in this particular instance—less of a change in the social class orientation of the clerical and sales strata of the working class than might be suspected. Kim Moody throws additional light on this point when he comments that "Clerical work, because it is low paying and repetitive, does not represent the proletarianization of formerly middle-class people so much as it is a channel for horizontal mobility within the working class and, even more, a second source of income for working-class families. In this sense, it has served as a safety valve for working-class discontent."[27]

Professional and Technical Workers. Professional and technical workers have grown more rapidly than any other sector of the labor force. Wage-paid professional and technical workers comprise 12.9 percent of the labor force, a total surpassed only by clerical and sales workers (23.6 percent) and semi-skilled operatives (17.6 percent).* Unlike the stratum of clerical and sales workers, the growth of the professional and technical sector cannot be accounted for by the influx of female workers into the economy; in fact, the percentage of all professional and technical jobs held by women has decreased since 1940 by 4.9 percent, falling from 45.3 percent in 1940 to 40.4 percent in 1970.[28]

* Government projections indicate, moreover, that there is a good possibility that by 1980 professional and technical workers will overtake semi-skilled operatives as the second largest grouping in the labor force.

Five central occupations represent the majority of all professional and technical workers: teachers, engineers, nurses, accountants, and technicians. Accounting for approximately 55 percent of the total category, the configuration of these occupational groupings provides us with considerable information about the character and direction of the contemporary "professional and technical labor force" understood as a changing historical totality.

Table 5

The Occupational Distribution of Professional and Technical Workers
(in thousands)

	1910	*1920*	*1930*	*1940*	*1950*	*1966*
1. Teachers	595	752	1044	1086	1254	2353
2. Engineers	77	134	217	297	527	1117
3. Nurses	82	149	294	376	486	637
4. Accountants	39	118	192	238	383	606
5. Technicians	0	4	20	84	185	485
6. Physicians	152	151	156	168	180	277
7. Draftsmen	45	67	98	114	120	270
8. Lawyers	115	123	161	182	172	260
9. Scientists	–	–	–	–	38	193
10. Clergymen	118	127	149	141	166	187

Data derived from Jay Mandle, "Some Notes on the American Working Class," *Review of Radical Political Economy* 2, no. 11 (Spring 1970), p. 67, and David L. Kaplan and M. Claire Casey, "Occupational Trends in the United States 1900 to 1950," Bureau of the Census, Working Paper no. 5, U.S. Department of Commerce, 1958, p. 10. Information on the early history of the stratum of scientists was unavailable.

Three of the occupational categories listed in Table 5 should be excluded from our analysis of the working class, on the grounds that they are made up primarily of men and women who do not function as wage labor. These three groupings are the physicians, lawyers, and clergymen. The bulk of the members of these groups have classically been considered "middle class" by Marxists because, instead of selling their labor power for a wage, they sell specific services for a price with no capitalist intervening to direct the uses of their labor power or extract a surplus from the exchange of the commodities produced. Since they control not only the uses of their labor power but the full exchange value of their products, these people cannot be considered workers. As Marx wrote, "They confront me as sellers of commodities, not as sellers of labor, and this relation therefore has nothing to do with the exchange of capital for labor."[29]

Subtracting these independent professionals from our category of professional and technical workers, we are still left with a total of 12.9 percent of the labor force represented by this designation. Not one of the three nonproletarian occupations eliminated from our analysis could be found among the top five occupations among professional and technical personnel, and all were growing slowly; in fact, in both absolute and relative terms, all three were the least dynamic of the occupations officially categorized as "professional and technical." As Szymanski comments, "Clearly the old independent professions, especially law and medicine, are now a small part of all professional jobs. These old professions have been greatly outdistanced by the rapid growth of such occupations as teaching, social work, engineering, nursing, scientific research, and various forms of technical work. Virtually all of these people must work for others. That is, they are proletarians. However great their pay, they do not control the conditions of their labor, but are subject to the will of someone else."[30]

Since 1940, of the various professional and technical occupations, teachers and engineers have grown the most rapidly in absolute terms, while scientists and technicians have grown by far the most rapidly in proportional terms. The members of these four occupations, together with accountants (who have almost tripled in number since 1940), represent the five professional and technical occupations most deeply and critically dependent upon higher education for the acquisition of job-related skills. Nurses and draftsmen, although to a lesser extent dependent upon various forms of specialized education, are not, like the other professional and technical occupations, necessarily products of the universities and related institutions. The workers in these five key occupations, therefore, together with a significant slice of managerial, sales, and service personnel, represent the true constituency of the college-educated, technical, and supervisory wings of the working class.[31]

Notes

1. Kim Moody, "The American Working Class in Transition," *International Socialism*, October-November 1969, p. 10.
2. Albert Szymanski, "Trends in the American Class Structure," *Socialist Revolution*, no. 10, July-August 1972, p. 103.
3. Ibid.
4. Michael Reich, "The Evolution of the United States Labor Force," in *The Capitalist System*, ed. Richard Edwards, Michael Reich, and Thomas Weisskopf (Englewood Cliffs, N.J.: Prentice-Hall, 1972), p. 175.
5. The Carnegie Commission on Higher Education, *College Graduates and Jobs* (New York: McGraw-Hill, 1973), p. 32.
6. Szymanski, op. cit., p. 107 (all data).
7. Department of Health, Education, and Welfare, *U.S. Manpower in the 1970s: Opportunity and Challenge* (1969).

8. Szymanski, op. cit., pp. 104-5.

9. Reich, op. cit., p. 178.

10. Karl Marx, *Grundrisse der Kritik der Politischen Okönomie* (Moscow: Foreign Languages Press, 1939), p. 486. Cited in Martin Nicolaus, "The Unknown Marx," *New Left Reader,* ed. Carl Oglesby (New York: Grove Press, 1969), p. 106. The *Grundrisse* has now been published in English for the first time, translated by Nicolaus.

11. Szymanski, op. cit., p. 106.

12. Moody, op. cit., p. 12.

13. Szymanski, op. cit., pp. 116-17 (all data).

14. Reich, op. cit., p. 180.

15. Szymanski, op. cit., p. 115. By "new working class," Szymanski is explicitly referring to professional and technical workers.

16. Reich, op. cit., p. 180.

17. Szymanski, op. cit., p. 120.

18. Ibid., p. 110.

19. Ibid., p. 111.

20. Ibid., p. 110.

21. Martin Oppenheimer, "What Is the New Working Class?" *New Politics* 10, no. 1 (Fall 1972), p. 39.

22. Ibid., p. 37.

23. Jay Mandle, "Some Notes On the American Working Class," *Review of Radical Political Economy* 2, no. 1 (Spring 1970), p. 56.

24. Szymanski, op. cit., p. 105.

25. Ibid. Szymanski defends this argument in the following manner: "Women tend to work irregularly, change jobs more often than men, define themselves less in terms of their jobs, join unions less frequently, and carry over job experiences to their non-working time less than men. The average job tenure of women workers is only 2.8 years, compared with 5.2 years for men. Only 42 percent of women workers compared with 70 percent of male workers who worked at all in 1967 worked full-time the year round. One in seven women workers compared with one in four male workers belongs to a union" (pp. 105-6).

26. Ibid., p. 106.

27. Moody, op. cit., p. 12.

28. Szymanski, op. cit., pp. 107, 112.

29. Karl Marx, *Theories of Surplus Value,* vol. 1 (Moscow: Progress

Publishers, 1969), p. 407; cited in Ian Gough, "Marx's Theory of Productive and Unproductive Labor," *New Left Review*, no. 76, November-December 1972, p. 54.

30. Szymanski, op. cit., p. 113.

31. Only 19.7 percent of the managerial work force is college educated. Moreover, from 1950 to 1968, fully 60 percent of the rise in employment for male college graduates occurred in the professional and technical sector, with no appreciable growth in the managerial sector. Although the situation has changed somewhat since 1968, with a fairly considerable rise in managerial employment, this is not considered likely to be a long-term trend. See, for example, The Carnegie Commission, op. cit.

10
Problems of Class Analysis

> *At the latest stage of economic and political concentration, the particular capitalist enterprises in all sectors of the economy are being subordinated to the requirements of capital as a whole. This coordination takes place on two interrelated levels: through the normal economic process under monopolistic competition (growing organic composition of capital; pressure on the rate of profit); and through "state management." Consequently, ever more strata of the formerly independent middle classes become the direct servants of capital, occupied in the creation and realization of surplus value while being separated from control of the means of production. The "tertiary sector" (production of services), long since indispensable for the realization and reproduction of capital, recruits a huge army of salaried employees. At the same time, the increasingly technological character of material production draws the functional intelligentsia into this process. The base of exploitation is thus enlarged beyond the factories and shops and far beyond the blue-collar working class.*[1]
>
> Herbert Marcuse
> *Counterrevolution and Revolt*

In this chapter, I'm going to make an effort to synthesize the ideas and information established in the last two chapters. In chapter 8, "The Myth of the Middle Class," I presented an abstract definition of the proletariat; in chapter 9, I offered a concrete portrait of the working class as it exists. Now I will try to blend these two approaches to class analysis and see if the results are harmonious.

The questions it will be important for us to answer are the following: (1) whether or not the proletariat as it actually exists is alienated and exploited in the Marxist sense; and (2) whether or not a precise line of demarcation can be drawn between the various elements of the proletariat and other clearly defined classes in the context of the hierarchical structure of the society. Answering these questions should, on the one hand, provide us with a deeper understanding of both the concrete and abstract nature of capitalist class relationships (i.e., the nature of the proletariat, the forms of exploitation, etc.), and, on the other hand, provide us with tangible information about the forward motion of capitalism and the class structure. If we can define the proletariat clearly and say how it has changed, we should be able to achieve at least partial insight into the direction of future change, which will in turn enable us to develop a political understanding sufficient to *make history* as we make ourselves in the course of struggle.

The Forms of Exploitation

Since Marx was concerned above all else with the historical motion of capitalism, he attempted to identify and analyze the class forces in capitalism which he felt both define capitalism and determine its forward motion. Structurally, Marx distinguished between two major forms of labor specific to the capitalist mode of production: productive wage labor and unproductive wage labor. Productive labor in general Marx defined as all useful labor, but since labor of this type is common to all forms of society, it tells us little about the specific nature of capitalism. Thus, when Marx used the terms "productive" or "unproductive" labor, he was referring not to the productivity of labor in general historical terms but to the structural importance each kind of labor possesses for capitalism.

What is productive labor from the standpoint of capital? Marx defined productive labor as labor productive of surplus value. As he wrote in *Capital,* "From the capitalist standpoint, only that labor is productive which creates surplus value."[2] Since surplus value is the source of all capital, it is thus structurally essential to capitalism. Without such productive labor, no capital accumulation would be possible, and thus capitalism itself would not be possible. Marx was keenly aware of this; as he pointed out in *Capital,* "Productive labor is only a concise term for the whole relationship and the form and manner in which labor power figures in the capitalist production process. The distinction from *other* kinds of labor is, however, of the greatest importance, since this distinction expresses precisely the specific form of labor on which the whole capitalist mode of production and capital itself is based."[3]

Productive labor in the capitalist sense is the quintessential form of labor under capitalism, making capital accumulation itself possible. Unproductive labor in some forms may at times be necessary to the continued maintenance of productive labor, but it does not define the character of the mode of production. Productive labor *is* the specifically capitalist mode of production, embodying the class relationship of exploitation in its purest and archetypal form. Unproductive labor—for example, the labor of state employees—may be necessary to capitalism and may occur within the context of capitalist relations of production, thus involving alienation and exploitation; but it is not, structurally, productive labor functioning as the motor of social development in capitalist society.

Productive wage labor, thus, is productive from the capitalist standpoint *only* because it produces surplus value. If the labor sold is productive of surplus value, then it is immaterial whether the labor is mental, manual, or some blurred amalgam of the two; it makes no difference whether the result of labor is a material or immaterial commodity, for as long as it is produced for exchange it will embody a greater quantity of value in exchange than the worker received in wages. Thus, as Marx wrote in *Theories of Surplus Value,* "The designation of labor as *productive* labor has absolutely nothing to do with the determinate content of that labor, its special utility, or the particular use-value in which it manifests itself. *The same* kind of labor may be productive or unproductive."[4] The key to the analysis is a question of social relations, for as Marx argued in *Capital,* "If we may take an example from outside the sphere of production of material objects, a schoolmaster is a productive laborer when, in addition to belaboring the heads of his scholars, he works like a horse to enrich the school proprietors. That the latter has laid out his capital in a teaching factory, instead of a sausage factory, does not alter the relation."[5]

All wage labor productive of surplus value is thus productive labor in the Marxist sense. Not all wage labor is productive of surplus value, however. Some—notably, the labor of state workers—is unproductive labor, in that no surplus value accrues directly to the employer as a result of the labor performed. The problem, therefore, is whether or not some forms of unproductive labor can be classified as proletarian labor. Specifically, can state workers be said to be exploited? If so, in what sense is this true? And what does this tell us about exploitation?

Marx differentiated between two different forms of what at first glance appear to be unproductive labor: first, labor sold for a wage but not productive of surplus value (such as the labor of state workers, who do useful work but produce no goods for exchange); and second, labor services exchanged directly for money with no capitalist as intermediary (such as the labor of independent physicians). Marx considered only the first of these two to be unproductive labor in the specifically capitalist sense, arguing that the direct exchange of labor services for money occurs outside the realm of capitalist relations of production, since those who perform labor services in a self-employed capacity are neither alienated from their labor nor exploited by a capitalist. "They therefore belong neither to the category of *productive* or *unproductive* laborers, although they are producers of commodities. But their production does not fall under the capitalist mode of production."[6] A worker is a worker only by virtue of his relationship to a capitalist. If a laborer is self-employed, he is not a "worker," no matter what kind of labor he (or she) performs.

Unproductive labor, therefore, is wage labor not productive of surplus value which nevertheless is performed in the context of an employer/employee relationship. The key question, from our standpoint, is thus whether or not the performance of such unproductive wage labor involves a relationship of exploitation and can be truly classified as proletarian. The direct extraction of surplus value is the archetypal form of exploitation, but is it the only one?

Marx argued that the direct extraction of surplus value is *not* the only form of exploitation which takes place in the context of capitalist class relations. In the third volume of *Capital,* he argues clearly and convincingly that commercial workers—the laborers of the consumption process—are exploited *without* producing surplus value. The crux of their exploitation is the performance of a quantum of unpaid labor. "The commercial worker produces no surplus value directly. But the price of his labor is determined . . . by its costs of production, while the application of this labor power, its exertion, expenditure of energy, and wear and tear, is as in the case of every other wage laborer by no means limited by its value [necessary living costs]. His wage, therefore, is not necessarily proportionate to the mass of profit which he helps the capitalist to realize. What he costs the capitalist and what he brings in for him are two different things. He creates no surplus value directly, but adds to the capitalist's income by helping him to reduce the cost of realising surplus value, inasmuch as he performs partly unpaid labor."[7] This argument is supplemented by the analysis presented in volume two: ". . . we shall assume that this buying and selling agent is a man who sells his labor . . . He performs a necessary function, because the process of reproduction itself includes unproductive functions. He works as well as the next man, but intrinsically his labor creates neither value nor product. . . . We shall assume that he is a mere wage laborer, even one of the better paid, for all the difference it makes. Whatever his pay, as a wage laborer he works part of his time for nothing."[8]

Surplus labor extracted from the commercial worker reduces the costs of circulation confronting the capitalist. This constitutes another form of exploitation based on the extraction of surplus labor paralleling the production of surplus value, which also involves the extraction of surplus labor. The direct creation of surplus value is thus not a necessary condition for proletarian status. When surplus labor is extracted from a worker, *whether or not surplus value is directly created*, exploitation takes place.[9]

Similar considerations arise in the case of state workers, who constitute the fastest growing sector of the work force. Although state workers generally sell their labor power and perform useful labor, they are not directly productive of surplus value since the state does not accumulate surplus value through the exchange of commodities. The unproductive wage labor they perform, therefore, though it may be necessary to keep the system of capitalist production intact, is not itself productive labor.

The labor of the majority of state workers employed as

manual and lower-level white-collar labor is certainly alienated in the classical sense. The question is whether or not they are exploited. While state workers are generally paid less than their counterparts in the private sector, this is not sufficient evidence to show that surplus labor is extracted from their labor. If productive workers are exploited for the surplus value they produce, and commercial workers are exploited for the reductions in the costs of circulation they make possible, how are state workers exploited? The answer, I think, is that state workers labor *to reduce the social costs of production.* They provide necessary social services which, on the one hand, pacify the working class and keep workers at an elastic and politically defined subsistence level (through welfare laws, unemployment compensation, social security, etc.), and, on the other hand, facilitate the processes of business (through the National Labor Relations Board, the Department of Commerce, the Department of Labor, the Federal Reserve Bank, etc.). If the public sector didn't provide these necessary social services, the private sector would be forced to do so. As James O'Connor points out, "The human costs of capital accumulation—unemployment, retirement, sickness, and so on—are shifted to the state budget, that is, to the taxpaying working class as a whole."[10]

The labor of state workers, therefore, *financed by the working class as a whole through the payment of taxes,* hugely reduces the social costs of production which the capitalist class would otherwise be confronted with. Universities, for example, spend large amounts of state money—revenue taken from wages—to provide college-educated workers with necessary training which the capitalist class would be forced to finance if the working class did not. Thus, although no surplus value is directly created by the surplus labor of state workers, huge sums of money are freed for use as capital as a result of this labor. State employees thus contribute indirectly but significantly to the process of capital accumulation. Their exploitation occurs through the extraction of a surplus from their labor by the capitalist class as a whole (through the state) for the purpose of reducing the social costs of production and thus freeing money for expenditure as capital.

State workers, however, are not the only ones whose function as unproductive labor is to reduce the social costs of production confronting capital. Housewives, too, perform necessary and exploited labor in this arena. As Mariarosa Dalla Costa comments, "We have to make clear that, within the wage, domestic work produces not merely use values, but is essential to the production of surplus value."[11] For the labor of housewives *does occur within the wage,* as Dalla Costa argues. In this society, the basic unit of wage labor is not an individual male wage-earner, but the family he represents, whose *total function* is the basis of his wage. This is true largely, as Selma James points out, because "the wage relation can exist only when the ability to work becomes a saleable commodity. Marx calls this commodity *labor power.* This is a strange commodity for it is not a thing. The ability to labor resides only in a human being whose life is consumed in the process of producing. First, it must be nine months in the womb, must be fed, clothed, and trained; then, when it works, its bed must be made, its floors swept, its lunchbox prepared, its sexuality not gratified but quietened, its dinner ready when it gets home, even if this is eight in the morning from the night shift. This is how labor power is produced and reproduced when it is daily consumed in the factory or the office. *To describe its basic production and reproduction is to describe women's work.*"[12]

Wages are paid, then, in exchange for the labor power of the wage earner, but they are designed to embrace women's work as well. Surplus value is the total amount of value accumulated by the capitalist over and above the wages paid to *families,* which must be understood as the basic units of wage labor. Women's work in particular is prized by the capitalist class (like the labor of state workers) because it contributes to reductions in the social costs of production. Explaining this point, Dalla Costa speaks "of the enormous quantity of social services which capitalist organization transforms into privatized activity, putting them on the backs of housewives. Domestic labor is not essentially 'feminine work'; a woman doesn't fulfill herself more or get less exhausted than a man from washing and cleaning. These are social services inasmuch as they serve the reproduction of labor power. And capital, precisely by instituting its family structure, has 'liberated' the man from these functions so that he is completely 'free' for *direct* exploitation; so that he is free to 'earn' enough for a woman to reproduce him as labor power. It has made men wage slaves, then, to the degree that it has succeeded in allocating these services to women in the family. . . ."[13]

At this point, it is vital for us to add another dimension to the discussion by identifying another key form of exploitation which has become central only in recent decades, what James O'Connor calls "tax exploitation." This is a form of exploitation through taxation which is characteristic of state monopoly capitalism, since "the problem of financing the budget . . . reduces itself to the problem of increasing taxes, specifically, the problem of intensifying tax exploitation of the working class, owners of small businesses, and self-employed professionals."[14] In the contemporary period, with the state playing a vital role in stabilizing the economy, state taxation of the working class has thus emerged as a form of the extraction of surplus value central to the continued functioning of capitalism.

While the higher wages granted to labor in the last thirty years have *apparently* reduced the amount of surplus extracted from the working class, this is more appearance than reality. In reality, higher levels of taxation continue to lower the real wages of workers, in a process directly analogous to the lowering of wages which formerly occurred on a firm-by-firm basis but which now occurs classwide. The state, by taxing workers in the interests of business, thus extracts a surplus from their labor. The withholding tax is the most obvious manifestation of this tendency, since it allows workers to acquire and spend only 80 percent of their wages, the remainder going to the state. O'Connor argues that this aspect of the income tax is "the highest form of tax exploitation," since 85 percent of income-tax returns are collected at the basic 20 percent withholding rate. Moreover, "The income tax in general has encroached more and more on wage and salary income since it was first introduced. The State has systematically reduced personal exemptions and credits for dependents from $4,000 (for a family of four) in 1913-1916 to $2,400 today. In 1913-1916, a single person was granted a $3,000 exemption; today, only $600. In terms of actual purchasing power, real exemptions have fallen even more," since steady inflation has eroded the value of the dollar for many years now. Also, "Since World War II, there has been a general upward movement of state and local taxes in comparison with per capita income, especially in the industrial states. Similarly, federal taxes take a larger and larger share of personal income."[15]

Taxation of the working class as a whole by the capitalist class as a whole through the agency of the state thus constitutes a major reduction in wages. The surplus which is extracted in this manner serves two essential purposes: first, insofar as state revenues are spent to bolster the economy through the purchase of large quantities of commodities, the surplus goes directly into the hands of leading capitalists and is transformed largely into capital; and second, insofar as state revenues finance the social services provided through the labor of state workers, the surplus is used as an *indirect* contribution to the accumulation of capital through reductions in the social costs of production resulting from the labor of state workers. Either way, the interests of the capitalist class are served. Moreover, the fact that this form of exploitation affects all workers (and independent professionals as well) provides a basis for common struggle by workers, *organized as a class,* against the state as the representative of the capitalists as a class. More will be said about this in the final chapter.

When Marx spoke of the emergence of state workers and other forms of necessary unproductive labor and productive service labor, he was expressing his awareness of the latent tendency inherent in capitalism to conquer "all spheres of . . . production," since, in his own time, "here the capitalist mode of production is met with to only a small extent, and from the nature of the case can only be applied in a few spheres. . . . All these manifestations of capitalist production in this sphere are so insignificant compared with the totality of production that they can be left entirely out of account."[16] It is only since Marx's death that the latent tendencies he identified and analyzed have become a major part of reality. Unproductive wage labor, especially the labor of state employees, has only in recent times blossomed as a significant branch of proletarian labor. The historical development of capitalism has thus led to the emergence of a truly diversified and independent proletariat in the years since Marx focused his attention on the problems of capital accumulation and proletarian class structure.[17]

The Problem of Managerial Labor

In *Capital,* Marx made an incomplete but profoundly suggestive effort to develop an understanding of the working class as a structural whole, an effort with significant implications for our analysis of the hierarchical and technical differentiation of the contemporary proletariat. "As the cooperative character of the labor process becomes more and more marked," Marx argued, "so, as a necessary consequence, does our notion of productive labor, and of its agent the productive laborer, become extended. In order to labor productively, it is no longer necessary for you to do manual work yourself; enough if you are an organ of the collective laborer and perform one of its subordinate functions. The first definition of productive laborer . . . still remains correct for the collective laborer, considered as a whole. But it no longer holds good for each member taken individually."[18] In another passage, Marx supplemented this analysis: "No longer the individual laborer but rather the socially combined labor power becomes the actual agent of the collective work process. The various competing labor powers which constitute the productive machine as a whole participate in very different ways in the immediate production of commodities. . . . One individual works with his hands, another with his head, one as manager, engineer, technologist, et cetera, the other as overseer, a third as direct manual laborer or mere helper. Thus more and more functions of labor power are being subsumed under the immediate concept of productive labor and the workers under the concept of productive workers. They are directly exploited by capital . . . and it is a matter of indifference whether the function of the individual worker, who is only a member of this collective laborer, is more remote or close to immediate manual labor."[19]

What this means is that the proletariat as a whole must be viewed as the agent of productive labor, and that the interdependence of the various forms of proletarian labor is more important for analysis than the fact that such labor is divided into productive and unproductive segments. It also raises the problem of managerial labor, that is, the problem of where the proletariat ends and other classes begin in the hierarchical structure of society. To what extent can managerial labor be defined as proletarian? Is it possible to establish a clear line of demarcation between the classes?

Marx did not hold a simple view of the class nature of managerial labor. He did not argue, as many theorists do, that all people occupying managerial positions in the economy are therefore members of a middle class, located in an intermediate position between capital and labor.[20] In *Capital,* he wrote that "The labor of supervision and management is naturally required whenever the direct process of production assumes the form of a combined social process, and not of the isolated labor of independent producers. . . . all labor in which many individuals cooperate necessarily requires a commanding will to coordinate and unify the process. . . . This is a productive job, which must be performed in every combined mode of production."[21] In another significant passage, in *Theories of Surplus Value,* he declared: "Included among these productive workers, of course, are those who contribute in one way or another to the production of the commodity, from the actual operative to the manager or engineer (as distinct from the capitalist)."[22]

The problem of managerial labor is thus complex, greatly complicated by the fact that no single occupation or sector of the economy accounts for a very large proportion of the ten million "laborers" classified by the government as "managers, owners, and proprietors." Within this jumbled and chaotic mass there are members of many different strata of the population, representing diverse (and often contradictory) class positions and interests. Not only the entire capitalist class but the entire "middle class" of small proprietors has been included in this grouping. Further, significant numbers of administrators from both government and industry are included, with no differentiation made between higher- and lower-level managers or administrative and technical managers. Finally—and incongruously—railroad conductors, union officials, department-store floor managers, and postal workers have been traditionally included in this category, along with several other clearly misplaced groupings. In order to consider the problem of managerial labor in its pure form, therefore, we will have to ignore all of these groupings except the category of administrative personnel employed by the state and business.

When considering managerial labor in this narrower sense, the first distinction that must be made is between supervisory workers employed in the technical wing of industry, who for the most part are comprised of lower-level managers immediately concerned with the problems of production, and administrative workers in both state and industry, who range from lower-level managers in the transportation industry to the president of General Motors.

The technical administrators, comprising a significant percentage of all scientists and engineers (29.4 percent in 1966), are not particularly difficult to classify. As Jacek Kuron and Karol Modzelewski argue, "The producer of national income in industry is 'aggregate labor,' that is, all workers who set up, carry out, and maintain the technical process of production, hence—in addition to directly or indirectly productive workers—the engineers and technicians, the technical intelligentsia."[23] With the exception of a handful of NASA and AEC officials whose labor is more purely administrative and political than technical, most technical administrators are steeped in the immediate work of production, functioning just over the heads of the scientists and technicians from whose ranks they are drawn. Their labor is *alienated* since they lack control over the purposes and results of production and they are *exploited* as a part of the "aggregate" technical mass producing either surplus value for a capitalist or reductions in the social costs of production for the capitalist class as a whole. In brief, they are workers.

Purely administrative labor is an infinitely more complex phenomenon, however, since most of the work carried out by these people involves reinforcing and streamlining the organization of the social relations of production necessary to the continued functioning of capitalism. Thus their primary responsibility, whether they are minor bureaucrats in the HEW hierarchy or top-level executives for General Electric, is to ensure that the structural relationship between the exploiting and exploited classes remains efficient and profitable.

For those administrators whose labor is both alienated and subject to exploitation—and I will argue that this is true of a large percentage of the administrative work force—this inevitably creates tensions and contradictions among them on the level of their subjective consciousness of class. While they are objectively part of a privileged stratum of the working class, their consciousness is likely to be "permanently and unremittingly" hostile to the interests of the class as a whole, much like the consciousness of policemen, professors, and professional soldiers. As the lieutenants of capital in the organization of production, they are less likely to join forces with the militant elements in the proletariat than any other sector of the working population.

While not all administrators are proletarian, the majority probably are. As the stratification of the labor force becomes more and more complex, involving an almost geological layering of responsibility and authority, the lower levels of administrative labor become more and more remote from the decision-making powers at the top, and thus increasingly alienated. From my standpoint, the decision-making power concentrated at the top entirely removes the upper echelons of "managerial labor" from the orbit of the proletariat, since their labor, although wage paid, cannot be said to be alienated. The presidents and vice-presidents of General Motors and the Chase Manhattan Bank exercise real control over the purposes and results of their labor. To a lesser extent, the bureaucrats below them share this decision-making power; the specific point in the hierarchy at which non-alienated labor becomes alienated labor is impossible for us to identify with precision, and is, moreover, inconsequential. As Kim Moody argues, "The question of whether or not certain marginal groups are or are not workers at any given time is somewhat beside the point. It is more a question of direction and process and the manner in which these affect consciousness that is relevant to a Marxist analysis. The so-called precision of bourgeois sociology at drawing lines of definition, based on income, education, etc., is not really precision since it obscures the reality of transition."[24]

When Marx began his systematic and incomplete analysis of classes in the last chapter of *Capital,* he commented that "middle and intermediate strata even here obliterate lines of demarcation everywhere. . . . However, this is immaterial for our analysis. We have seen that the continual tendency and law of development of the capitalist mode of production is more and more to divorce the means of production from labor, and more and more to concentrate the scattered means of production into large groups, thereby transforming labor into wage-labor and the means of production into capital."[25]

What it is important for us to recognize is that, since the majority of managerial workers are never likely to rise to positions of real authority in the economic structure, they are thus locked in the vise of false consciousness when they identify their interests with those of the capitalist class. As alienated labor, they confuse their class interests when they identify not with other workers but with the capitalists who are their masters. For in contemporary capitalist society, even a large percentage of managerial labor—formerly the sole province of capital and the direct lieutenants of capital—has been proletarianized. Capital thus continues to concentrate the means of production and to "transform labor into wage labor."

On the other hand, the real leaders in the managerial structure are *not* mistaken when they identify their personal interests with those of the ruling class. Although frequently not capitalists themselves, these men (rarely women) comprise a power elite which functions in a symbiotic relationship with the capitalist class. Much of the ruling class of the future originates in this sector of the population, gathering the wealth and prestige necessary for membership as a concomitant of their decision-making power. Their children are likely to attend the elite schools reserved for the children of the ruling class, and their high wages are likely to be amply supplemented by large quantities of stocks and bonds. The capitalists in the managerial structure rely on their *possessions for the acquisition of positions,* while the power elite relies on their *positions for the acquisition of possessions.* The confluence of these two groups is easily visible in the upper reaches of American social life.

Notes

1. Herbert Marcuse, *Counterrevolution and Revolt* (Boston: Beacon Press, 1972), pp. 9-10.

2. Karl Marx, *Theories of Surplus Value,* vol. 1 (Moscow: Progress Publishers, 1969), p. 153, cited in Ian Gough, "Marx's Theory of Productive and Unproductive Labor," *New Left Review,* no. 76, November-December 1972, p. 50. For the rest of this section, I have relied deeply on the whole of Gough's article and on the essay "Productive Labor" by Isaac Ilyich Rubin, from his book, *Essays on Marx's Theory of Value,* originally published in the Soviet Union in 1928 and recently republished by Black and Red, Detroit (1972). While Gough's analysis is more extensive, Rubin is bolder in his conclusions and more concise in his presentation. Together, the two articles are an excellent introduction to the subject.

3. Marx, *Theories of Surplus Value,* p. 396, cited in Gough, pp. 51-52.

4. Ibid., p. 401, cited in Gough, p. 52.

5. Marx, *Capital,* vol. 1 (Moscow: Progress Publishers, 1961), p. 509, cited in Gough, p. 52.

6. Marx, *Theories of Surplus Value,* p. 407, cited in Gough, p. 54.

7. Marx, *Capital,* vol. 3 (New York: International Publishers, 1967), p. 300.

8. Marx, *Capital,* vol. 2, pp. 131-32.

9. If it isn't entirely clear why Marx defined commercial workers as unproductive laborers, I. I. Rubin presents a brief explanation: "Why," he asks, "does Marx not consider the labor of salesmen and store clerks, organized in a capitalistic commercial enterprise, productive? To answer this question, we must remember that whenever Marx spoke of productive labor as labor which is hired by capital in *Theories of Surplus Value,* he had in mind only *productive capital.* The addendum to the first volume of *Theories of Surplus Value,* which has the title 'The Concept of Productive Labor,' begins with the question of productive capital. From here, Marx moves on to productive labor. This addendum ends with the words: 'Here we have been dealing only with *productive capital,* that is, capital employed in the *direct process of production.* We come later to capital in the *process of circulation.* And only after that, in considering the special form assumed by capital as *merchants' capital,* can the question be answered as to how far the laborers employed by it are productive or unproductive." (Rubin, op. cit., pp. 267-68.)

Without attempting a full-scale analysis of Marx's categorizations of capital, it can nevertheless be said that Marx believed that labor engaged solely in the transfer of ownership rights over commodities (the labor of commercial workers) adds nothing to the exchange of values of those commodities and thus is not productive of surplus value. This analysis may be disputed, and it has been disputed in the past, with regard to commercial workers, but it should nevertheless be clear that unproductive wage labor is a meaningful category: state workers, for example, are definitely unproductive wage laborers insofar as their labor does not result in the direct production of commodities embodying exchange value. This does not mean that these workers are inessential to capitalism—but they are not themselves directly productive of surplus value. The importance of this point is most apparent in terms of understanding questions relating to the overall production of surplus value, the problems involved in assessing rates of profit and capital accumulation, etc.

10. James O'Connor, "The Fiscal Crisis of the State," *Socialist Revolution,* no. 2, March-April 1970, p. 65.

11. Mariarosa Dalla Costa, "Women and the Subversion of the Community," in Mariarosa Dalla Costa and Selma James, *The Power of Women and the Subversion of the Community* (London: Falling Wall Press, 1972), p. 31.

12. Selma James, Introduction to Dalla Costa, op. cit., p. 7.

13. Ibid., pp. 31-32.

14. O'Connor, op. cit., p. 65.

15. Ibid., pp. 71-72.

16. Marx, *Theories of Surplus Value,* vol. 1, pp. 410-11.

17. To my knowledge, among contemporary Marxists only Martin Nicolaus and Nicos Poulantzas argue that the working class is made up solely of productive laborers. Nicolaus, in his essay "Proletariat and Middle Class in Marx," comments that "it should be clear that to Marx, the proletariat meant productive workers only. If the proletariat is defined to include all those who work for wages, then many corporation executives and managers are proletarians, too." (This statement was made in a footnote, without elaboration, in *Studies on the Left* 7, no. 1 [January-February 1967]). Poulantzas, in his essay "Marxism and Social Classes," comments that "while every worker is a wage earner, not every wage earner is a worker, since not every wage earner is necessarily a productive worker, i.e., one who produces surplus value (commodities)" (*New Left Review,* no. 78, March-April 1973). It should be clear by now that both men are mistaken. Aside from the fact that Poulantzas wrongly equates commodity production with the production of surplus value (in fact, nonproletarian independent producers also produce commodities, but do not produce surplus value), both writers base their arguments on the premise that wage earners are not necessarily workers in the Marxist sense. Although this is clearly true, especially in terms of such strata as wage-paid managerial decision-makers (whose labor is far from alienated), it is nevertheless insufficient evidence to justify the conclusion that only *productive* labor is *proletarian* labor. For top managers are neither productive nor unproductive laborers. Unproductive wage laborers, on the other hand, such as state

workers, commercial workers, etc., are both alienated and exploited. While not directly productive of surplus value, they are, nevertheless, indirectly *necessary* to such production. It would thus make little sense for us to deny the proletarian status of such workers, either logically or politically. If, as Nicolaus argues, this means that "many corporation executives and managers are proletarian, too," so be it. Marx explicitly indicated that this was true for many lower-level managers, as will be seen in the following pages.

18. Marx, *Capital,* vol. 1, pp. 508-9, cited in Gough, p. 50.

19. Marx, in a passage drawn from an early version of chapter 6 of *Capital,* published as *Resultate des Unmittelbaren Produktionsprozesses* in Frankfurt in 1969; cited in Herbert Marcuse, *Counterrevolution and Revolt* (Boston: Beacon Press, 1972), pp. 12-13; also cited in Ernest Mandel, *The Leninist Theory of Organization* (Great Britain: International Marxist Group, n.d.), p. 23, n. 60.

20. Bourgeois theorists are the most consistent sinners on this point, since they exercise a virtual monopoly on the "free marketplace of ideas" which ostensibly exists in the universities, the media, etc. For a useful survey of the literature in the field, see Leonard Reissman, *Class in American Society* (Glencoe, Illinois: The Free Press, 1959). Standing virtually alone among non-Marxist sociologists, C. Wright Mills disputed this thesis in his important work, *White Collar: The American Middle Classes* (New York: Oxford University Press, 1956). As Mills saw it, "In terms of property, the white collar people are not 'in between Capital and Labor'; they are in exactly the same property-class position as the wage workers. They have no direct financial tie to the means of production, no prime claim to the proceeds from property. Like factory workers—and day laborers, for that matter—they work for those who do own such means of livelihood" (pp. 71-72). In saying as much, Mills came closer to a Marxist analysis of the class position of white-collar workers than many avowed Marxists. For an excellent and sympathetic Marxist critique of Mills, see Fredy Perlman, *The Incoherence of the Intellectual* (Detroit: Black & Red, 1970).

21. Marx, *Capital,* vol. 3, p. 383, cited in Gough, p. 58.

22. Marx, *Theories of Surplus Value,* vol. 1, pp. 156-57, cited in Gough, p. 55.

23. Jacek Kuron and Karol Modzelewski, *Revolutionary Marxist Stu-*

dents in Poland Speak Out (New York: Merit Publishers, 1969), p. 21.

24. Kim Moody, "The American Working Class in Transition," *International Socialism*, October-November 1969, p. 23.

25. Marx, *Capital*, vol. 3 (New York: International Publishers, 1967), p. 885.

Part IV
An End to Ruling-Class Control

11
The Student Revolt

. . . it would be hard to understand the dimensions and importance of the universal student revolt in the imperialist countries without taking into account the tendencies which we have sketched here: the growing integration of intellectual labor into the productive process; the growing standardization, uniformity, and mechanization of intellectual labor; the growing transformation of university graduates from independent professional and capitalist entrepreneurs into salary earners appearing in a specialized labor market. . . . What do these trends mean but the growing proletarianization of intellectual labor, its tendency to become part and parcel of the working class?[1]

Ernest Mandel
"Workers Under Neo-Capitalism"

One of the most important results of the contemporary transformation of the universities has been the striking growth of the student population in America. Reflecting the shifting class origins and status of students, this process of growth has taken place under the careful guidance of the representatives of capitalism on the boards of trustees of the universities. In their effort to remake the working class in the image of their own needs, they have succeeded in reorganizing the universities as an integral part of capitalist production—and in so doing have sown the seeds for new forms of revolt and new dimensions of class struggle. The student revolt which began during the sixties was the first visible manifestation of this tendency; but it is not likely to be the last. Taking place in the lacerated context of an institution reshaped to train and socialize young college-educated workers, the struggles in the universities are likely to have been little more than a prelude to the symphony of struggles which will unfold when capitalism tries to absorb and exploit these new college-educated workers in the larger institutions of the economy.

The dimensions of recent growth in the size of student populations have been staggering. Forty years ago there were no more than 1.2 million college students in the United States; even as late as 1960 there were barely three million students attending college-level institutions. Currently there are more than eight million students attending institutions of higher education, representing fully 50 percent of the 18-21-year-old age group in America.[2]

The 1960s were the turning point in this process of growth. The number of students soared, more than doubling in a single decade. According to the Department of Health, Education, and Welfare, "Between 1955 and 1965, the number of high school graduates increased more than 85 percent; the number of those graduates going on to college increased 110 percent. Today, more than half of our young people enter college; yet twenty years ago less than 25 percent entered."[3]

If economist H. R. Bowen is accurate in his projections, "By 1977 the number of college students will probably be about 64 percent of all persons of ages 18-21."[4] This prediction is corroborated by the Department of Labor in its pamphlet, *College Educated Workers:* "U.S. colleges and universities are expected to turn out record numbers of graduates each academic year through the 1970s. The number of bachelors degrees awarded between 1968 and 1980 will increase 48 percent and the number of masters and doctorate degrees will increase even more rapidly, 95 percent and 117 percent respectively."[5] The *Monthly Labor Review* further confirms this projection when it reports that "the Nation's colleges and universities—principal suppliers of our most highly trained manpower—are now turning out record numbers of graduates and are expected to continue to do so throughout the 1970s."[6]

These statements were made toward the end of the 1960s, when war prosperity was at its height. When the bubble of war prosperity began to burst in late 1969 and 1970, newly trained college-educated workers began to experience significant employment difficulties for the first time, leading government analysts to moderate their previous optimism about the potential growth of the universities. It became apparent that college-educated workers were being produced in too great an abundance for the economy to absorb, and that steps would have to be taken to prevent the emergence of a significant sector of unemployed intellectual workers. Thus, although the number of students continues to rise significantly, what was previously a headlong rush has now slowed to a brisk forward march. The problem of surplus labor and its absorption has re-emerged, in other words, in a new context but with similar implications for the stability of capitalism. Thirty years ago, faced with a potential surplus of blue-collar workers, the ruling class diverted millions of workers into the white-collar sector of the economy—and now the white-collar sector is overflowing as well.*

What is important is that the quantitative leap forward in the size of student populations reflects qualitative changes in the social role of students. As Michael Kidron accurately points out, the vast growth which has taken place in the number of students "has been in response to capital's prodigious and growing appetite for technical and social-manipulative skills. It has been an uncoordinated and explo-

* The full meaning of this development will be explored in the next chapter.

sive growth that has wrenched most of the established patterns in higher education out of shape."[7] Formerly, students were the peaches-and-cream white Protestant children of the ruling and middle classes, preparing for the assumption of leadership roles in society; now they are for the most part members-in-training of the college-educated strata of the working class. Students have been *proletarianized,* in other words, by natural developments intrinsic to monopoly capitalism, and although a ruling-class elite is still being trained, it is a proportionately shrinking minority of the general student population, restricted to expensive private universities and minority representation at major public universities. The process of social transformation which led to this situation will be documented in the following pages.

The Changing Class Origins of Students

Although he somewhat oversimplifies matters, Ernest Mandel is essentially correct when he argues that "the function of the university during the two preceding phases of capitalism was primarily to give the brightest sons—and, to a lesser extent, also the daughters—of the ruling class the required classical education to equip them to administer industry, the nation, the colonies, and the army efficiently."[8] Mandel is correct when he delineates the essential purpose of the early universities. He oversimplifies when he fails to mention that the children of the majority of two other branches of the population were also trained in the early universities: the middle-class stratum of independent professionals, then much larger than at present, and the working-class stratum of engineers and accountants, then much smaller. Together, these three groups comprised the basic constituency of the universities before World War II.

Samuel Bowles describes the process of class differentiation which took place in the educational system during the early years of this century: "A system of class stratification developed within this rapidly expanding educational system. Children of the social elite normally attended private schools. Because working-class children tended to leave school early, the class composition of the public high schools was distinctly more elite than the public primary schools. And as a university education ceased to be merely training for teaching or the divinity and became important in gaining access to the pinnacles of the business world, upper-class families used their money and influence to get their children into the best universities, often at the expense of the children of less elite families."[9]

At the University of Michigan in 1902, a poll revealed that 30 percent of students' fathers were businessmen (merchants and manufacturers), 22 percent were farmers (resulting from the heavy emphasis on agrarian subjects at Michigan), 17 percent were either independent professionals or professional/technical workers, and, of the remainder, only 5.21 percent were mechanics, craftsmen, or manual laborers of any kind.[10] Even in this relatively early period, in other words, in an unusually agrarian environment, the children of businessmen stood out as the leading element of the student population. "In general," as one commentator points out, university classes at the turn of the century "were made up of the future owners and managers of the country, intent upon present social and athletic success before they entered the competitive world of which life in college was a miniature reflection. . . . As the manager sought to promote and educate his heirs into positions of profit and power, he found higher education in general, and business education in particular, to be increasingly useful."[11] As Mabel Newcomer shows, the relatively small number of female students attending college in this period also came from elite backgrounds: ". . . the families that sent their daughters to college were likely to be those in which the father had been sent to college. This meant that they were, for the most part, from the professional and wealthy business class."[12]

This remained the situation in the universities until the social transformation occurring in the years after the Second World War. In 1920, only 2 percent of all college-level students were of nonprofessional working-class origin; in 1940 only 5 percent were the children of manual, service, or lower-level white-collar workers.[13] Since then the class index defining student origins has shifted rapidly to the proletarian end of the spectrum.

In an important and hitherto little-known empirical study published in 1960, Robert J. Havighurst made the following vital observations: "Before World War I the colleges were attended by sons and daughters of upper-middle- and upper-class families, who were seeking positions in the professions and, to a limited extent, in business and government. . . . Until World War II, the proportion of children of working-class families in college was very small, but it has been increasing since the war until at present about 20 percent of the children of the upper working class enroll, which means that in absolute numbers there are in college today more youth from the working class than from the upper and upper-middle class. Thus, there has been a veritable social revolution in American higher education since 1920."[14] In 1960, fully 25 percent of the male children and 18 percent of the female children of the nonprofessional working class were attending institutions of higher education, to say nothing of the children of professional and technical workers. Moreover, in an attempt to extrapolate into the future, Havighurst pointed out that "any major expansion [in student populations to come during the sixties] would have to come about through the attendance of more lower-middle- or working-class youth," since the majority of all "upper- and upper-middle-class youth" were already enrolled in institutions of higher learning.[15] The vast growth which occurred during the sixties, in other words, took place not because more children of the ruling class chose to go to school but because children of the expanding and diversifying working class found themselves channeled, for the good of the economy, into a system of higher education restructured to produce a technical and supervisory work force.

Bettina Aptheker adds empirical strength to this analysis when she argues that "this phenomenal numerical increase" in student populations "is indicative of the changing class origins of the students. In 1966, for example, 37 percent of California's college students in public institutions came from families with an annual parental income of $8,000 or less (which is an admittedly conservative figure for the annual income of the traditional sectors of the working class)."[16]

Aptheker's figures, impressive as they are, nevertheless represent only a single instance of a more impressive general situation, as illustrated by the following table:

Table 6

College Attendance in 1967 Among 1966 High School Graduates

Family income	*% who attended college*	*% who did not*
Total	46.9%	53.1%
under $3,000	19.8%	80.2%
$3,000-$3,999	32.3%	67.7%
$4,000-$5,999	36.3%	63.7%
$6,000-$7,499	41.1%	58.9%
$7,500-$9,999	51.0%	49.0%
$10,000-$14,999	61.3%	38.7%
$15,000 and over	86.7%	13.3%

Samuel Bowles, "Unequal Education and the Reproduction of the Social Division of Labor," *Review of Radical Political Economy* 3, no. 4 (Fall-Winter 1971). The initial source of this data was the U.S. Department of Commerce, Bureau of the Census, *Current Population Report*, Series P-20, No. 185 (July 11, 1969), p. 6.

Fully a third of all high school students from families with an annual income ranging from $3,000-$4,000 went directly to college upon graduation from high school in 1966. More than 40 percent from families with incomes ranging from $6,000-$7,500 did so, while more than 50 percent of the children of families in the $7,500-$10,000 bracket went directly to college. Thus, while it remains true that families with higher incomes are more likely to send their children to college than families with lower incomes, it is also true that this differential is falling as greater and greater proportions of the wage-labor forces encourage their children to attend more advanced levels of schooling. In absolute terms, therefore, since the working class continues to expand, the majority of contemporary students must be understoood to come from working-class families.

Some students, of course, continue to function as the children of the ruling class have always functioned, especially those attending elite private universities. As William DeVane comments, "By and large, the students in the colleges of the Ivy League and in the smaller private colleges of the region major in history, English and American literature, philosophy, political science, and economics, and the larger part of the talent of these colleges is headed for law and industry. These students look forward to being the managers of our society in government, business, and industry, as their fathers have been before them and are now."[17] The percentage of these students, however, in proportion to the general student population, is small and shrinking. Thus, when Ernest Mandel describes students as "a social layer in transition," saying that from this layer "there arises on the one hand an important part of the future capitalist class and its main agents . . . and on the other hand a growing proportion of the future working class," it is clear that the latter category of students is far more important, both numerically and structurally, than the first.[18]

Marx foresaw the likelihood of this shift in the class status of students. In an important passage in the third volume of *Capital,* he argued that "because the necessary training, knowledge of commercial practices, languages, etc., is more and more rapidly, easily, universally and cheaply reproduced with the progress of science and public education, the more the capitalist mode of production directs teaching methods, etc., towards practical purposes. The universality of public education enables capitalists to recruit such laborers from classes that formerly had no access to such trades and were accustomed to a lower standard of living. Moreover, this increases supply, and hence competition. With few exceptions, the labor power of these people is therefore devaluated with the progress of capitalist production. Their wage falls, while their labor capacity increases."[19]

While Marx is speaking here of public education in general, the applicability of his broader framework of understanding to the specific historical evolution of the universities is clear. Students are members-in-training of the working class in the contemporary period because capitalists need workers with special abilities in diverse fields. Thus, as Calvert and Neiman conclude, "The old 'liberal arts' university which once trained 'professionals' and gave a facade of culture to the sons of the rich has been transformed (largely since the Second World War) into a new kind of institution—the multiversity. The primary function of the multiversity in advanced capitalist society is to train the highly skilled personnel which are necessary to the functioning of advanced industrial capitalism. Students are told that they are (or will become) members of the middle class. This is a lie which obscures their real position in the society. In fact, students are not middle class—they are pre-workers, trainees for the new jobs created by advanced industrial technology."[20]

The Alienation of Students as Apprentice Workers

At the present time, most students are being prepared for supervisory and technical or scientific jobs not of their own choosing and serving not their own interests but the interests of the ruling class. The root of the oppression of students can be identified as the authoritarianism built into the structure of the universities which prevents students from exercising meaningful control over the purposes and final social results of their studies. This relationship of authoritarian control and alienated study is typified by the relationship between students and trustees, which is in the deepest sense a *class* relationship. As the basis for the calculated control and use of students' lives, this relationship provides the context for the essence of what takes place in the universities. For college graduates have no more control over the kinds of jobs available to them or the kinds of lives they can lead than other workers have over the structure of the job market. College-educated workers and other workers both fill slots in an economy over which they have no control. Powerlessness—the class-determined inability to define the direction of their own lives—is the social link joining college-educated workers to the more traditional sectors of the proletariat. For exploitation, as we have shown above, is not a one-dimensional relationship which can exist in one and only one pure form, as some rigid "orthodox" Marxists seem to believe. On the contrary, as E. P. Thompson has pointed out, "It is a relationship which can be seen to take distinct forms in different historical contexts, forms which are related to corresponding forms of ownership and control."[21] In the contemporary period, the forms of exploitation have expanded and diversified in step with the expansion and diversification of the working class itself.

Students are allowed no control over the institution which not only defines their lives on a day-to-day basis but also prepares them for the jobs which will define their lives on a long-term basis. Although they are the essential constituency of the university, students are allowed no more than at best a token role in the decision-making process of the university. In much the same way, members of the working community as a whole are deprived of any meaningful role in the running of the university, although they finance it with their taxes. Power over higher education in America is vested entirely in the hands of those who sit on the boards of trustees of the universities. These men are not only the current supervisors of the universities but the future employers of the majority of students, for students are the human raw material from which the skilled intellectual labor force of the future will be drawn.

The leading effects of the class relationships prevailing in the universities are several, varied, and interrelated. First of all, the content of our education—*what* we study—is decided for us.* What this has meant in the past decade is (1) that students have been channeled into technical/scientific fields of study against their wishes; and (2) that ideas dangerous to the rule of capitalism have been stifled.

In confirmation of the first point, we note that of the $16 billion distributed to the universities by the federal government in 1969, 60 percent went to projects in the physical, environmental, and engineering sciences; 30 percent went to the life sciences; and 3 percent went to the social sciences (the remainder going to a variety of "other" disciplines). A similar emphasis has been placed on the development of technical/scientific skills at the University of California, as a

* I am writing this as a student myself, at the University of California.

result of pressure exerted by the Regents in opposition to the expressed wishes of the students on the nine University campuses. In the Academic Plan for the years 1969-1975, the Regents, although they acknowledge the fact that "in the past five years enrollment in the social sciences has increased 200 percent, while in the natural and physical sciences the figures have dropped or remained the same," nevertheless call, "in spite of this trend . . . for increased allocations and enrollments in the natural and physical sciences and for diminished allocations and enrollments in the humanities and social sciences. Concretely: the Psychology Department had 303 majors in the fall of 1957, 675 by fall of 1965, and 995 by winter of 1969. The plan now calls for 680 majors by 1975. Chemistry, on the other hand, which had 420 majors in 1965 and 439 in 1969, is scheduled to have 615 in 1975."[22]

Further evidence of the widespread nature of this trend is readily available, and the motivation underlying it is transparently clear. According to the chairman of the board of the University of Rochester—who happens also to be the president of the Xerox Corporation—it's a simple business matter: "To put it as crassly as possible, it's a matter of sheer self-interest—dollars and cents. Xerox will live or die by technology."[23]

Confirmation of the second point—that ruling-class control of the universities allows the suppression of ideas dangerous to the ruling class—can be found in a cursory examination of the course catalogues of any of the major universities. Almost invariably, although thousands of courses will be offered in engineering, business, and the physical sciences, few courses concerned with the social implications of these disciplines will be found. Furthermore, although thousands of social science courses are offered, classes focusing on critical discussions of Marxism, the labor movement, or the war in Vietnam are extremely rare, despite the significance of the subject matter. Even more difficult to find is a class taught by someone with a Marxist or radical perspective. Almost invariably, social science classes are oriented toward the defense of "liberalism," a fact *not* representative of the inner workings of the "free market of ideas," nor of accidental developments.[24] Students do not decide who will teach them; this is decided for them. Few radical or Marxist scholars are tolerated for long. Generally speaking, only instructors consciously or unconsciously willing to be ideologues for capitalism are hired or tolerated by any significant university; and since only bourgeois social science is taught in the universities, it is also extremely difficult (1) for people to develop a comprehensive Marxist perspective in the first place, or (2) for people *with* a Marxist perspective to remain in the confines of the university system long enough to emerge as instructors. And then, even if they do remain and are finally hired, they face the dismal choice of either reconciling themselves to the probability of being fired or diluting their political views. Either way, the likelihood of Marxist views being expressed in the university for any length of time ends up being very small.

Another of the consequences of ruling-class control of the universities is that the structure of our educational experience—*how* we study—is determined for us. Competitive, individualistic, solitary studies with the awarding of a grade as the ultimate goal is the oppressive mode of learning favored and enforced by the businessmen who control the universities. As Herb Gintis comments, "The authority relations and structure of incentives in schools mirrors the work-environment. Learning is not a result of the student's intrinsic interest in the process of learning, nor in the goal of this process—the possession of knowledge. The student must learn to operate efficiently in an educational environment unmotivated by either the process or the product of his activities—in short, in an alienated educational environment in which the rewards are in all cases external: grades, the threat of failure, or more subtle interpersonal sanctions."[25] This authoritarian, hierarchical structure is not accidental. Not only does authoritarian control of the university give the business community free reign to satisfy its needs at the expense of the students; it also teaches students the most important lessons they learn in the university: submissiveness to authority, conscientious and unquestioning work habits, goal and status orientation, passivity, and so on. For as the Carnegie Commission points out, "The college graduate has demonstrated his willingness to accept functional authority, to postpone gratification, to work steadily. . . ."[26]

Roger Harris has defined two further personality traits imbued in students by the stifling regimen of university studies: social incompetence and cynicism. "*Social incompetence* and an individualistic mentality are acquired in the competitive educational system. Collective action, as opposed to personal status climbing, becomes more difficult as a consequence. *Cynicism* is learned from doing meaningless assignments and busy work. This serves to negate any serious political thought. As long as the worker does not take himself seriously and is cynical about his world, it does not matter much what his politics are."[27]

The two most important personality traits imprinted on students during their twenty years of schooling are submissiveness to authority and the internalization of work discipline. The acquisition of these traits is highly valued by the corporations; H. R. Bowen, making a point that almost all manpower analysts have agreed on, declares that businessmen "sometimes place more emphasis on degrees and other educational qualifications than is genuinely required for the positions being filled. Yet the discipline and experience of college education is absolutely vital to many positions and an important asset in many more."[28] Eli Ginzberg, one of the leading manpower analysts in the nation, confirms this analysis when he says, "Educational requirements for employment continue to rise. Employers are convinced that, by raising their demands, they will be more likely to recruit an ambitious, disciplined work force that will be more productive than workers who have terminated their schooling earlier."[29]

The terminology is slightly different in Bowen and Ginzberg's analysis than in mine, slanted toward a more neutral, apolitical interpretation, but the meaning is the same. As the Department of Labor announced, "a college degree is necessary in many jobs once performed by workers with less education. The proportion of jobs requiring college degrees in professional, technical, and kindred occupations is expected to increase from about three-fifths to about two-thirds between 1968 and 1980."[30] University experience is thought to be desirable for workers because of the socializing, pacifying effects it has on them. *External* control becomes less and less necessary as workers are taught to *internalize* the rules, roles, and goals established for them by their employers.

Further, the *conditions* of education have grown steadily more and more oppressive and unsatisfying. According to June O'Neill and Alice Rivlin, during the past decade, while the size of student populations rose rapidly, "the bulk of the increase was accommodated, not by founding new institutions, but by enlarging existing ones."[31] In other words, huge numbers of students have been jammed into the universities. (In 1970, the average public university served 23,000 students.) In addition, the amount of teaching time expended by instructors has been increasingly diminished as the research and development demands of the state and industry have climbed skywards. One result of this expansion of student population concurrent with the contraction of teaching efforts has been that the ratio of students to teachers in the average classroom situation has risen enormously, resulting in what one economist has called an "efficiency gain."[32] As Peter Shapiro and Bill Barlow comment in their book on the student strike at San Francisco State College, "All this has had a profoundly disillusioning and dehumanizing effect on the lot of the individual student caught up within the system. The central feature of his education consists of seeing himself reduced to a commodity; the final direction his education takes is determined ultimately by its degree of profitability to those to whom he will eventually sell his labor."[33]

The sense of alienation from their own labor experienced by students as a consequence of their lack of control over their studies is matched by an equally potent sense of alienation from other students. The vast impersonality of the university bureaucracy and authority structure extends even into the relations among students. Isolated from one another and pitted against each other in a competitive struggle for grades and jobs, students have found no established mechanisms for any kind of collective or cooperative effort. Social interaction on a level beyond boyfriend/girlfriend relationships or occasional sports activities is tacitly discouraged by the atomizing and individual-centered structure of grading and study in the university. All of these problems, intensified by the accelerated growth of student populations, have contributed greatly to student loneliness and frustration. Representing a marked deterioration in our working conditions, they have led to a marked deterioration in the quality of our lives. Among other things, this has helped produce an increasing incidence of emotional disturbance and suicide among students. In addition to the more severe problems experienced by students, the nationwide ferment and protests of the past decade, directed largely against impersonal and degrading study conditions, provide eloquent evidence of the oppressive nature of authoritarian and overcrowded institutions of higher education. "Not the university," as Bogdan Denitch declares, "but their own new position in society is a major cause of student alienation, just as not the machine but the new social organization of production changed the role of the old craftsman."[34]

The Student Revolt

> *The meaning of being a college student and the nature of the work that college-trained people did after graduation changed dramatically with the rapid expansion of higher education. Students, most of whom two decades earlier were from or entering the middle classes (small entrepreneurs, independent professionals, upper-level management), now, by and large, were faced with becoming employees in corporate or government bureaucracies. How students felt about this, what it meant to their lives, was dramatically expressed in the Free Speech Movement in Berkeley.*[35]
>
> James Weinstein
> "The Left, Old and New"

The proletarianization of the bulk of students reached its first high-water mark in the early years of the 1960s, leading directly to the emergence of a massive and volatile student movement in the subsequent decade. As Michael Miles shows, ". . . the student movement became a national phenomenon . . . in the 1967–68 school year, when over one hundred colleges and universities experienced protests. The movement leaped to a new level of significance in 1968–69, when over five hundred institutions experienced disruptive protests. In 1969–70, protests were just as numerous, spreading to many colleges, community colleges, and universities which had never had student protest."[36]

Three major factors combined to produce the seeds, shoots, and ultimate germination of this New Left rooted so largely in the universities: (1) the socialization of students as an emergent stratum of the working class; (2) the proliferation of student grievances resulting from the latest transformation of the university system; and (3) the contradictions of global capitalist hegemony, most sharply illustrated by the wars in Vietnam and Algeria and the emergence of racial struggles on the home front.[37]

Although the structural reorganization of the universities and the new class status of students provided the immediate context for the emergence of this New Left, the antiwar and black liberation struggles played equally important roles in galvanizing students into action. SDS, the highest organizational expression of early student radicalism, had its roots deeply implanted in the struggle of Southern and, subsequently, Northern ghetto blacks, and antiwar organizing served as its primary point of reference and *raison d'être.* What the New Left lacked, however, in its early years was a consciousness of the class nature of the oppression of students, for although students were quick to decry the authoritarianism and imperialist role of the universities, no clear consciousness of self and class crystallized as an integral part of the struggle. As Bettina Aptheker points out, "The intellectuals, still attached to the superstructure of the society, tended to see first its social injustices; and their protests tended to center on issues such as racial oppression and the war in Vietnam. The inability of the social order to resolve these crises—and in fact official resistance to their resolution—forced many intellectuals to reevaluate their previous assumptions about the system itself."[38]

Throughout the first decade of its existence, two tendencies within the student movement struggled with one another in partially conscious battle for hegemony within the New Left. The first of these tendencies can be described as anti-imperialist, the second as socialist. Each grew from the antiwar, student power, and black liberation struggles of the mid-sixties, but differed substantially in their consciousness of class and in their strategic perspectives for the emerging left. While the anti-imperialist activists acknowledged the reality of imperialism as a system, they denied the class nature of the student struggles of which they themselves were a part, restricting their militance to the key issues of social injustice of the mid-sixties and failing to broaden their perspective to include an understanding of their own new role in the class struggle. The socialist perspective, on the other hand, acknowledged precisely the new role of students in the class struggle, emphasizing the *class* nature of the battle to be waged. In its sharpest outlines, therefore, the difference between the two positions must be understood as a matter of class consciousness.

Anti-imperialist consciousness was the first higher form of student radicalism to appear, stressing the importance of the worldwide struggle against imperialism and drawing its inspiration from the heroic struggles of the Vietnamese people and from the liberation struggles of black people in this country. As Angela Davis explains, "The emergence of an anti-imperialist consciousness among the intelligentsia is immediately attributable to the *combination* of their moral outrage against the war and the new Black consciousness, the new Brown consciousness, engulfing their institutions."[39] The limitation of this form of consciousness, however, in Bettina Aptheker's words, is that "the intellectuals develop an anti-imperialist consciousness devoid of class consciousness. Their sole affinity is with the movements for national liberation at home and abroad. They do not generally conceive of the national liberation movements as an essential component of the class struggle";[40] when they do, they misunderstand their own role as being extraneous to the class struggle.

Thus, while the reality of their existence was a *class* reality, contingent upon the social transformation of the universities, the consciousness of students in this early period remained limited to consciousness of the *moral* issues involved in their own oppression and the oppression of others. Like most of the working population as a whole, they thought of themselves as middle class. When they directed their activism against the universities, therefore, it was frequently not on the basis of their recognition of the oppression of students but on the grounds of university involvement in war research and racial discrimination.* Their "anti-imperialist" struggles, moreover, usually did not demand the elimination of *all* forms of alienation and exploitation; instead, *partial* demands were presented calling for the elimination of specific forms of oppression affecting groups suffering from what was conceived of as *special* oppression. Lacking class consciousness, their struggles lacked a unified focus, appearing fragmented, partial; a conception of the *class* nature of the struggle and their own participation in that struggle eluded them, preventing them from broadening their perspective to include an awareness of the diversity of the potentially revolutionary class forces.[41]

It would be false, however, to draw a hard-and-fast line between the emerging forms of radical consciousness that arose during the sixties. Although in retrospect the latent polarities are apparent, in the context of the struggle itself the specific rationales for action at any given moment were at best partial, fluid, and indefinite. The roots of a socialist vision firmly anchored in class consciousness were as much present in early anti-imperialist struggles as they were in early struggles directed against the oppression of students, and the fruits of this vision began to emerge from both sources toward the end of the 1960s. For in order for the polarization of more clearly defined "anti-imperialist" and "socialist" perspectives to take place, it was necessary first for the socialist position to be coherently articulated.

The first theoretical expression of revolutionary class con-

* This statement must be immediately qualified, however, for as Michael Miles points out, "In its survey of 1969 student protests, the Urban Research Corporation found that student power issues were raised in 44 percent of the cases of protest, second only to issues of black recognition. The principal student power issues raised were student participation on decision-making committees and a student role in the hiring and firing of faculty members. The third major category

sciousness among students took shape in the context of internal debates within Students for a Democratic Society. Carl Davidson, David Gilbert, Greg Calvert, and John and Margaret Rowntree emerged as some of the first recognized proponents of the new perspective, which attracted immediate and widespread attention.[42] Calvert and Neiman summarize this position as follows: "Essentially, the new viewpoint argued that the traditional analysis of students as petit-bourgeois intelligentsia was incorrect. Since the Second World War, the American university had been transformed into the multiversity. It was no longer an institution which trained a narrow stratum of 'middle-class professionals' and gave a facade of culture to the sons of the ruling class. The needs of the new technology had forced the transformation of the old liberal arts institution into a new kind of institution which had as its primary task the training of scientific, technical, and professional workers to fill the labor needs of advanced industrial capitalism."[43]

As this perspective began to spread throughout SDS, gaining widespread popularity, it came into open conflict with the emerging "Marxist" version of the anti-imperialist perspective, which had for long been the reigning orthodoxy of the Communist party and was now championed within the ranks of the New Left by the Progressive Labor party, the Maoist organization which eventually tore SDS apart. The argument presented by these "Marxist-Leninist" groups was the following: Only the working class can make a revolution, and the working class consists primarily of industrial workers. Students remain what students have always been, middle-class intellectuals, and as such must direct their attention to

of protest was "quality of student life," which ranked ahead of war-related protest in frequency. The major demand raised under this heading was for revision of the system of grades and courses." Michael Miles, *The Radical Probe* (New York: Atheneum, 1971), p. 99. The same results were obtained in an American Council on Education study.

the industrial proletariat if they hope to transcend their retrograde class origins and contribute to the "real" working-class struggle.

The problems with this analysis, however, are legion, since within it everything that is new and vital in both theory and reality is denied in the name of a rigid and schematic Marxism which has not kept pace with reality. Calvert and Neiman make a stinging and accurate analysis of this position when they argue that "not only did this Old Left viewpoint ignore the fundamental alterations in class structure and work which had been transforming the nature of the labor force for a generation, it demanded that students see themselves as mere adjuncts to other movements. This time the politics of guilt and missionary activity were not to be directed at the black community but rather in the direction of industrial workers. Not only was the Old Left blind to the real role of the multiversity in the transformation of the labor force and the training of a new and vitally important sector of the work force to fit the needs of the new technology, but it was attempting to enforce false consciousness within one group in the society—a group which was beginning to develop a revolutionary class consciousness of its relationship to the means of production. Old Left ideological categories centering on 'the industrial proletariat' hindered rather than aided the development of socialist consciousness among students. In calling students 'middle class,' the Old Left was promoting a false picture which was precisely the same as that promoted by the governing ideology."[44]

Since the split in SDS in 1969, the organized student left has been virtually nonexistent. Since the massive but short-lived outcry over Nixon's invasion of Cambodia in 1970, the student movement has been dangerously quiescent. As the media have been eager to inform us, the raging waters of dissent have stilled—and yet they have also deepened, in some senses, as students and former students have for the first time seriously begun to confront the question of power. While the Cambodian crisis showed us the full measure of our powerlessness in legal and institutional terms, it showed us also the full measure of our potential *strength* in class terms. During the last three years, although lacking its former effervescence, the student movement has slowly become more serious as it has moved consciously to the left. Carl Davidson once commented that "apathy is the *unconscious* recognition students make of the fact that they are *powerless.*"[45] In the contemporary period, however, the relative quiescence which passes for apathy is the *conscious* recognition of students that they are institutionally powerless and reflects their search, halting and uncertain though it may be, for new methods of struggle and new forms of organization for the expression of their continuing disenchantment with American society.

Marxist-Leninist anti-imperialist perspectives and class-conscious socialist perspectives now rival each other as the leading tendencies within both the student left and the left in general, represented on the one hand by the Communist party and the various Leninist sects (both Maoist and Trotskyist), and, on the other, by independent Marxist working collectives and democratic Marxist organizations such as the New American Movement. The spectacular quality of the old student movement has disappeared, along with its massive organizational forms, but the seedbed of alienation and authoritarian power relations at the root of the student rebellion remains intact. Temporarily halted, the disorganized left is now searching for new methods of organization to replace the strategy-of-impulse and tactics-of-outrage which characterized the old student movement. Among disaffected students, recognition is slowly growing that "since students are essentially white-collar workers-in-training, the university is no longer an elite, irrelevant body, but an important institution for the reproduction of capitalist relations of production."[46] On the level of day-to-day practice, what this means is that students must no longer confine themselves to supporting struggles of other sectors of the international working class but must work among students; for in order to *truly* support other branches of the working class and make a shared revolution possible, students must be an organized force in their own right. If socialism means *democratic* working-class control of society, then all potentially revolutionary elements of the working class must be prepared to participate in the creation of such a society.

Notes

1. Ernest Mandel, "Workers Under Neo-Capitalism," *International Socialist Review*, November-December 1968, pp. 8-9.

2. June O'Neill and Alice Rivlin, "Growth and Change in Higher Education," in *The Corporation and the Campus*, ed. Robert Connery (Washington: Praeger, 1970), p. 66.

3. Department of Health, Education, and Welfare, *Report on Higher Education* (Newman Report), March 1971, p. 1.

4. Howard R. Bowen, "Financial Needs on the Campus," in *The Corporation and the Campus*, op. cit., p. 77.

5. Department of Labor, Bureau of Labor Statistics, *College Educated Workers*, 1970, p. 3.

6. *Monthly Labor Review*, "The U.S. Economy in 1980," April 1970, p. 32.

7. Michael Kidron, *Western Capitalism Since the War* (Baltimore: Penguin, 1968), p. 165.

8. Ernest Mandel, "The Changing Role of the Bourgeois University," speech delivered at Rijks University, Leiden, Holland, published as a pamphlet by the Spartacist League of Great Britain (n.d.), p. 3.

9. Samuel Bowles, "Unequal Education and the Reproduction of

the Social Division of Labor," *Review of Radical Political Economy* 3, no. 4 (Fall-Winter 1971).

10. Lawrence Veysey, *The Emergence of the American University* (Chicago: University of Chicago Press, 1965), p. 43.

11. William C. DeVane, *Higher Education in Twentieth Century America* (Cambridge, Mass.: Harvard University Press, 1965), p. 16.

12. Mabel Newcomer, *A Century of Higher Education for American Women* (New York: Harper and Brothers, 1959), p. 130.

13. Robert J. Havighurst, *American Higher Education in the 1960's* (Columbus: Ohio State University Press, 1960), p. 35.

14. Ibid., p. 33.

15. Ibid., p. 57.

16. Bettina Aptheker, *The Academic Rebellion in the United States* (Secaucus, N.J.: Citadel Press, 1972), p. 34.

17. DeVane, op. cit., p. 177.

18. Mandel, "Workers Under Neo-Capitalism," op. cit., p. 9.

19. Karl Marx, *Capital,* vol. 3 (New York: International Publishers, 1967), p. 300. Later, Paul Lafargue echoed and amplified this idea when he said, in 1900, "The capitalist class, which to increase its wealth is in pressing need of inventions, is in even more imperative need of intellectuals to supervise their application and to direct its industrial machinery. The capitalists, before they equipped invention factories, had organized factories to turn out intellectuals." From *Socialism and the Intellectuals,* p. 15. Lafargue also commented: "On the platform of the Constituent Assembly of 1790, the Marquis of Foucault could declare that to be a laborer it was not necessary to know how to read and write. The necessities of industrial production today compel the capitalist to speak in language altogether different; his economic interests and not his love of humanity and of science force him to encourage and to develop both elementary and higher education." Ibid., p. 16.

20. Greg Calvert and Carol Neiman, *A Disrupted History: The New Left and the New Capitalism* (New York: Random House, 1971), p. 56.

21. E. P. Thompson, *The Making of the English Working Class* (New York: Random House, 1963), p. 203.

22. Philosophy Strike Central, "On University Neutrality," Berkeley, California, May 1970, p. A8.

23. Cited in G. William Domhoff, *Who Rules America?* (Englewood

Cliffs, N.J.: Prentice-Hall, 1967), p. 78.

24. For an excellent critique of liberalism, see Robin Blackburn, "A Brief Guide to Bourgeois Ideology," in *Student Power,* ed. Robin Blackburn and Alexander Cockburn (Baltimore: Penguin, 1971), pp. 163-213.

25. Herb Gintis, "The New Working Class and Revolutionary Youth," *Socialist Revolution,* no. 3, May-June 1970, p. 30.

26. The Carnegie Commission on Higher Education, *College Graduates and Jobs* (1973), p. 13.

27. Roger Harris, "The University: Love It or Seize It!" in *Slate,* a radical student journal at the University of California, Berkeley, Spring 1972, p. 97.

28. Bowen, op. cit., p. 78.

29. Eli Ginzberg, Foreword to Ivar Berg, *Education and Jobs: The Great Training Robbery* (Boston: Beacon Press, 1971), p. xiii.

30. Bureau of Labor Statistics, *College Educated Workers,* op. cit., p. 3.

31. O'Neill and Rivlin, op. cit., p. 67.

32. Bowen, op. cit., p. 78.

33. Peter Shapiro and Bill Barlow, *An End to Silence: The San Francisco State College Student Movement in the 60's* (New York: Pegasus Books, 1971), pp. xiv-xv.

34. Bogdan Denitch, "Is There a New Working Class'?" in *Workers' Control,* ed. Garson, Hunnius, and Case (New York: Random House, 1973), p. 432.

35. James Weinstein, "The Left, Old and New," *Socialist Revolution,* no. 10, July-August 1972, p. 43.

36. Michael Miles, *The Radical Probe* (New York: Atheneum, 1970), p. 43. To show the depth as well as the breadth of radicalism during the student movement, Miles makes the following two points: (1) "Some 28 percent of all students, according to a Gallup poll, have already demonstrated for some cause or another"; and (2) "According to the Yankelovich firm, 3.3 percent of *all* college youth considered themselves 'revolutionaries,' while another 9.5 percent were self-described 'radical dissidents' and 39.3 percent were 'reformers.' " Ibid., pp. 17-18.

37. Insights into the international dimensions of the emergent New Left are provided by Barbara and John Ehrenreich, speaking about

Germany, and Eric J. Hobsbawm, speaking about Great Britain. As their comments show, the conditions which gave rise to a New Left in each of these nations were largely parallel in certain key areas relating to the growth of higher education. Interestingly, the Ehrenreichs show us that the context for the development of the German New Left largely paralleled the context in which the American New Left arose: "The mid-1960s," they say, "also saw the emergence of a crisis in the universities, a crisis intimately linked to the changes in the economy. The rapid growth of the economy and the development of the high technology and the sales effort characteristic of an advanced capitalist industrial economy had led to a growing need for a variety of highly educated workers. Teachers, engineers, chemists, advertising men, computer programmers, etc.—all were in demand, and the university would have to supply them. But the university was neither ready nor willing. It had been designed to train an elite for nineteenth-century professions, not a mass for twentieth-century jobs. By the mid-1960s the crisis was evident. The universities were overcrowded. The curriculum was obsolete . . ." B. and J. Ehrenreich, *Long March, Short Spring: The Student Uprising at Home and Abroad* (New York: Monthly Review Press, 1969), pp. 24-25.

Hobsbawm comments: ". . . the origin of the 'intellectuals' as a special social group can be traced back to the period before 1914. The sheer increase in the numbers of brain-workers—overwhelmingly salaried, or the non-manual equivalent of casual labor—emphasized their collective problems. Their relative lack of involvement in management and government, their lack of traditional status, made them less conservative than others in their income bracket.

"They could no longer be recruited merely from the existing upper and middle classes, and the mass emergence of intellectuals from the lower-middle- and working-class backgrounds in the 1950s produced tensions which were reflected in the sometimes rather superficial 'leftism' of the later years of this decade. The rapidly growing universities focused their political dissidence. For the first time in British history 'students' became both a political force and a fairly predictably left-wing group." Eric J. Hobsbawm, *Industry and Empire* (Baltimore: Penguin, 1969), p. 292.

38. Aptheker, op. cit., p. 160.

39. Angela Davis, Introduction to Aptheker, op. cit., p. 15.

40. Ibid., pp. 161-62.

41. An interesting parallel to this form of revolutionary consciousness minus class consciousness was identified by Lenin in his 1903 essay, "The Tasks of the Revolutionary Youth." "If certain reports are to be credited, a further divergence of the unlike elements among the students is becoming increasingly marked, namely, dissociation of the socialists from political revolutionaries who refuse to hear of socialism. It is said that this latter trend is very pronounced among the students exiled to Siberia." Indicating his own position on the matter, Lenin added: "A certain section of the students want to acquire a definite and integral socialist world outlook. The ultimate aim of this preparatory work can only be—for students who want to take practical part in the revolutionary movement—the conscious and irrevocable choice of one of the two trends that have now taken shape among revolutionaries. Whoever protests against such a choice on the plea of effecting ideological unity among the students, of revolutionizing them in general, and so forth, is obscuring socialist consciousness and is in actual fact preaching absence of ideological principles." *Collected Works,* 4th edition, vol. 7, p. 55.

42. See especially John and Margaret Rowntree, "The Political Economy of Youth," *International Socialist Review,* February 1968, and Carl Davidson, "Campaigning on Campus," in Blackburn and Cockburn, op. cit.

43. Calvert and Neiman, op. cit., pp. 22-23.

44. Ibid., pp. 23-24.

45. Davidson, op. cit., p. 328.

46. New American Movement, New York, *The Open Road: Socialist Strategy in the Corporate Liberal State,* chapter 1 (pamphlet, 1973), p. 25.

12
Future Contradictions

What possibility is there that the profoundly radical spirit of the student movement of the sixties will continue to advance in the coming years? Will college-educated workers find themselves as deeply disenchanted with the system as students did earlier, expressing their disenchantment through radical activism, or will they accept their roles with a minimum of protest, as the ruling class would like? In brief, what role will students and college-educated workers play in the developing class struggle, and what paths will that struggle take?

For a provisional answer to these questions, we must begin with an exploration of the future contradictions which are likely to emerge in the coming years, not only in the context of the job market and the economy but in terms of working-class consciousness. For a complex dialectic of rapid but irregular development has taken place (and continues to take place) both in the objective structure of capitalism and in the consciousness of the classes at the base of capitalism. If we are to grasp the meaning and implications of the objective analysis which has been offered so far, we must go further and address ourselves to the complexities of this dialectic of consciousness in its concrete manifestations: if the working class is diversified, in other words, what impact will this diversification have on working-class struggles? Are highly educated workers likely to accept the alienated nature of their labor as readily as most trade unionists have in the past, or will they be more susceptible to revolutionary ideas? And finally, can the working class—diversified and divided as it is—be united in a common struggle for an end to alienation, workers' self-management—in other words, socialism?

These are the questions which will be examined in the final two chapters of this work.

Contradictions in the Job Market

As long ago as 1892, in his book *The Class Struggle,* Karl Kautsky made a prescient analysis of the rise of an educated proletariat in Germany which remains relevant to the contemporary situation. "The result of this whole development," Kautsky argued, echoing Marx's fragmentary insights in *Capital,* "is that the number of educated people has increased enormously. Nevertheless, the beneficent results which the idealists expected from an increase of education have not followed. So long as education is a merchandise, its extension is equivalent to an increase in the quantity of that merchandise, consequently to the falling of its price and the decline in the condition of those who possess it. The number of educated people has grown to such an extent that it more than suffices for the wants of the capitalists and the capitalist state. The labor market of educated labor is today as overstocked as the market of manual labor. It is no longer the manual workers alone who have their reserve army of the unemployed and are afflicted with lack of work; the educated workers also have their reserve army of idle, and among them also lack of work has taken up its permanent quarters. . . . The condition of the educated workers deteriorates visibly; formerly people spoke of the 'aristocracy of the intellect,' today we speak of the 'intellectual' or 'educated' proletariat. The time is near when the bulk of these proletarians will be distinguished from the others only by their pretensions. Most of them still imagine that they are something better than proletarians . . ."[1]

Kautsky's analysis is relevant to the contemporary period because the situation he identified in Germany in 1890 parallels the present situation in the United States. During the last decade, millions of young people emerged from the universities as college-educated workers. In 1960, accurately foreseeing the situation which was to develop, Robert Havighurst commented that within ten years "the market for college graduates will change character, shifting from a scarcity of the commodity to a surplus." From the standpoint of big business, moreover, he noted that "conditions will change from famine to feast . . . though in terms of economic opportunity, the young people themselves may experience it as a shift from feast to famine."[2]

Fully 53 percent of the growth of the labor force during the sixties was accounted for by workers 16-24 years old. "These young adults," the Department of Labor comments, "were born during the post–World War II baby boom. In the '60s, they crowded into high schools, colleges, and entry jobs. In the '70s, they will be moving beyond entry positions in the workforce and will account for almost one-half of total labor force growth."[3]

Table 7

Age Group	*Percent change in the labor force* 1960–1970	1970–1980
16-24	53	19
25-34	16	49
35-44	-1	13
45-54	15	-4
55-64	21	14
65-	-8	6
Total labor force	18	18.3

Department of Labor, *U.S. Manpower in the 1970's: Opportunity and Challenge,* 1969, p. 2.

Youth thus continues to be the leading new force in the working class, but it is becoming a more mature and better educated sector. What kinds of labor will these youthful workers perform in the future? According to the Department of Labor, "In this decade, as in the last, the fastest growing occupations are professional and technical, the ones requiring the most educational preparation. This occupational group will increase by 50 percent by 1980. Service occupations (excluding private households) will rank second only to professionals with a growth of 45 percent. By 1980, for the first time, there will be as many professional and technical workers as blue collar operatives."[4] This is not to say, however, that manual workers will disappear. Thirty-one million workers will remain employed in blue-collar occupations, an impressive figure—yet more than twice that number will be employed as white-collar workers.

Recently, surveying a job situation which has grown increasingly bleak for college graduates since 1968, the Carnegie Commission on Higher Education made a sober and thorough assessment of job opportunities for college graduates. The future, as the Carnegie Commission sees it, is not likely to be rosy. Along with a host of other analysts, they predict an extended period of insufficient and unfulfilling employment for college-educated workers. Not enough jobs will be available, they say, and a large percentage of those jobs which are available will fail to make use of the talents of highly educated workers.[5] In confirmation of this point, they observe that "the U.S. Bureau of Labor Statistics has estimated that 'a high school education will be sufficient for eight out of every ten jobs' during the 1970s. Stated the other way around, only 20 percent of the jobs will require education beyond the high school. Yet today, more than one-third of the 18-21-year-old age group is in college at any one moment of time, and one-half attend college at some point; our Commission also estimates that two-thirds of this age group will take post-secondary educational training of some sort in the foreseeable future."[6]

In other words, as they state explicitly, fully 47 percent of the members of the current 18-21-year-old age group are likely to find themselves employed below the level of their educational training when they enter the labor force (or, as the Carnegie Commission expresses it, "occupationally downgraded") and therefore potentially disgruntled.[7] "Some persons," the Commission announces, "will go into jobs that *will* not and perhaps *cannot* be raised to the level of their capacity. Some of this happens already. Nearly 30 percent of four-year male college graduates are now in blue-collar, sales, and clerical jobs, many of which do not make full use of their education."[8]

The outlook is particularly disheartening for female college graduates, since teachers at all levels will be the professional workers least in demand during the 1970s. "The impact on women will be particularly important, because, as we have seen, about one-half of all employed female college graduates have been engaged in teaching. To some degree, women will doubtless choose other careers without counseling . . . but, significantly, the BLS points out: 'Over the 1968-80 period, the number of women graduates is expected to increase two-thirds, or twice the rate for men.' "[9]

These facts are important, in the Commission's eyes, for their political implications. A more and more consciously alienated and thus dangerous stratum of the working class is growing rapidly. If little is done to allay the disenchantment of these workers, the consequences could be explosive. In the Commission's words, "If inadequate adjustments are made, we could end up . . . with a political crisis because of the substantial number of disenchanted and underemployed or even unemployed college graduates—as in Ceylon or in India or in Egypt. . . . *Higher education will then have become counterproductive.*"[10] The Commission takes this danger very seriously, not only because of the ripening possibilities of explosive alienation among college-educated workers, but because "frustration may extend to other groups as well: to young persons without college experience who are pushed down by the pressure of college graduates in the market—even pushed into unemployment—and to older persons who are passed over by younger and more educated persons. These strains on society will be increased."[11]

If the Carnegie Commission is correct, then it is likely that the productive role played by college-educated workers will remain as deeply alienating to them as their student role was previously, and thus will be a source of continuing social tension. Whereas students are estranged in the context of a training and socialization process centered in the universities, college graduates are likely to be equally estranged in the context of the job market itself, an environment which not only deprives them of control over their hard-won creativity but allows them few opportunities to exercise their talents as educated workers.

The contradictions in the class role of highly educated workers are thus present on the objective level, in terms of the *structural* role of educated workers in the society; the question remaining to be answered, therefore, is whether these contradictions will provoke struggle—and, if so, what kind of struggle?

Contradictions at Work

It is far from speculative to argue that working-class consciousness of alienation will sharpen in the immediate future. As numerous recent studies have shown, such consciousness is already emerging at a quickening pace, among numerous sectors of the working class.[12] White-collar workers, blue-collar workers, and managerial workers alike are exhibiting the symptoms of a growing job-centered malaise. Thus, while consciousness of their alienation is particularly intense among young workers and highly educated workers, it is not limited to the young or the highly educated. While women and Third World groups are most sharply affected by the requirements and contradictions of the job market, revolt against alienation is not restricted to their ranks. Isolated from one another, denied creativity, and deprived of control over their destinies, the members of the fragmented proletariat have one thing at least in common with one another: they all lead lives of quiet desperation. If, in the coming years, their growing consciousness of alienation leads them to recognize their *common* oppression, it will not be long before their desperation loses its voicelessness.

Work in America, a recent study by the Department of Health, Education, and Welfare provides a thorough and revealing analysis of the growing dissatisfaction among American workers. Although its proposed solutions to the problems of alienation are reformist and half-hearted, its analysis is penetrating and comprehensive. As a reference work on the current situation of the American working class, it cannot be recommended too highly.

It is in the arena of production, the authors announce, that "we find the 'blues' of blue-collar workers linked to their job dissatisfactions, as is the disgruntlement of white-collar workers and the growing discontent among managers. Many workers at all occupational levels feel locked-in, their mobility blocked, the opportunity to grow lacking in their jobs, challenge missing from their tasks. Young workers appear to be as committed to the institution of work as their elders have been, but many are rebelling against the anachronistic authoritarianism of the workplace."[13] Generalized discontent prevails, and appears to be growing. What is the cause of the problem?

According to HEW, "What the workers want most, as more than a hundred studies in the past twenty years show, is to become masters of their immediate environments and to feel that their work and they themselves are important—the twin ingredients of self-esteem."[14] What the workers want most is to *control* their environment—which means, first and foremost, the *social purposes* and *results* of their labor. What the "workers want most," in other words, is an end to alienation.

To HEW, this situation of alienation and latent class-consciousness is both a paradox and a danger. "On the average, no workers have ever been as materially well-off as American workers are today. What, then, is wrong? . . . It may be argued that the very success of industry and organized labor in meeting the basic needs of workers has unintentionally spurred demands for esteemable and fulfilling jobs."[15] What is "wrong" is that, now that the trade-union struggles of the past century have been essentially successful, it is possible for the working class to see precisely how limited and unsatisfying (though necessary) those successes have been. *For alienated labor remains alienated.* Higher wages, no matter how desirable, cannot compensate for the fundamental loss of autonomy and creativity intrinsic to the alienation of labor at the root of the capitalist labor process. Increasingly, different elements of the proletariat are awakening to this fact.

From the standpoint of capitalist authority, this tendency is a fearful one: the "danger" mentioned above. For as HEW observes, "The result of alienation is often the withdrawal of the worker from community or political activity or the displacement of his frustrations through participation in radical social or political movements. . . . It seems fair to conclude that the combination of the changing social character of American workers, declining opportunities to establish independence through self-employment, and an anachronistic organization of work can create an explosive and pathogenic mix."[16] Like the Carnegie Commission, HEW takes the dangers in the current situation with the utmost gravity. They point to striking increases in sabotage, absenteeism, and turnover rates as manifestations of mounting working-class dissatisfaction: in recent years the number of man-days lost yearly as a result of strikes has doubled.

It is in the context of this fear of an awakening proletariat that the "solutions" offered by HEW must be evaluated. They propose that jobs be "redesigned" in order to give workers a greater sense of autonomy, more prestige, and a greater sense of self-worth. Nowhere, however, do they propose that the alienation of labor itself be eliminated. Nowhere do they propose that workers' self-management replace the authoritarian and exploitative relationship currently existing between capitalists and workers. Their proposals, in other words, are classically reformist: they advocate changing the *appearance* of alienation without altering its essence; they advocate changing the form of alienation without altering its content. How? By providing workers with greater latitude for independent action *within the framework of alienated labor*—labor which remains alienated by virtue of the fact that its purposes and results remain under the control of the capitalist class. The authors of *Work* thus advocate a palliative solution which does not strike at the root of the problem, hoping thereby to dispel the gathering clouds of dissatisfaction and emerging class-consciousness which threaten bourgeois hegemony. As they express it, "Citizen participation in the arena where the individual's voice directly affects his immediate environment may do much to reduce political alienation in America."[17] In other words, if "job redesign" is necessary to dissolve the possibility of proletarian class-consciousness, then such "redesign" must be undertaken in the best interests of capitalism.

In the eyes of HEW, young workers in particular constitute a potential wellspring of activism. "Traditionally, lower-level white-collar jobs in both government and industry were held by high-school graduates. Today, an increasing number of these jobs go to those who have attended college. But the demand for higher academic credentials has not increased the prestige, status, pay, or difficulty of the job. For example, the average weekly pay for clerical workers in 1969 was $105 per week, while blue-collar production workers were taking home an average of $130 per week. It is not surprising, then, that the Survey of Working Conditions found much of the greatest work dissatisfaction in the country among young, well-educated workers who were in low-paying, dull, routine, and fractionated clerical positions. Other signs of discontent among this group included turnover rates as high as 30 percent annually and a 46 percent increase in white-collar union membership between 1958 and 1968."[18]

Since the Carnegie Commission predicts that "young, well educated workers . . . in low-paying, dull, routine"[19] jobs will increase significantly as a category of the labor force in the coming decades, it is reasonable for the authors of *Work* to conclude that this form of dissatisfaction will diffuse itself through larger and larger sectors of the working class. For example, in the medical care industry—which the Carnegie Commission identifies as the potentially most dynamic sector of the economy as a whole for the foreseeable future[20]—"the phenomenal growth in employment over the past decade or so has occurred largely in lower-level occupations. This growth has been accompanied by an attempt to increase the efficiency of the upper-level occupations through the delegation of tasks down the ladder of skills. This undoubtedly results in a greater efficiency in the utilization of manpower, but it rigidifies tasks, reduces the range of skills utilized by most of the occupations, increases routinization, and opens the door to job dissatisfaction for a new generation of highly educated workers."[21]

The danger of this situation is clear to HEW: "For many of the new workers, the monotony of work, [the] scale of organization, and their inability to control the pace and style of work are cause for a resentment which they, unlike older workers, do not repress." The distance between open resentment and revolt is not great enough to provide the decision-makers in capitalism with a very considerable sense of security. For working-class anger ripening beneath the surface of events is as formidable a force as anything actually in motion in capitalist society. "More than any other group, it appears that young people have taken the lead in demanding better working conditions. Out of a work force of more than 85 million, 22.5 million are under the age of thirty. As noted earlier, these young workers are more affluent and better educated than their parents were at their age."[22]

Ominous changes are occurring in the outlook of young people. According to a survey conducted by Daniel Yankelovich, Inc., "In 1968 over half (56 percent) of all students indicated that they did not mind the future prospect of being 'bossed around' on the job. By 1971 only one out of three students (36 percent) saw themselves willingly submitting to such authority." A striking shift also occurred during this three-year interval in the proportion of students believing that "hard work always pays off": in 1968, 69 percent of all students responded affirmatively to this statement, while only 39 percent did so in 1971.[23]

Another way of approaching the problem of youthful allegiance to alienated labor is to consider the changing positions and attitudes of different sectors of the working class, especially white-collar workers, managerial labor, and young manual workers. How have their roles changed, and how has their consciousness developed?

Speaking of white-collar workers in general, the authors of *Work* comment that "secretaries, clerks, and bureaucrats were once grateful for having been spared the dehumanization of the factory. White-collar jobs were rare; they had higher status than blue-collar jobs. But today the clerk, and not the operative on the assembly line, is the typical

American worker, and such positions offer little in the way of prestige. Furthermore, the size of the organizations that employ the bulk of office workers has grown, imparting to the clerical worker the same impersonality that the blue-collar worker experiences in the factory."[24] In this increasingly factory-like atmosphere, class attitudes among office workers have changed considerably, especially since the beginning of a rupture with the earlier phases of capitalism at the start of the Second World War. "Loyalty to their employers was once high among this group of workers who felt that they shared much in common with their bosses—collar color, tasks, place of work. Today, many white-collar workers have lost personal touch with decision-makers, and, consequently, they feel estranged from the goals of the organizations in which they work."[25]

This process of increasing disaffection from hierarchically structured work has permeated many sectors of the working class, including the most improbable and most tenuously "proletarian" groupings. Thus, "One finds evidence of increasing dissatisfaction with jobs even among such traditionally privileged groups as the nation's four-and-a-half million middle managers. For example, where this group once represented a bulwark of company loyalty, today one out of three middle managers indicates some willingness to join a union. Another striking indicator of discontent is the apparently increasing number of middle-aged middle managers who are seeking a mid-career change."[26]

In modes of analysis borrowed from rigidly orthodox Marxists or bourgeois theorists, these developments would be virtually inexplicable, posing well-nigh insoluble problems for schemas which have grown fossilized from the narrowness and inflexibility of their applications. In terms of an analysis focusing on the *forward motion* of the class structure, however, these developments make a great deal of sense. Unintentionally, but accurately, the authors of *Work* parallel this kind of Marxist analysis. Thus, their report, as a careful study of the forward motion of capitalism, is Marxist in implication because it *is* accurate.

"Why," they ask, "should there be job dissatisfaction among people earning $20,000 a year? Some trained observers say that the new values of the counterculture have had a noticeable effect even on these workers. . . . Management scientists [however] point to the inherent qualities of the jobs of middle managers as the prime source of their dissatisfaction. Characteristically, middle managers perceive that they lack influence on organizational decision-making, yet they must implement company policy—and often without sufficient authority or resources to effectively carry it out. They must then compete to gain the attention of top management for support for their particular projects or functions."[27] Middle management, like the rest of the white-collar work force, has been reduced to an insignificant fragment of the hierarchy of decision-making power, significantly removed from the nerve centers of authority but entrusted with responsibility for the transmission of decisions made above. Like puppets, these managerial workers often speak with the voice of authority—yet neither the voice nor the authority is their own. For the authority which animates them rules them as much as it achieves expression through them. A conveyor belt for decisions, middle management is separated from the formulation of those decisions and is thus alienated in a fundamental sense.

Young manual workers are also a cause for alarm. "Young blue-collar workers also are better educated than their parents. In 1960, 26 percent of white and 14 percent of black craftsmen and operatives had completed a secondary education. By 1969, 41 percent of whites and 29 percent of blacks in those jobs had completed four years of high school. . . . These better educated workers, quite clearly, are not so easily satisfied as their forebears with the quality of most blue-collar jobs—a fact verified by the Survey of Working Conditions. . . . many young union members are challenging some basic assumptions about 'a fair day's work for a fair day's pay.' In the past, unions concerned themselves with establishing what a fair day's pay would be, while the employer's prerogative was to determine what constitutes a fair day's work. Young workers are now challenging both unions and management by demanding a voice in the setting of both standards."[28]

The prospect, then, is one of increasing dissatisfaction among wide sectors of the working class, and an expanding proletarian consciousness of alienation. What this will mean in the long run is not yet clear. Socialist revolution may or may not become a possibility depending upon the configuration of future events and the play of future contradictions. In the final chapter, therefore, I will make a provisional effort to explain the new dimensions of class struggle which have opened up as a result of the forward motion of the working class in advanced capitalist society. I will try to explain the possible consequences of the contradictions at work in America, portraying the proletariat not just as an *objective structure* but as a *potentially revolutionary subject.* For classes define themselves first and foremost in action. Class analysis would be empty if it failed to refer in every instance to the *subjectivity* and *activity* of the classes involved. If the diversified working class is not a potentially revolutionary subject, its objective identity as a class is stripped of its real interest and historical significance.

Let us see, then, what can be said about the revolutionary potential of the diversified working class.

Notes

1. Karl Kautsky, *The Class Struggle* (New York: Norton & Co., 1971; originally published in 1892), pp. 39-40.

2. Robert J. Havighurst, *American Higher Education in the 1960's* (Columbus: Ohio State University Press, 1960), p. 33.

3. Department of Labor, *U.S. Manpower in the 1970's: Opportunity and Challenge* (1969), p. 2.

4. Ibid., p. 12.

5. As Bettina Aptheker comments, "Professional, social, technical and scientific workers are overproduced, underemployed, misemployed, and unemployed. Increasingly, they must sell their intellectual and technical skills whenever, wherever, and however the market permits." *The Academic Rebellion in the United States* (Secaucus, N.J.: Citadel Press, 1973), p. 129.

6. The Carnegie Commission on Higher Education, *College Graduates and Jobs: A Report and Recommendations* (April 1973), p. 2.

7. Ibid., p. 3.

8. Ibid., p. 4.

9. Ibid., pp. 70-71.

10. Ibid., pp. 4-5 (emphasis added).

11. Ibid., p. 14.

12. See, for example, Patricia and Brendan Sexton, *Blue Collars and Hard Hats* (New York: Random House, 1971).

13. *Work in America: Report of a Special Task Force to the Secretary of Health, Education, and Welfare* (Cambridge, Mass.: MIT Press, 1972), p. xvi.

14. Ibid., p. 13.

15. Ibid., pp. 11-12.

16. Ibid., pp. 22-23.

17. Ibid., pp. xvii-xviii.

18. Ibid., p. 39.

19. Ibid.

20. Carnegie Commission, op. cit., p. 83.

21. Department of Health, Education, and Welfare, op. cit., p. 19.

22. Ibid., p. 43.

23. Ibid., p. 44.

24. Ibid., p. 38.
25. Ibid., p. 40.
26. Ibid.
27. Ibid., pp. 40-41.
28. Ibid., pp. 46, 34.

13
The Struggle for Socialism

The point of the theory of the new working class is not simply to say what is *but rather to point in the direction of what is* becoming *and to elaborate a political strategy that will not be made inadequate by the objective evolution of the capitalist system.*[1]

Dick Howard
"New Situation, New Strategy"

The focus of this work so far has been on what I have called the forward motion of the working class. I have argued that the working class is now a vastly different entity than it was in its early days of formation, altered in innumerable ways by the structural evolution of capitalism. It is now a diversified class, an expanded class: the question remaining to be answered, therefore, is whether or not the forward motion of the working class has brought it nearer to the realization of its destiny as the agent of revolutionary socialism, as prophesied by Marx. So far, the working class has made no revolution. Will the diversified working class now prove to be the embodiment of the revolutionary aspirations of earlier socialists? Or will it remain quiescent, reformist, like the bulk of the traditional proletariat during the earlier stages of capitalism?

In *The Holy Family,* Marx declared that "the question is not what goal is envisaged for the time being by this or that member of the proletariat as a whole. The question is *what is the proletariat* and what course of action will it be forced historically to take in conformity with its own nature."[2] Earlier in this work, I have attempted to say what the proletariat *is*. Now we must ask ourselves whether or not the proletariat as it has actually developed will be "forced historically . . . in conformity with its own nature" to engage in the struggle for socialism, as advocated by all Marxists. Or will it remain divided, incapable of transcending the limited perspective of its trade-unionist past? Is it possible that alienation cannot be surpassed, and that socialism cannot be created? What tendencies exist? What futures do we face?

From Trade Unionism to Socialism

When Lenin first developed his seminal theory of the vanguard party at the turn of the century, he postulated that the working class could not, "purely by its own efforts," sufficiently transcend trade union consciousness to reject the accommodation with capitalism inherent in the idea of trade unionism.[3] Such a rejection was essential if the working class was ever to break with the reformist strategies of the past and struggle against capitalism as a total system.

Since the proletariat itself was not likely to become spontaneously socialist, Lenin argued that historical actors external to the working-class would be necessary to bring socialist consciousness to at least leading elements of the proletariat, thus making the eventual completion of the working class struggle possible as well as necessary. These historical actors Lenin identified as the members of the revolutionary wing of the intelligentsia then emerging in agrarian Russia, the children of bourgeois and petit-bourgeois families who, renouncing their class heritage, aligned themselves with the potentially revolutionary forces slowly gathering strength in the belly of the Tsarist regime.

The central reason Lenin considered it crucial for this vanguard of "intellectuals and advanced workers" to exist was that, without such a vanguard, workers themselves would evolve "naturally" only to the level of "economism"—trade-union consciousness divorced from an awareness of the necessity of political struggle and the proletarian seizure of power. In a sense, therefore, what Lenin was maintaining was that the emancipation of the working class would not fully be the work of the proletariat itself, as Marx had envisioned. Instead, revolutionary intellectuals from the nascent bourgeoisie—equipped by their superior education to comprehend the necessity of the socialist revolution—would be required to step in, recruit the "advanced sectors" of the proletariat, and organize for socialism.

The subsequent experience of the Bolshevik party under Lenin's leadership seemed to confirm the truth of this proposition, and it has since come to be viewed as an infallible axiom by orthodox Marxists, despite the vast differences of the situations these Marxists have faced and despite Lenin's own warnings against blind imitation of the forms of struggle undertaken in Russia.[4] Nevertheless, the continuing reformism and trade-union consciousness of the working classes in the advanced Western countries, combined with the reign of Stalinist orthodoxy among Communist parties, have together continued to reinforce this principle.

The problem of class consciousness, however, must be approached historically, not as a question of faith in Leninist pronouncements. The evolution of classes and of class consciousness must be viewed as just that: a process of evolution, of change, involving precise study of the specificity and forward motion of any given structure of relations. If trade-union consciousness was the "natural" consciousness of the working class at one stage in its evolution, then we must ask ourselves if it *remains* the natural mode of proletarian consciousness. *Has* consciousness changed? If so, how have the "objective conditions" underpinning consciousness changed? Where are we going now?

When Lenin developed his theory, the Russian proletariat was still in its infancy, barely out of the womb of agrarian Russia. It was still a minority class, greatly outnumbered by the peasantry and possessing little experience of struggle. It was largely correct, therefore, given the realities of the situation in Russia and the reformist tendencies in Western Europe, to believe that the Russian proletariat would be unlikely, *in that period,* to develop socialist class consciousness purely as the result of the objective evolution of capitalist social relations. Since a substantial part of the intelligentsia had been fundamentally Marxist in outlook since Plekhanov first introduced Marxism to Russia in the 1880s, it was reasonable to theorize that intellectuals would be among the vanguard in the creation of socialist consciousness. In fact, the revolutionary wing of the intelligentsia *did* ultimately prove itself vital to the revolutionary process as a profoundly significant agent of consciousness and political struggle.

This does not mean, however, that trade-union consciousness is the inevitable outcome of working-class struggle at all times and in all places, or that a revolutionary intelligentsia external to the proletariat must constitute the vanguard of the struggle for socialism. It is true that, in advanced capitalist societies like the United States, the first experience of the proletariat has taken place within the framework of trade-union consciousness—an experience prolonged by the ability of the capitalist class to make concessions to the working class in terms of wages, etc., on the basis of the vast profits reaped from imperialism. It does not necessarily follow, however, that this form of consciousness is unalterable. In fact, just the reverse appears likely. Unions have been institutionalized in the United States as an accepted part of the power structure since the late 1940s. Since then, the AFL-CIO has largely achieved what it set out to achieve—increasingly higher and higher standards of living (in material terms) for the workers represented by its component unions. Unionized workers now see themselves almost universally as members of the "middle class." In terms of consumption and consciousness, thus, they have apparently elevated themselves from their former degradation; or have they? For if trade unionism seems to have realized its goals, then a working class limited to trade-union consciousness should be satisfied with its lot. Is this actually the case? According to most authorities, it is not: workers remain dissatisfied with their lives, particularly with the fact that they are denied self-management and denied creativity. Will more money dispel this gathering consciousness of alienation? For a time—perhaps. And then again, perhaps not.

It seems likely that trade-union consciousness can and will be transcended—slowly perhaps, but steadily—as it becomes increasingly apparent that trade unions are insufficient either to put an end to the root cause of social discontent, the alienation of labor, or to permanently ensure the working class a high level of wages and material well being. Before embarking on the crucial struggle for unionization, the working class could have had no clear perception of the overall inadequacy of such a tactic. Not until the battle had been "won" and it became increasingly clear that the essence of the struggle had eluded capture (as is becoming increasingly clear today), could trade-union consciousness be transcended. It had to be completed first, and then shown to be inadequate, before it could be negated. It has now been largely completed. It is beginning to be seen as inadequate. Will it be negated?

If trade-union consciousness is transcended, it will be replaced by the beginnings of socialist consciousness. This is not, as it may appear, an arbitrary statement, for it flows directly from the inner logic of the relationship between trade unionism and socialism. The essence of trade unionism is its focus on small, quantitative improvements in the material conditions of life for elements of the working class. Socialism, on the other hand, is characterized above all else by its *qualitative* concerns: rather than focusing exclusively on the achievement of marginal gains *within* capitalism, it represents the desire of the working class for an *end* to alienation and exploitation.

If it is correct, therefore, to say that alienation is the root cause of working-class discontent, then it is also correct to say that it cannot be eliminated by trade-union gains. As workers become increasingly conscious of this fact, they are bound to substitute socialist modes of consciousness for their earlier trade-unionist ideals. For as Ernest Mandel comments, "Even more important than the basic instability and insecurity of the proletarian condition which neo-capitalism hasn't overcome and cannot overcome is the inherent trend under neo-capitalism to push the class struggle to a higher plane. As long as the workers were hungry and their most immediate needs were unattended to, wage increases inevitably stood in the center of working class aspirations. As long as they were threatened by mass unemployment, reductions in the work week were essentially seen as means of reducing the dangers of surplus labor. But when employment is relatively high and wages are constantly rising, attention becomes gradually transferred to more basic aspects of capitalist exploitation."[5] Or, more tersely, as Serge Mallet phrases it, "Precisely because its elementary demands are largely satisfied, the new working class is led to pose other problems which cannot find their solution in the sphere of consumption."[6]

These problems are the problems of alienation—alienation from the social processes of decision-making and from the purposes and results of proletarian labor. Their solution can be found only in the realm of socialism—workers' democratic self-management.

The Special Role of College-Educated Workers

> *The working class has not been replaced, nor has its proletarian core been eliminated. On the contrary, its constituency has been expanded, immeasurably adding to its political power and revolutionary potential.*[7]
>
> Angela Y. Davis

While it would be historically shortsighted for us to deny the vast revolutionary potential of manual and clerical workers, it would be equally mistaken to deny the special role of students and college-educated workers in the evolution of the class struggle. Class consciousness does not develop evenly or uniformly in any society; its development is, in Trotsky's words, both "uneven and combined."[8] *Uneven,* because classes are uneven; *combined,* because no stratum of a class can evolve independently of the other strata. A class made up of authentically independent units would be a class in words only—it would have no *social* reality.

The special role of students and college-educated workers in the evolution of the class struggle first evidenced itself during the turbulent years of the sixties, but remains far from exhausted historically. Its most important manifestation was the emergence of what became known as the New Left—the anti-authoritarian force, made up largely of students, which placed apparently forgotten issues of alienation on center stage of the unfolding social drama. In sometimes chaotic but universal and authentic expressions of their concerns, the students, college-educated workers, and black people at the center of the New Left raised fundamental issues of decision-making power, issues which had been neglected for decades in the reformism and trade unionism of earlier movements for social change. Tenaciously, the New Left worked to shift the focus of struggle from material to social issues, from narrower issues of material oppression and inadequate purchasing power to broader issues of alienation and exploitation. Following the lead of the students in particular, the New Left began posing its demands not as attacks merely on the oppressiveness of conditions but on the condition of oppression itself. From the implicit reformism of the early civil rights and antiwar movements, the New Left advanced by giant steps to an emerging class and socialist consciousness.

This advance has, however, apparently been halted. The student movement (to say nothing of the left in general) has been far less vocal and far less explosive in the 1970s than it was in the 1960s. Seemingly—as the media report—all is quiet on the campuses, all is calm in the cities. But the calm is deceptive; the appearance is more illusion than reality. As most ruling-class analysts agree, we are experiencing at most a temporary lull in the process of struggle.[9] For the amorphous left has been halted by its confusion and by its inability to grasp fully the protracted, class nature of the struggle—not by bewildered apathy or by grudging acceptance of an intractable reality. Consciousness of alienation is as strong now as it has ever been, but its expression has not yet crystallized into highly developed organizational forms or theories of struggle. Faced not by the urgency of ending a genocidal war but by the complex problems involved in the transformation of society, the left—in this sense, the elements of the working class gaining consciousness of the struggle—needs time to reorient itself and develop a strategy sufficient for the eventual success of socialism. When more thinking has been done and more organizational work completed, the socialist left will lack neither issues nor targets to transform its theories into material forces—for theory *becomes* a material force when it grips the masses, as Marx wrote.[10]

The early, formative years of the New Left are largely over. One phase of the struggle has thus been completed—yet the special role played by students and college-educated workers is far from ended. The emergent New Left of the sixties is now transforming itself from a *youth* movement centered principally in the arenas of higher education into a *class* movement centered increasingly in the arenas of the production process. As it transforms itself, it is likely to grow in strength. For as Herb Gintis comments, "The power of a youth movement is both considerable and indirect; considerable because of the proximity of youth to the crucial instrument in the generation of alienated labor—the educational system—and indirect because its influence on the social system must operate primarily through the educational system."[11]

The influence of college-educated workers in the production process has not yet been felt in any profound way. Their social weight as a newly significant element in the working class has not yet registered on the seismic scale by which social forces are measured in this society, yet the gathering power and combustible ingredients are present. Overshadowed by their predecessors belonging to the student movement, college-educated workers are nevertheless intensely dissatisfied with their labor and accustomed, from their student past, to think in terms of social justice and revolt.

If a revolt is brewing, then, given the almost crisis conditions in the job market, it is not likely to be far off. When the first tremors of the earthquake are felt, a new period of struggle will be in the process of beginning. It will almost inevitably draw in additional layers of the work force, young manual and clerical workers especially, and rekindle smoldering coals of dissent still lingering among the ashes of the student movement.

What more can be said about the special role of college-educated workers in the struggle for socialism? What special features of their class identity can we locate which will make college-educated workers more or less likely to participate in the revolutionary struggle?

First, we must acknowledge that *the potentially revolutionary intelligentsia is no longer an agency external to the proletariat.* Such an intelligentsia now exists in nascent form not only on a much broader scale than in the past, but as a vital and growing stratum of the working class itself. It is thus likely to develop a form of consciousness which is doubly revolutionary because it is also *class* consciousness. As a significant element of the working class, moreover, this intelligentsia is also a far more formidable force than any previous intelligentsia, both in terms of numbers and in terms of its key position in the labor process. Capitalism thus continues to plant the seeds of its own destruction. If Lenin was correct in his belief that revolutionary intellectuals are crucial to the process of socialist revolution, then we are not far from correct today in our belief that capitalism continues to supply its own gravediggers—this time, in the shape of a diversified working class. For contemporary capitalism has been forced, as a result of its internal contradictions, to divert tens of millions of potentially blue-collar workers from industrial production into the technical and supervisory wings of the production process. It has thus created, as part of the proletariat itself, an active and vital intelligentsia which has demonstrated time and again its potentially revolutionary inclinations.

Consciousness does not develop smoothly or evenly among all sectors of the working class. Since college-educated workers in the present era are likely to develop a broader view of the system than less completely educated workers, they are thus likely to have a special role to play in the development of revolutionary consciousness. Equipped by the relative leisure of their schooling with an opportunity to contemplate and judge the social system, they are likely to develop a more comprehensive understanding and critique than other sectors—an understanding rooted in a more deeply considered awareness of the possibilities confronting us. Part of their special role will thus be to convey a sense of this understanding to other intellectuals and other elements of the working class which find themselves awakening to the realities of their own oppression. Further, highly educated workers are likely to have less patience with narrowly trade-unionist struggles than other groups of working people, since they have been trained to *expect* material well-being as a direct result of their education. Great expectations are the rule and not the exception among college-educated workers, making their probable future frustrations that much more volatile and severe as a result. Since highly-educated workers are trained to use their creativity and judgment, their dissatisfaction is likely to be explosive when they enter the labor force and find that ultimately all creativity and judgment flows from the decision-making powers of capital. With no real autonomy possible, consciousness of alienation is the logical result.*

Another important feature of the contemporary situation is that there is an increasing concentration of abilities among the different sectors of the proletariat, equipping it now more fully than ever before to exercise control over the direction of society. At the same time, there has been a parallel concentration of authority in the state and the giant corpo-

* This is not to say, however, that there will necessarily be a smooth transition from alienated modes of consciousness to coherent forms of socialist consciousness. One of the key facts about alienation is that it poses false problems and engenders false consciousness even among a large percentage of those workers who arrive at a dawning awareness of the oppressiveness and systemic nature of capitalist social relations. Thus, although working people may become increas-

rations, leaving the agencies of capitalist decision-making power more and more concretely unified and identifiable. The question—who shall rule?—can now be posed with greater clarity and force than in the past. No longer is the working class a class of "machine tenders" lacking the technical and supervisory skills necessary to organize a society. No longer is capitalist authority diffused among thousands of anarchically competing and uncoordinated agencies. Instead, the antagonisms of the rival classes can now be clearly articulated as a matter of decision-making power and class rule. As Moody argues, with "the interpenetration of industry and the State that was required by the arms economy . . . the enemies of the working class became more centralized and visible."[12] Far more workers have been hired in the state sector of the economy during recent decades than in any other sector, and projections for the future indicate that this trend will continue. The political importance of this fact is that, as Jay Mandle comments, "Any effort by these employees on any governmental level to improve their standard of living through wage increases is likely to be politicized. Wage increases usually can only be financed through increased taxation, and hence the class nature of the tax structure may become a significant issue."[13]

On one level, thus, the extraction of surplus value through taxation may become an important issue, as the needs and interests of state workers are translated into political terms in the arena of the state. On another level, the entire relationship between the working class and the state may itself become deeply politicized and hostile as the state increasingly

ingly conscious of their alienation, it is likely that their initially alienated consciousness will present serious obstacles to the development of socialist consciousness. Specifically, tendencies toward individualism, self-denial, cynicism, escape through consumption, passivity, etc., all work against the full flowering of socialist consciousness.

intervenes in the economic affairs of the working class. (This is especially likely in conjunction with events such as the recent state promulgation of wage controls, energy controls, etc.) For as the state more and more directly exercises control over the socioeconomic life of the working class, the working class is less likely to focus its attacks on fragments of the problem and increasingly likely to engage itself in struggle with the state, understood as the *locus* of capitalist authority. The issue of the class nature of government is thus likely to become increasingly prominent, and debates over the possibility of socialism—working-class control of society—will figure more and more prominently in the arena of public controversy. The fact that the working class is now more fully equipped than ever before to assume control over and transform the directing processes of society can only add fuel to this controversy. For as Bogdan Denitch comments, "Today a new meaning can be given to demands to extend democracy to all aspects of social and political life—and the technical skills and education of the new working class equip it to challenge the monopoly of expertise of the old elites."[14]

Always before, Marxists had placed great stress on the revolutionary capabilities of special sectors of the working class which find themselves in a position to "paralyze the economy at a single stroke": transport workers, communications workers, etc. Now, however, Marxists of the New Left are beginning to stress the importance of working-class abilities not just to paralyze the economy but to restructure it. As Frank Ackerman comments, "Perhaps a handful of terrorists, the transit or sanitation workers of a few major cities, or several other small groups could singlehandedly shut down America; but to shut it down and open it up again as a socialist democracy requires a mass movement from all strata of society."[15]

The Experience of France in May 1968

The general strike which rocked France in May 1968 is the most important mass struggle to have taken place in an advanced capitalist society in recent times. As such it provides us with a valuable test of the validity of our hypothesis about the diversified working class. What role did highly educated workers play in this massive upheaval? Were they a revolutionary force, or a reactionary force? How did their actions express their class identity, and what does this tell us about the working class in the United States?

The best analysis of the French general strike can be found in the book *Prelude to Revolution* by Daniel Singer. A participant in the strike, an independent Marxist of undeniable talent, and an eyewitness reporter of almost every facet of the struggle, Singer has written an illuminating analysis as well as a vivid account of the events. In the pages that follow, therefore, I will be relying almost entirely on his analysis—not because it differs so sharply from other interpretations, but because it is more incisive, more cogent and many-sided in its understanding of the *meaning* of the struggle.[16]

Singer begins by throwing the events into bold relief, reducing them to their essence. Who initiated the strike, he asks, and where did it go? "It started not among industrial workers but among students, and it is among them that it found its most radical expression. The politically conscious students rebelled against society as a whole, against its hierarchical structure, against the foundations of private property on which the edifice rests, against its vulgarly aggressive commercial facade. Only when the rebellion spread throughout the country, when it gathered political momentum, switching from university to factory bench, did it lose its revolutionary impetus. The labor unions, admittedly after some delay and frantic efforts, had managed to turn a struggle *against* the system into a battle *within* it."[17]

Drawing upon the concrete experience of the strike, Singer observes further that "during the general strike, the traditional dividing line between wage and salary earners was blurred. Salaried employees, whether in technical, scientific, or managerial jobs, did not this time rally collectively to the employers' side. Many, as usual, did act as the upholders of capitalist law and order, but quite a few did not. Siding this time with the workers, they took an active part in the strike. The emergence of such an activist minority marks a break with the past and an interesting pointer to the future. Interesting, because these *cadres,* as the French call them, are the fastest growing section of the labor force, and because the rapid expansion of this professional intelligentsia is a common feature of all advanced countries. Everywhere numerical growth is coupled with social differentiation. A fraction of the newcomers can be absorbed at the top of the establishment and get real executive functions. The majority must resign themselves to jobs increasingly distant from the real centers of decision-making, to being the recipients of orders handed down from above, to a narrowing scope for genuine initiative; in short, to a form of alienating work that was once thought to be the exclusive prerogative of the laborer. Gradually, they lose the feeling, or rather the illusion, that they are an integral part of the ruling class."[18]

What special importance does this have from the standpoint of our concern with the revolutionary potential of highly educated labor? Singer answers: "The malaise of the *cadres* resulting from these frustrations is international, though under normal circumstances it is difficult to gauge how widespread and deep this feeling is. The French upheaval provided a unique opportunity for seeing how these pent-up passions express themselves in a time of crisis and for drawing distinctions between the behavior of various groups lumped together under the generic name professional intelligentsia."[19]

Singer points out that the movement was ignited and spearheaded by "would-be cadres," university students "who rejected the future that society offered them." He then divides the professional and technical sector into three categories: first, those who functioned as "more or less active strikebreakers"; second, those comprising the relatively inert and vacillating mass of "passive strikers," which, while numerically the largest group and ostensibly in support of the strike, took no revolutionary initiative; and third, those who joined with the students and manual workers as active participants in the revolutionary effort. "The activists were still a minority. By itself, however, this fact in no way invalidates the thesis that a new revolutionary class has appeared on the horizon. A movement must start from somewhere, and political class consciousness is not acquired overnight."[20]

Who among the cadres were the most active strikers? According to Singer, scientists and technicians on the lower levels of the decision-making hierarchy proved to be the most explosive of the cadres, although scientists at higher levels, in supervisory roles, proved to be relatively inert and passive in their response to the great events of 1968. Managerial employees and workers in circulation also remained somewhat distant from the strike, but much of the rest of the professional work force did not. Thus, "If sales managers and salesmen stayed aloof, or were hostile to the strike, economists, sociologists, and statisticians working in market research or other economic and social institutions were among the most radical participants in the movement."[21] This was especially true of those state workers engaged in social administration, who adopted as their own the student slogan, "We don't want to be the watchdogs or servants of capitalism."

While the situation in France is, of course, different from the situation in the United States, there are important similarities between the two. Each has entered the stage of state monopoly capitalism (or "neocapitalism"); the United States, however, has progressed much further than France has so far. Thus, while the earliest statements of "new working-class" theory were articulated by French Marxists, this was not because their class structure was the most advanced, but because their Marxism was—a paradox arising from the uneven development of proletarian struggles. It is thus intriguing and plausible when Singer suggests that "maybe the theory is not destined for France. If teachers and technicians, scientific and social workers, are the revolutionary class of today or tomorrow, then North America should figure at the top of the revolutionary agenda. It is in the United States . . . that the premises of the theory are fulfilled. There, with no untapped reserves of farm labor to draw upon, the relative share of industrial employment is actually declining. The technological transformation has gone farther there than anywhere else, and the number of white-collar workers is rising fast. The proportion of college-trained graduates in the economy is also much larger. . . . Projecting current American trends into the future, it is not impossible to imagine a situation in which the apathy of the traditional American working class would cease to be a major obstacle to revolutionary developments. If continued economic concentration and the connected streamlining of organization reduce the growing mass of white-collar employees to conditions of work that, at least in terms of lack of initiative, were hitherto associated with the factory; if scientific progress and the spread of automation reduce drastically the number of unskilled, and even skilled, workers in industry and replace them with a college-trained labor force, then these scientific and technical workers—the new producers, newly alienated—could become the driving force of historical change."[22]

The logic of the argument seems inescapable. For if the history of the past thirty years provides us with any basis for prediction, it seems likely that highly educated workers will become both more numerous and more conscious of their alienation as workers—and thus very likely to be among the "driving forces" of social change moving us in the direction of socialism.

Anti-Authoritarian Socialism

> *Socialist democracy is not something which begins only in the promised land after the foundations of socialist economy are created; it does not come as some sort of Christmas present for the worthy people who, in the interim, have loyally supported a handful of socialist dictators. Socialist democracy begins simultaneously with the beginnings of the destruction of class rule and of the construction of socialism. It begins at the very moment of the seizure of power by the socialist party. It is the same thing as the dictatorship of the proletariat.*[23]
>
> Rosa Luxemburg, 1918

The proletarian struggle for socialism has been developing, in one form or another, for more than a century. Inspired by the clash of class forces at the base of capitalism, it has advanced alternately by great leaps and painfully small steps; it has been crushed again and again, only to be reborn, like the phoenix, with a wealth of new experience and fresh strength. As Marx wrote in the *Eighteenth Brumaire*, "Proletarian revolutions . . . criticize themselves constantly, interrupt themselves continually in their course, come back to the apparently accomplished in order to begin it afresh, deride with unmerciful thoroughness the inadequacies, weaknesses, and paltrinesses of their first attempts, seem to throw down their adversary only in order that he may draw new strength from the earth and rise again, more gigantic, before them, recoil ever and anon from the indefinite prodigiousness of their own aims, until a situation has been created which makes all turning back impossible, and the conditions themselves cry out: 'Here is the rose, here dance.' "[24]

In terms of the construction of international socialism, we are still light-years from "a situation . . . which makes all turning back impossible," but we are also infinitely further advanced than we were in Marx's day. Since the red flag was first raised over the Paris Commune in 1871, thousands of battles have been fought and untold mountains of experience have accumulated. Consider the experience of German Social Democracy; the world-shaking drama of the Bolshevik Revolution; the failure of the German Revolution; the birth and traumas of international communism during the 1920s; the failure of the Chinese Revolution in 1927; the bitter experience of fascism; the defeated revolution in Spain in the 1930s; Stalinist consolidation in the USSR; the revolutionary success in China; the spread of Marxism throughout the Third World; revolution in Cuba, Vietnam, Angola; the experience of the Communist parties since World War II; the rise of the New Left; and so on. All this and much more is now water under the bridge for the Marxist left, part of the vast heritage of revolutionary struggles to have taken place during the twentieth century.[25]

Capitalism, meanwhile, has reached the autumn of its existence. As Marx wrote in the *Critique of Political Economy,* "No social order is ever destroyed before all the productive forces for which it is sufficient have been developed."[26] While it would be foolhardy for me to argue that capitalism has now fully exhausted itself, it is nevertheless considerably more than an act of faith to declare that the larger part of its life is now behind it. As a world system, capitalism has embraced every continent and every civilization, only to be repelled now in increasingly large areas of the world: not just in Russia and China, but in Vietnam, Cambodia, Laos, Korea; Angola, Mozambique; South Yemen; Cuba; etc. Moreover, if not yet defeated, capitalist social relations have been significantly challenged in innumerable other areas of the world, from Chile to France. In short, the struggle continues—and while the final outcome is far from determined, the forward motion is clear: for socialism has gained far more than it has lost in the last century, as the logical result of proletarian struggle.

In the course of the struggle, however, no general agreement has emerged about the specific meaning of the concept "socialism" itself. While it is agreed that socialism would be a form of society characterized by public control of the means of production, little more can be said with an assurance of unanimity among socialists.

For a long time the Stalinist conception of socialism, as practiced in the USSR, was endorsed by the leading communist forces of almost every nation. Recently, however, this conception has been challenged by the amorphous international movement of the left which began to sink roots in the capitalist countries in the last decade. No longer is the authoritarian Soviet state universally acceptable as a model for socialists in other countries. New and democratic approaches to socialism have begun to be explored, inspired principally by the strongly anti-authoritarian ideas of the largely college-educated New Left. *This is one of the most important results of the emergence of college-educated labor and its revolutionary expression, the New Left.* For socialism is now no longer the private property of tiny sects and reformist parties. It stands open once again for fresh development, as the potential consciousness of a diversifying working class.

The Stalinist conception of socialism must be understood as a narrow, one-dimensional interpretation of Marxism vastly exaggerating the importance of the economic side of society at the expense of an awareness of the richness and complexity of the "ensemble of social relationships" comprising the real subject matter of Marxist political economy (as defined by Marx in the *Critique of Political Economy*). The Stalinist conception is that socialism consists of state ownership of the means of production combined with comprehensive economic planning. The assumption implicit in this, as Paul Sweezy has shown, "is that once socialism in this sense has been firmly established, *its own inner dynamic will automatically propel it forward on the next leg of the journey to communism.*"[27]

What this implies is that a revolutionary change in the economic structure of society is not only necessary but sufficient for the successful completion of the journey to communism, which will result automatically from the implementation of socialist economic policies. What this theory fails to take into account, however, is that class rule has a political dimension inseparable from its economic dimension. Authority—*power*—is fundamental to all class relationships. If the goal of socialists is to overthrow capitalism and to establish democratic working-class control of society, then the working class must assert control over the political processes of society and establish democratic relations *in every arena.* It is not simply a question of public ownership of the means of production. For as Vittorio Foa comments, some people "think that oppression arises exclusively from private appropriation of the means of production, and that once public expropriation of capital has been achieved, the workers' liberty will be automatically ensured. This . . . seems to us inexact: socialist power can expropriate the private capitalist and create in this way the *premises* of workers' liberty; but if the organization of production in the enterprise and in the total economy remains bureaucratized with a rigid system of centralized decision-making, then the workers will continue to experience social production as an alien process and will find themselves in a subordination in certain ways similar to that in the capitalist countries."[28]

Under Stalin, authority in the Soviet Union was concentrated in the hands of an all-powerful bureaucracy, not in the hands of the working class. Nothing resembling socialist democracy has emerged in the USSR, and all efforts to achieve workers' self-management have been defeated. Social equality has thus been halted, not only in practice but in theory as well—for as Stalin put it, equality is nothing more than "reactionary, petty-bourgeois absurdity worthy of a primitive sect of ascetics but not a socialist society organized along Marxian lines."[29] It is the question of political and economic democracy, therefore, which serves as the dividing line between Stalinist conceptions of socialism and those advanced by the Marxists of the New Left, whose choice has been to reaffirm Rosa Luxemburg's views on the issues of democracy in explicit opposition to the views of the Stalinist parties. For as Paul Sweezy recently declared, "We must decisively reject the idea . . . that egalitarianism is foreign to 'a socialist society organized along Marxian lines.' This idea is in fact an ideological rationalization for privilege and ultimately class rule. It is necessary to proclaim, on the contrary, that egalitarianism is the most fundamental principle of a socialist society organized along Marxian lines."[30]

What does it mean to speak of a democratic movement for socialist democracy? How would such a movement differ from previous revolutionary efforts?

First of all, it means that socialist consciousness cannot remain restricted to a "vanguard" of committed revolutionaries. In the eyes of orthodox Communists, the function of the "vanguard party" has classically been understood in the following terms: the vanguard, composed as much as possible of advanced sectors of the proletariat, should work in the context of bread-and-butter reform issues to arouse the working class to militant class-consciousness and an awareness of the fundamental oppressiveness of a system of exploitation, reserving, however, correct socialist consciousness for the party cadres. When the moment of crisis comes, the masses will hurl the ruling class from the helm of state and seize power, placing faith in—and delegating much of its power to—the vanguard party itself, which has proven its iron will, sincerity, and capacity for leadership during the struggle.

This vision crumbles, however, if we question either of its two central premises: first, that the working class is incapable of achieving socialist consciousness in its own right; or, second, that power should be concentrated "after the revolution" in the hands of a centralized vanguard party instead of in the hands of representative workers' councils (or comparable organs of proletarian power).

If we oppose bureaucratic rule, then it is clear that we must struggle for a "dictatorship of the proletariat" in which the proletariat actually rules. In order for the proletariat to rule, it is vital for the majority of the proletariat to share the goals and understand the purposes of the socialist revolution. In other words, in order for socialism to mean *democratic* working-class control of society, the bulk of the proletariat must be consciously socialist. This is not only necessary, it is also possible. For the working class today is not the working class we encounter in history books and in the rhetoric of the various vanguard parties. It is a growing and diversifying class, with a full history of trade-union struggles behind it and a growing, potentially revolutionary intelligentsia within it. It has a vast amount of information and experience at its disposal. Whether or not a mode of revolutionary organization transcending the archaic formal notions of the "vanguard party" of the past will emerge is unknown, but it will be necessary if socialism is to be achieved. An organization such as the New American Movement, which is explicitly committed to the building of a mass movement for socialist democracy as a non-Leninist revolutionary party, is a step in the right direction. In order for that step to become a long forward march, however, much work must be done. The present members of the New Left will bear key responsibility for that work.[31]

The New Left can be distinguished from the Old Left chiefly by its emergence among newly forged sectors of the working class which are chained neither to reformist strategies of struggle nor to trade-union views and institutions. In a context of this sort, it makes sense that various forms of class and socialist consciousness should begin to emerge as a replacement for the traditional reformism of the organized working class.

While it is true that beginning forms of socialist consciousness have occurred first among "new working-class" elements, it is not likely that such consciousness will remain unique to them. In the future, as trade unionism proves itself to be more and more thoroughly bankrupt—and as consciousness of alienation grows increasingly strong—the emergence of socialist consciousness is increasingly probable among all sectors of the proletariat. Socialist intellectuals, thus, are not a vanguard in the sense of being the sole source of revolutionary consciousness in the contemporary period. However, since their consciousness is in some ways more advanced than the consciousness of other elements of the working class (including a large percentage of their fellow professional workers, who lack even minimal class consciousness), they do have a highly modified, historically specific "vanguard" role to play. As they are increasingly successful in communicating their revolutionary message to other working people, however, and as trade unionism demonstrates its exhaustion, they will be increasingly able to transcend their vanguard role and emerge as equal participants in a diversified mass movement. They will be aided in this process by the autonomous development of socialist consciousness among other sectors of the working class, which will occur as a result of the transcendence of necessary—but insufficient—trade unionism.

When consciousness rises to high enough levels, the social weight of the working class will be embodied in the formation of autonomous organs of proletarian power (factory councils, people's assemblies, etc.). The stage will then be set for increasingly high levels of class polarization and confrontation, and socialist revolution will become a clear possibility.

As the issues of the struggle are clarified—not only in theory but in practice as well—the diverse elements of the proletariat will increasingly stand ready to recognize their essential unity as a class. Thus, in Marx's words, when they finally act not just as a class *in* themselves but as a class *for* themselves, socialism will have become the order of the day.

In other words, if an end to alienation *is* possible, the emancipation of the working class will be the conscious achievement of the workers themselves—college-educated and less educated alike.

Notes

1. Dick Howard, "New Situation, New Strategy: Serge Mallet and André Gorz," in *The Unknown Dimension: European Marxism Since Lenin,* ed. Howard and Klare (New York: Basic Books, 1972), p. 400.

2. Karl Marx, *The Holy Family,* in *Werke,* vol. 2, p. 38, cited in George Lukács, *History and Class Consciousness* (Cambridge, Mass.: MIT Press, 1972), p. 46.

3. V. I. Lenin, *What Is to Be Done?* in vol. 5 of the *Collected Works,* 4th ed. (Moscow: Progress Publishers, 1964).

4. For the best history and analysis of the revolutionary process in Russia, see Isaac Deutscher, *The Prophet Armed, The Prophet Unarmed,* and *The Prophet Outcast*—his famous Trotsky trilogy (New York: Random House, 1965). Also, see his *Stalin: A Political Biography* (New York: Oxford University Press, 1969), and the seven-volume history by E. H. Carr (Baltimore: Penguin, various years).

5. Ernest Mandel, "Workers Under Neo-Capitalism," *International Socialist Review,* November-December 1968, pp. 11-12.

6. Howard, op. cit., p. 390.

7. Angela Davis, Introduction to Bettina Aptheker, *The Academic Rebellion in the United States* (Secaucus, N.J.: Citadel Press, 1972), p. 17.

8. Leon Trotsky, *History of the Russian Revolution,* vol. 1 (London: Sphere Books, 1967), pp. 22-24.

9. See, for example, Frederick G. Dutton, *Changing Sources of Power* (New York: McGraw Hill, 1971).

10. Karl Marx, "Introduction to the Critique of Hegel's Philosophy of Right," from the *Early Writings,* ed. T. B. Bottomore (New York: McGraw-Hill, 1963), p. 52.

11. Herb Gintis, "The New Working Class and Revolutionary Youth," *Socialist Revolution,* no. 3, May-June 1970, p. 36.

12. Kim Moody, "The American Working Class in Transition," *International Socialism,* October-November 1969, p. 10.

13. Jay Mandle, "Some Notes on the American Working Class," *Review of Radical Political Economy* 2, no. 1 (Spring 1970), p. 66.

14. Bogdan Denitch, "Is There a 'New Working Class'?" in *Workers' Control,* ed. Case, Garson, and Hunnius (New York: Random House, 1973), p. 438. Moreover, as Bettina Aptheker points out, "The *private* appropriation of *socially* produced wealth . . . presents itself in a new and particularly striking way to students and intellectuals in the present era. They are aware of the material capabilities of the society in scientific and technical detail. They *know* that scientifically and technically the social problems are solvable; and they can therefore see clearly and *concretely* the inability of the social order to realize its material capabilities in terms of human need." Aptheker, op. cit., p. 25.

15. Frank Ackerman, "The University and Socialism," *Upstart,* Winter 1971, p. 12.

16. The highly touted work by Alain Touraine, for example—*The May Movement or Utopian Communism*—proved to be a big disappointment. Pregnant with the obscurantist and indecipherably phrased concepts of bourgeois sociology, its analysis was far from rigorous, and decidedly unhelpful. Even Henri Lefebvre's *The Explosion,* while un-

abashedly Marxist by contrast, nevertheless also proved to be largely opaque in the imprecision and grandeur of its terminology.

17. Daniel Singer, *Prelude to Revolution* (New York: Hill and Wang, 1970), p. 244.

18. Ibid.

19. Ibid., pp. 244-45.

20. Ibid., pp. 245-46.

21. Ibid., pp. 246-47.

22. Ibid., pp. 253-54.

23. Rosa Luxemburg, "The Russian Revolution," in *Rosa Luxemburg Speaks,* ed. Mary Alice Waters (New York: Pathfinder Press, 1970), pp. 393-94.

24. Karl Marx, *The Eighteenth Brumaire of Louis Bonaparte* (New York: International Publishers, 1968), p. 19.

25. Karl Marx, *A Contribution to the Critique of Political Economy* (Moscow: Progress Publishers, 1970), p. 21.

26. Ibid.

27. Paul Sweezy, "On Studying the Transition Process," *Monthly Review,* February 1972, p. 3 (emphasis in original).

28. Vittorio Foa, cited in André Gorz, *Strategy for Labor* (Boston: Beacon Press, 1964), p. 38.

29. Cited in Sweezy, op. cit., p. 5.

30. Ibid., p. 10.

31. For a more detailed analysis of the implications of a democratic approach to socialist revolution, see "Revolution and Democracy" by Frank Ackerman and Harry Boyte, to bepublished in *Socialist Revolution* in early 1974.